D1061422

# The new novel in Latin America

## Politics and popular culture after the Boom

*Philip Swanson*

Manchester University Press

Manchester and New York

distributed exclusively in the USA by St. Martin's Press

PQ
7082
.N7
S96
1995

*Published by* Manchester University Press
Oxford Road, Manchester M13 9NR, UK
*and* Room 400, 175 Fifth Avenue, New York, NY 10010, USA

*Distributed exclusively in the USA*
*by* St. Martin's Press, Inc;, 175 Fifth Avenue, New York, NY 10010, USA

*Distributed exclusively in Canada by*
UBC Press, University of British Columbia, 6344 Memorial Road,
Vancouver, BC, Canada, V6T 1Z3

*British Library cataloguing-in-publication data*
A catalogue record for this book is available from the British Library

*Library of Congress cataloging-in-publication data*
Swanson, Philip, 1959–
        The new new novel in Latin America : politics and popular culture
    after the boom / Philip Swanson.
            p.     cm.
        Includes bibliographical references (p.      ).
        ISBN 0-7190-4038-8
        1. Latin American fiction—20th century—History and criticism.
    2. Politics in literature. 3. Popular culture in literature.
    I. Title.
    PQ7082.N7S96    1995
    863—dc20                                                    95-1713

ISBN 0 7190 4038 8 *hardback*
ISBN 0 7190 5361 7 *paperback*

First published 1995

99 98        10 9 8 7 6 5 4 3 2

Typeset in Great Britain
by Koinonia, Manchester

Printed in Great Britain
by Bookcraft Ltd, Midsomer Norton

# Contents

# Acknowledgements

The Fulbright Commission generously awarded a fellowship which allowed me to spend a year in the USA, where I did much of the work for this book, enjoyed opportunities to develop my ideas in preparing for speaking engagements on topics related to it, and was fortunate enough to make many kind and rewarding American friends. The British Council and the Chilean Ministry of Education were also good enough to provide funding for a visit to Santiago to talk about the subject of one of the chapters of this book.

A number of individuals invited me to write or speak about topics that permitted me to explore areas of inquiry which would eventually contribute to or form part of this book: Peter Beardsell, Catherine Davies, Ricardo de la Fuente, Alan Deyermond, Lynne Diamond-Nigh, José Donoso, Steven DuPouy, Evelyn Fishburn, Stephen Hart, Nancy Kason, Donald Shaw, Barbara Weissberger, Edwin Williamson. Related lectures or papers were given at: University of Georgia, Georgia State University, University of Virginia, Old Dominion University, Universidad de Valladolid, Universidad de Chile, University of Edinburgh, University of St. Andrews, Queen Mary and Westfield College (University of London), Association of Hispanists of Great Britain and Ireland (Belfast), Society for Latin American Studies (Bradford), South Atlantic Modern Language Association (Knoxville, Tennessee), Kentucky Foreign Language Conference (Lexington), Louisiana Conference on Hispanic Languages and Literature (New Orleans), Twentieth Century Literature Conference (Louisville, Kentucky), Friends of Women's Studies Work in Progress (Norfolk, Virginia). Versions of parts of this book have been published by: *New Novel Review*, *Studies in Twentieth Century Literature*, *Romance Quarterly*, *Bulletin of Hispanic Studies*, Támesis.

Finally, I would like to thank John Gledson for encouraging me to write about Clarice Lispector, Elaine Dawson for her help in the preparation of the manuscript, Anita Roy and her staff at MUP for their patience and, above all, Barbara Weissberger who hindered and helped me in the best possible ways.

London, 1994                                                                                              P.S.

# Chapter 1

# The Boom and beyond: Latin America and the not so new novel

The adjective 'new' has formed part of a number of terms routinely used in literary criticism to categorise modern Latin American fiction, most notably 'new novel' or 'new narrative' – 'nueva novela' or 'nueva narrativa'. However, such terms, though providing an often useful and undeniably attractive label, may, on closer inspection seem loose and perhaps even misleading. One problem is that the whole notion of the Latin American new novel has become bound up with the phenomenon of the so-called 'Boom', that is the eruption in the 1960s of a 'new' kind of experimental Latin American fiction onto the international scene. But what was so new about it? And if it was so 'new', did it ever become 'old'? And is the expression 'new novel', by definition, inapplicable to much subsequent fiction, say since the 1960s? While the Boom is associated with the sixties, many major examples of the new narrative were published in the 1940s and fifties. Borges' *Ficciones* came out as a collection in 1944. Asturias' *El Señor Presidente* appeared in 1946, having been started back in 1922. Rulfo's *Pedro Páramo*, one of the most important pieces of new narrative, dates from 1955. Carpentier and Onetti were already publishing major works in these decades too, while a number of precursors of the Latin American new novel had written their finest works earlier still. Indeed the 'new novel' of the sixties seems somewhat less 'new', when it is recalled that Macedonio Fernández's extraordinarily modern text *Museo de la Novela de la Eterna*, though published (posthumously) at the height of the Boom in 1967, was in fact written much earlier (Macedonio actually died in 1952). Anybody reading or overhearing a description of Macedonio's 'belarte' – in which the ideas of a fixed identity and a fixed reality are under-

mined through the use of depthless characters, fifty-six prologues
and an open ending which invites readers to use the present text to
recreate their own – might be forgiven for thinking it was a writer
of the Boom who was being described. Equally it might be argued
that many significant 'new novels' appeared after the 1960s: Roa
Bastos' *Yo el Supremo* in 1974, Fernando del Paso's *Palinuro de
México* in 1975, and Fuentes' *Terra Nostra* in 1977. At the same
time, the now common term 'post-Boom' implies some kind of
rupture in the chronology of the new novel. The novels of Manuel
Puig, for instance, are usually regarded as marking a break of sorts
with the mainstream of Boom narrative, yet they clearly also
continue in a vein very typical of the new novel. The works of
Donoso and Vargas Llosa in the 1970s and early eighties differ
sharply from their earlier production: does this mean their later
fiction cannot be examples of the new novel? And what about
writers like the three (rather different) Cubans, José Lezama Lima,
Severo Sarduy and Guillermo Cabrera Infante, all of whom had
major novels published in the 1960s but, though 'associated' with
the new novel, would not always be automatically linked to the
Boom?

Clearly, playing the dating game does not necessarily get us
much closer to defining the new novel. In this sense the sixties are
more interesting for what they connote rather than what they literally denote. The sixties *represents* newness, change, breaking with
tradition. Steven Boldy pinpoints this when he talks of Cortázar's
*Rayuela*, the most quintessentially 'sixties' novel of the Boom (and
consequently perhaps the most dated), as 'the cosmopolitan novel
of the 1960s', 'excitingly of the 1960s in its hail of cobblestones
against the *gendarmerie* of moral, vital and verbal automatisms and
conformity'.[1] Yet of the big Latin American novels of the 1960s,
this is the one which is closest to Macedonio's *Museo de la Novela
de la Eterna*. The Boom, then, is merely an exemplification of the
sense of 'break with tradition' that has come to be associated with
the new novel. In this way, while the term 'new novel' may cover a
wide range of differing types of text, it can be used to categorise a
kind of modern fiction in Latin America which is 'new' insofar as it
rejects the premises and formal structures of conventional realism.
The argument runs basically as follows. Conventional realism is
based on the assumption that reality is a readily observable and
knowable phenomenon that can be observed and documented in

writing. This is all the more true in Latin America where fiction in the first half of the twentieth century was largely social realist in nature, attempting to paint authentically local or regional social, economic or geographical conditions. Generally, the 'new novelist' perceives realism as fundamentally flawed in its simplistic supposition that reality is essentially observable, comprehensible and transferable to a written medium (and, by implication, therefore, ordered and coherent) and, more specifically, perceives Latin American social realism as misleading in its attempt to present to its readers a socially or politically skewed or slanted vision of society as a mirror of reality. In the new novel, therefore, regional issues give way to universal epistemological or ontological scepticism and the ordered narrative form which reflected an ordered world view gives way to a fragmented, distorted or fantastic narrative form which reflects a perception of a contradictory, ambiguous or even chaotic reality. Hence the new novel is a literary space in which the reader plays an active rather than a passive role, seeking (as a reader as in life) an order in an apparently formless world rather than simply accepting a previously given version of it.

If there is anything which defines the new novel in Latin America or unites its disparate manifestations, it is this desire somehow to re-evaluate or reject the values, belief systems and formal or stylistic patterns that lie at the roots of traditional realism.[2] Yet even this claim is fraught with complications or inconsistencies. Critics of Balzac, Galdós (or, worse, Flaubert or Machado de Assis) would be dismayed to see their authors so accused of reductivity or of being free of ambiguity. After all, Galdós' *Tristana*, for example, ends with the words: '¿Eran felices uno y otro? ... Tal vez'.[3] What is this if not a crucial ambiguity at the very point of closure and completion of a supposedly traditional realist text? What is Machado's *Dom Casmurro*, with its complex and still controversial narratorial stance, if not a masterpiece of ambiguity? Latin American regionalism is no less closed or certain. In fact, a novel like Rivera's *La vorágine* shows a considerable degree of psychological awareness and complexity, while even the most seemingly obvious example of social realist naivete like Ciro Alegría's *El mundo es ancho y ajeno* reveals a tension or ambiguity between the indigenous world it seeks to portray and the position of the narrator who is plainly from without that tradition. A similar problem occurs with Azuela's *Los de abajo*, in which a middle-class liberal writing about

peasant revolution portrays his protagonists as an ill-defined
mixture of rugged hero and aimless delinquent. In Gallegos' *Doña
Bárbara*, the hero Santos Luzardo is as attracted to the enticing
world of the villain Bárbara as she is to him. The crude distinction
between 'civilisation' and 'barbarism' often used to characterise
this novel is not so clear cut, nor indeed was it ever: even
Sarmiento's seminal 1845 essay on the theme, *Facundo*, romanti-
cises the gaucho culture of the pampas at the same time that it identifies them irrevocably with the lawless forces of barbarism that
were thought to be undermining the new Republics' movement
towards progress and civilisation. And if Güiraldes' 1926 gauch-
esque novel, *Don Segundo Sombra*, seeks to reassess Sarmiento's
notion of 'civilisation-versus-barbarism', it generates an equal,
though inverse, pattern of ambiguity. In a similar way to Alegría
and Azuela, Güiraldes loses himself in the paradox of being a
'culto' author using a latterly cultivated narrator to describe a
rustic, rough-and-ready cowboy lifestyle, undermining – according
to Carlos J. Alonso in his interesting re-reading of the autochthonous novel – 'the assumed organicity between writing and its referent'.[4] Earlier, Beardsell had perceptively drawn attention to the
crucial importance of the episode of the knife duel involving
Antenor Barragán in the twenty-third chapter of the novel.[5] Here,
the otherwise idealised gaucho hero, Don Segundo, effectively
forces an innocent young man into a fight that ends in a gruesome
death for his opponent, ruining the young man's life and provoking
horror and astonishment in Don Segundo's young disciple, Fabio,
who represents the young Argentina which must learn its future
values from its own gaucho past. Hero and ruffian, threat and
example, merge into a heady, possibly dangerous, and certainly
thoroughly ambiguous cocktail.

Now, of course, this ambiguity in the telluric novel is precisely
the sort of limitation that the 'break-with-tradition' theory alludes
to when it accuses the 'traditional' Latin American novel of offering a biased or misleading version of reality: the idea that authors
like Alegría, Azuela, Gallegos and Güiraldes purport (or at least it
is claimed they purport) to offer an objective, 'realistic' account of
the outside world, when in fact they are steering their readers
towards their own particular sociopolitical interpretation of the
outside world. The ambiguities noted above, then, would be nothing more than the inevitable inconsistencies of their own inconsis-

tent ideological position. It is interesting that ambiguity is dismissed as ideological inconsistency in regionalist fiction while it is prized above all else in the so-called 'new novel'. Could it be that the new novel has more in common with early twentieth-century Latin American fiction than it sometimes likes to claim? Could it even be that the new novel itself is just as inconsistent or ideologically inconsistent as it is ambiguous?

When one compares some of the themes and contexts of the 'traditional' and 'new' novel, one notices that they are not really always all that different. A facile distinction is sometimes made between the traditional novel as rural and the new novel as urban. But, like the notion of the 'sixties', the 'urban' is, in part at least, essentially an image or representation of modernity or 'break-with-tradition'. There were, anyway, urban social realist novels in Latin America before the Boom, like Manuel Rojas' *Hijo de ladrón*, and, what is more, as far as the new novel is concerned, for every *La ciudad y los perros*, there is a *La casa verde* or a *Pedro Páramo* or an *Hijo de hombre* or a *Cien años de soledad*. Indeed these novels all dwell on the same concerns of many 'novelas de la tierra': man's struggle with his natural environment and the exploitation of rural areas, peasants and Indians. So, to some extent, what is new about the 'new novel' is not its content. This would seem to suggest that the 'newness' of modern Latin American fiction is largely a matter of form. Yet formal experimentation is usually justified on the grounds of the 'newness' of content. If form and content ought to be indistinguishable, then the Latin American new novel may seem to be little more than a showcase for flashy formal games. It is frequently argued that the ludic element in writers like Cortázar or Sarduy serves some kind of social or political function (a problematic claim, in itself), but the formal poses of those novels with a more obviously concrete social, political or historical background may be more difficult to justify. It is a commonplace of Vargas Llosa criticism to view the labyrinthine structures of his earlier novels as a plastic symbol of a corrupt society, though essentially they are simply realist novels presented in a fragmented form – and often, a rather contrived one at that (consider the artificial scene-setting of the final chapter of *La casa verde* or the structurally-dependent twists involving Jaguar in *La ciudad y los perros* or don Fermín in *Conversación en la Catedral*). In Fuentes' *La muerte de Artemio Cruz*, the somewhat arbitrary and certainly mechanical rotation of narrative viewpoint adds little to a largely conventional portrayal of Mexican society: indeed the twelve fragments of third-person narration which provide the backbone of the text are pretty straightforward in themselves. And while no one would doubt the sincerity of Roa Bastos in *Hijo de hombre*, it is difficult to reconcile fully (beyond a discussion of the narrative's formal dramatisation of the relationship between the intellectual and the masses) the tradition of protest fiction which informs much of the novel's content and the work's fragmentary narrative form which problematises the whole question of our ability to understand reality, thus problematising the element of sociopolitical comment. What makes the new novel 'new', then, is the way it looks: which suggests that its allure may lie at the surface rather than at any truly deeper level.

Of course, it would be wrong to deny any profundity of ideas in the new novel. The point is that there is nothing especially unusual about them – both at the social or political level in someone like the early Vargas Llosa or at the existential or metaphysical level even in someone like Borges. The novelty really lies in the presentation. However, this is a rather embarrassing admission for educated middle-class readers or, worse, for professional literary critics and so, not surprisingly, much of the debate on the new novel has concentrated on what the novels have to say. There are usually two broad areas of concern, each broadly in conflict with the other. In a review published in 1989 Gerald Martin refers to this basic 'divergence of perspective' and 'permanent bone of contention', which he sums up as 'the *BHS-BLAR* debate', referring to the traditionally liberal humanist *Bulletin of Hispanic Studies* and the more sociopolitically oriented *Bulletin of Latin American Research*.[6] Essentially, he is differentiating between those critics who approach texts from an existential, supposedly 'universal' angle, seeing them as explorations of the wider human condition, and those critics who choose to see or have to see such texts in the specific, local context of Latin American history and politics. Martin's crusading 1989 book, *Journeys Through the Labyrinth: Latin American Fiction in the Twentieth Century* (published by Verso, the 'imprint of New Left Books'), leaves us in no doubt about which side his sympathies lie with. But, of course, the distinction drawn by Martin is exactly that drawn by his current critical polar opposite, Donald Shaw, in the latter's well-known survey of the criticism of *Cien años de soledad* published in *Ibero-Amerikanisches Archiv* in 1977. Shaw's article boils down to a complaint about 'the contradiction which subsists between seeing *Cien años de soledad* as primarily a novel about Latin America, and therefore in some degree a novel of protest with a positive intention, and seeing it as a novel about the changeless tragedy of the human condition'.[7] Shaw's own position is made clear in his book on the new novel, *Nueva narrativa hispanoamericana*, where he explicitly argues 'la desaparición de la vieja novela "comprometida" y la emergencia de la novela "metafísica". En vez de mostrar la injusticia y desigualdad sociales con el propósito de criticarlas, la novela tiende, cada vez más, a explorar la condición humana y la angustia del hombre contemporáneo ...'[8]

There are big problems here. The sociopolitical approach carries the inevitable implication that the new novel is not particularly new because it is broaching the same sort of themes as earlier fiction. Yet, plainly, there is a difference between the new novel and the earlier traditional novel (and many major works of authors like Borges, Donoso, Onetti and Sabato are not obviously political in any strong sense). The 'universal' or existential approach inevitably disrupts any level of sociopolitical critique. Yet, plainly, the Latin American new novel is highly political (and the major novels of the so-called 'Big Four', Cortázar, Fuentes, García Márquez and Vargas Llosa can hardly be considered unpolitical). Martin and Shaw represent the best in both approaches, but what is interesting is that they both lay the blame, in large part, on the literary critics rather than the literary authors. The problem seems to be that certain critics (i.e., those who do not agree with them) choose to read the way they do rather than that certain authors choose to write the way they do. Yet surely many, if not most, modern Latin American novels can be read both ways. To be sure, they must be read both ways. And many more ways too. It is often a feature of criticism, which likes boxes and categories, to try and fit relatively random phenomena into an ordered pattern. But the reality is that the whole history of the new novel in Latin America is riddled with contradictions, contradictions which may be ultimately mutually exclusive.

The biggest problem for critics of the new novel is how to reconcile the political dimension with the issue of the problematisation of reality and literature's relation to it. For instance, we are often

told that one of the factors which, historically, allowed the Boom
to take place, what gave it unity and cohesion, was the sense of
solidarity and hope generated in Latin American writers by the
Cuban Revolution. Yet equally we are repeatedly told that the theoretical basis of the new novel is a rejection of the simplistic, black-
and-white view of traditional Latin American social realism, a
development which, at the very least, complicates, at worst, undermines the possibility of a positive political analysis of reality.
Perhaps this is why Cortázar's story on the Cuban Revolution,
'Reunión', is tucked away rather disconcertingly in the otherwise
totally contrasting collection of semi-surreal fantasies in his book
*Todos los fuegos el fuego*. Perhaps this is why Vargas Llosa, the
young author of the biting social and political satire on modern
Peru, *La ciudad y los perros*, should declare of the Big Bang of the
Boom that: 'la novela deja de ser "latinoamericana", se libera de
esa servidumbre'.[9] Maybe this is why we are told so many times of
the towering and inescapable influence of Borges as another deci-
sive factor in the growth of the new novel and the emergence of the
Boom, while that same author is so often awkwardly shoved to one
side and dismissed as an unfortunate reactionary blip on an otherwise impeccably Latin Americanist screen of political fiction. Then
there is the whole question of Carpentier and Asturias' forging a
genuinely Latin American, Third-World consciousness – but only
after they have imported from France the lessons of a European
Surrealism. Carpentier's notion of 'lo real maravilloso', though
attempting to promote an authentically Latin American identity,
risks shutting out the Latin American reader by encouraging him or
her to 'marvel' at their own Latin American reality and thereby
adopt what is effectively a non-participatory, external, even
European perspective.[10] As for Asturias' *El Señor Presidente*, whose
opening pages have been described as the first pages of the new
novel,[11] it is a political novel, a novel of dictatorship, but one which
takes place nowhere and at no particular time; where the political
revolution crumbles as soon as it starts, and the only real rebellion
is that of a presidential favourite marrying an enemy's daughter.
And above all, a novel, whose expressionistic (often comic) technique, mixed with an attempt to recreate the feel of a subjectively-
constructed reality, risks fracturing the link with external reality
and any consequent faith in an ability to assess it objectively. That
other major milestone along the road to the Boom, Rulfo's *Pedro*

*Páramo*, is equally difficult to pin down: an attack on *caciquismo* and a critique of the Mexican Revolution, it is frequently claimed, yet the *cacique* is viewed internally as well as externally, the question of his responsibility problematised by his humanisation, while the Revolution is of little interest to him (one of its principal targets!) and of little relevance as far as most of the rest of the characters are concerned. And the contradictions are not resolved by the Boom itself. Continuing the trend of *Pedro Páramo, La muerte de Artemio Cruz*, for example, presents the journey through life of its protagonist from ardent revolutionary to corrupt capitalist as a pathetic attempt at self-justification, but also as an inevitable fight for survival in an unavoidably tough world and even as a transient irrelevancy in the eternal scheme of inevitable oblivion. The great speaker, thinker and Latin Americanist, Carlos Fuentes offers what can only be described as a highly ambivalent moral standpoint here. One might even be forgiven for suspecting that the new novel, of the Boom in particular, depends on ambivalence and ambiguity for its literary appeal, yet needs attractive political certainties for its promotion and marketing. Moreover, in terms of world literature at the time of the Boom and after, there is nothing especially different or exciting about ambiguity and technical experimentation, suggesting that the success of the new novel in translation owes much to the exoticism factor of Latin America and its politics – despite the efforts of so-called 'Marvellous' or 'Magical Realism' to develop a non-eurocentric Latin Americanist viewpoint. Selling the new novel, then, appears to involve denying what it seems to be all about.

The author who most obviously shares the Fuentes-like split between public persona and literary persona is, of course, the most successful of them all, Gabriel García Márquez. Yet the publication of *Cien años de soledad* in 1967 marks a kind of watershed in the history of the new novel. García Márquez is the biggest of the Big Four and is often blithely included amongst lists of the 'typical' new novelists of the Boom. Yet the linear structure and, above all, the popular tone of *Cien años de soledad* have little in common with the intellectual posturing of *Rayuela*, the structural complexity of Vargas Llosa's first three novels, or the attempts at portentous verbal pyrotechnics by Fuentes. Indeed, by the late 1960s/early 1970s the Boom was effectively over. The split caused by the arrest of the Cuban poet Heberto Padilla in 1971, on the grounds of

counter-revolutionary activities, dissolved the illusion of creative
unity centred around the Cuban Revolution, while the schism
within the Seix Barral publishing house at the turn of the decade
partially derailed one of the most influential instruments in the
promotion and internationalisation of the Latin American new
novel in the 1960s. In fact, the novel which would have received the
1970 Premio Biblioteca Breve from Seix Barral, had it not been
suspended due to this rift, was Donoso's *El obsceno pájaro de la
noche*, a long, tortuous, massively difficult work, perhaps the
pinnacle of the new narrative's penchant for complex structures –
and, curiously, not really a very new 'new novel', more like 'more
of the same', a work which is in some ways emblematic of the
climax and exhaustion of the new novel's ability to shock and
surprise and an indication of the need for a change in direction. As
José Promis Ojeda has remarked, 'con esta novela se cierra y se
cumple un ciclo, más allá del cual no existe otra posibilidad expre-
siva. Como en el caso de *Cien años de soledad*, la novela de Donoso
es el broche que cierra una etapa, después de la cual sólo cabe
cambiar de rumbo'.[12] Donoso himself makes the same point about
this need for change. Referring to his fiction after *El obsceno pájaro
de la noche*, he says: 'Lo que me interesa ... es hacer una batida
contra la aceptada novela clásica: no la novela clásica antigua sino
la contemporánea... . Es decir la novela que bajo el disfraz de una
libertad narrativa forja una serie de reglas de las cuales no es posible prescindir. Por ejemplo, todas las reglas terribles que me parece
que usa Cortázar: *Rayuela* es un muestrario de reglas encubiertas
que forjan toda una teoría de la novela: esta teoría pretende
destruir la novela clásica pero forja otra novela clásica'.[13] Indeed,
change was underway and on the way. This is not a clear-cut
process, but suffice it to say for present purposes that a key feature
of this stage of development in the new novel was a movement away
from complexity towards more popular forms. *Cien años de soledad*
is a case in point. But round about the same time *Vista del amanecer
en el trópico* was shedding its hard-edged political concerns and
transforming itself into Cabrera Infante's playful tongue-twister,
*Tres tristes tigres*. While Cabrera Infante celebrated the world of
films, songs, night-clubs and fast cars, along came Manuel Puig
with *La traición de Rita Hayworth* and *Boquitas pintadas*, focusing
on the *cursi*, small-town middle-classes, and engaging in a bitter-
sweet revelry in tangos, soap opera and B-movies. Established

authors soon changed tack too. Donoso himself never returned to the tone of *El obsceno pájaro*, and produced works like the deceptive soft-porn detective novel *La misteriosa desaparición de la marquesita de Loria*. Even Vargas Llosa, the man who had declared that there was no place for humour in literature, started writing funny, accessible novels in the 1970s, trying his hand at manipulating soap opera à la Puig in *La tía Julia y el escribidor*. The Boom, it seems, had gone 'pop' and, before long, a post-Boom of sorts was in full swing.[14]

However, it is the introduction of popular culture or mass culture into the equation which rips the new novel apart at the same moment as it revitalises it: it may be enriching on a literary level, it may even sell more books, but on the ideological level it opens up a huge fissure in the new novel's intellectual basis, to such a degree that the 'text' seems to collapse in on itself at the very point of its artistic culmination. The problem really is one of playing politics with the popular (especially since the relative accessibility of the post-Boom is frequently identified with a tendency towards greater political directness). Is the liberation of the popular really a triumphant blow against fixed bourgeois traditional models? Is the dissolution of the boundary between the serious and the useful, on the one hand, and the popular and the playful, on the other, really an effective attack on the utilitarian ethic of productivity which underlies western and capitalist thought and, likewise, an attack on institutionalisation and closed sign systems? Or is it a nonsense to say that fiction can be politically useful by being useless on a literary level? Does not the dissolution of the gap between High Culture and Popular Culture undermine the very popular quality of popular culture and generate a new form of elitism? Does not the urge to situate popular culture in a 'new novel' framework imply the hierarchical superiority of the framework over the popular element contained within it? And is not popular culture (or mass culture at least) actually dangerous anyway, since it denies individuality and promotes given role models? And does the new 'new novel' draw attention to this danger at the very same time that it glorifies mass culture?

Now, of course, popular culture and mass culture are not always the same thing. It is as we get closer to the 'mass' end of the scale in Puig, Donoso, Vargas Llosa and many of the so-called 'younger' (i.e., less known) writers of the post-Boom that the ideological

implications or complications become most apparent. García
Márquez moves towards the 'mass' end later in his career, but in
*Cien años de soledad* popular culture is not a question of TV,
Hollywood or youth cults, but of writing an entertaining book for
wide consumption and, more problematically, recreating the popular viewpoint of a Third-World community. The difficulty of reconciling a serious political or negative existential position with a text
written for popular, mass consumption is an obvious one: back in
1977 Shaw was already talking of 'the contradiction between the
content of the work, which is generally negative however we interpret it, and the flippant, frivolous, sometimes even hilarious tone,
which is consistently maintained …' (326). The question of recreating the popular point of view is even more problematic and
suggests a link between the inconsistencies of García Márquez's
brand of Magical Realism and the dichotomy apparent later in the
works of writers like Puig. Magical Realism in García Márquez is
basically a matter of presenting extraordinary events in a natural
way, thus allowing the reader to share the perspective of the characters. This, though, goes against the idea that the novel's undermining of conventional notions of reality and its well-known play
of literary games and in-jokes constitute a negation of reality.
Rather, then, it must be a political question of a reinterpretation of
reality. Utilising the oral style inherited from his grandmother's
fantastic story-telling, García Márquez seems to want to reproduce
a traditional, popular rural perspective – challenging the hegemony
of the alien, dominant, imported culture and reinstating the value
of the community's own cultural perspective. The 'magical' element
therefore represents freedom of imagination and consequently
revolution: that is, the freedom to imagine an alternative destiny.

However, a similar conclusion can be reached by inverting
totally the whole concept of Magical Realism. It can be argued that
the magical is a construct of alien, imperialist, dominant or
exploitative forces which transform simple realities into myths. The
alien imagination is an agent of repression which suppresses historical truths and encourages the masses to languish in a kind of
submissive, unquestioning stupor. In *Cien años de soledad*, the
young literature buff Gabriel (who goes off to Paris with the
complete works of Rabelais and is the grandson of Gerineldo
Márquez) clearly represents the author, and his great friendship
with the last of the Buendías, Aureliano Babilonia, is founded on

their mutual faith in the historical truth of the banana massacre: 'de modo que Aureliano y Gabriel estaban vinculados por una especie de complicidad, fundada en hechos reales en los que nadie creía, y que habían afectado sus vidas hasta el punto de que ambos se encontraban a la deriva en la resaca de un mundo acabado, del cual sólo quedaba la nostalgia'.[15] The author's 'nostalgia', then, is for 'hechos reales', not the 'magical' community perspective and certainly not the self-indulgent notion of fiction as fiction, literature as play.

The conclusion that has to be drawn from all this is that far from creating a fusion of narrative and popular perspective, the novel is based on a direct distinction between the two. Hence, while there is much talk in the novel of the circularity of time, the narrative structure, as experienced by the reader, is largely logical, straightforward and linear. It is as if the author wants the reader to see through the magical and confront reality. Indeed, as Edwin Williamson has pointed out, Magical Realism depends on irony.[16] The reader may experience, like José Arcadio Buendía, a sense of wonderment when faced with 'un enorme bloque transparente, con infinitas agujas internas en las cuales se despedazaba en estrellas de colores la claridad del crepúsculo': but the reader knows it is only ice and does not share the character's belief that it is 'el diamante más grande del mundo' or 'el gran invento de nuestro tiempo' (23). In this respect, there is an important distinction to be drawn between Melquíades' manuscripts (which are mixed-up, 'magical' or non-historical, and with which the characters are obsessed) and García Márquez's text (which is linear and historical, the version of Macondo experienced by the readers). And so there is a significant parting of the ways between Aureliano Babilonia and the author-figure Gabriel. The final Buendía immerses himself in the labyrinthine world of the old gypsy's parchments as Macondo collapses, while Gabriel *leaves* the magical world of Macondo, following the advice of the '*sabio* catalán' (my italics), who 'perdió su maravilloso sentido de la irrealidad, hasta que terminó por recomendarles a todos que se fueran de Macondo' (348). The popular perspective, then, is a myth, a reflection of a state of submission. Realism is more important than magic.

Now, in a sense, that last statement is a necessary one for a historical or political reading of the novel. And it is fairly obvious that *Cien años de soledad* is a novel which has to be read historically or politically. Yet, in another sense, that statement is clearly a nonsense, for the appeal and success of the novel depend more than anything else on its creation of a 'magical' world view stemming from the popular perspective of a rural Latin American community. Yet the only possible resolution of the contradiction is to make a highly selective or reductive reading of the text. The alternative is to say that the novel can be read or must be read in many different ways (but then these contradictory readings must wipe each other out) or to say that the novel is only a fiction and not reality (but that is to conclude that the novel has nothing to say except to tell its own tale). Where does this lead us? Unfortunately, it would seem to lead us nowhere in particular.

The attempt to subsume popular mass culture into the sophisticated world of the new novel, particularly in the 1970s, led the Latin American novel even deeper into a literary and ideological minefield. Puig's *El beso de la mujer araña* is an important case in point and will occupy our attention in the next chapter. Though the novel's pattern of inconsistency will be emphasised here, Puig did, nonetheless, along with Cabrera Infante (the subject of the third chapter), influence decisively the direction of the new novel from the early 1970s onwards. Perhaps the most obvious example is *La tía Julia y el escribidor*, by the previously well-established Vargas Llosa. Like *Cien años de soledad* to some degree, and certainly like *El beso de la mujer araña*, this novel seems to wish to insert popular discourse into 'high culture' but ends up demonstrating a clear hierarchical distinction between the two levels, though, as the fourth chapter will argue, in a different and in some ways less problematic way. Even so, the ideological implications of such textual obfuscation are quite serious. Robin Fiddian has commented that 'in Latin America, ... writing and politics go hand in hand'.[17] Undoubtedly true. But just where is it that they are going together? Vargas Llosa's previous novel, *Pantaleón y las visitadoras*, for example, is more of a problem. Here, the absurd military scheme of the Special Service of whores to service the randy and unruly soldiers posted in remote jungle garrisons is clearly a parody of the outlandish schemes developed and imposed by the central authorities in Latin America (often to quell disorder created by them in the first place). It is an inversion of the traditional civilisation-versus-barbarism ethic. But at the same time the novel reaffirms that ethic. The story of the dangerous fanatical sect of Hermano Francisco basically tells us that the interior *is* barbaric and needs to be tamed for civilisation to progress. This is why the story of Captain Pantoja and his Special Service is funny, while that of Hermano Francisco is decidedly not. The popular tone is undone by a lack of any apparent popular identification. Another established author, Carlos Fuentes, gets into similar difficulties in his stab at a popular form in his 1978 spy thriller *La cabeza de la hidra* where once more, the popular form is undermined and the text betrays an unresolved tension between the desire to comment on reality and a tendency to break the link between fiction and reality (a topic to be considered in the fifth chapter). When questioned by me regarding a similar gap between the deliberately artificial form of his *Casa de campo*, with its self-expressed mistrust of the mimetic properties of narrative, and his avowed intention of writing a political novel, José Donoso's reply was: 'It certainly is a contradiction'. He went on to say that 'the best novels contain this negation, this ambiguity, this contradiction'. True perhaps, but where does such 'negation', such 'contradiction', leave the politics? His conclusion was simply that 'things can be and not be at the same time'.[18] Of course, one could trot out again the familiar but, frankly, feeble argument that the attack on bourgeois literary norms is a coded attack on bourgeois social and political values. There is no automatic connection between literary revolution and revolutionary literature. The point about many of the later novels of the Boom or post-Boom is that they are the sort of novels readers want to consume. Many may quite simply appeal to an established bourgeois readership or market, offering them a series of accessible entertainments, spiced with a dash of experimentalism and garnished with a political topping. The reader can therefore be entertained while enjoying an apparent sense of intellectual challenge and the vicarious thrill of armchair political engagement. The market's power to normalise may be stronger than the new novel's power or willingness to fight norms.

It may not be entirely surprising, then, that someone like García Márquez – who seems to present the public face of a highly committed political figure – could end up writing something like *El amor en los tiempos de cólera*. Robin Fiddian and Stephen Minta have written some good work which presents the novel in a social, political and historical light.[19] But this is no modern *Madame Bovary*, as some would like to see it. It is not a parody of the sentimental novel, but revels in its sentimentality in a way that probably would have

horrified Flaubert. One cannot really see the novel as an elaboration of a popular triumph over the positivist rationalism and eurocentrism of Dr Juvenal Urbino. After all, Juvenal Urbino's scientific
rationalism does help stave off a plague of cholera and his wife does
love him. Her relationship with Florentino Ariza at the age of
nearly eighty years, after a wait on his part of more than fifty years,
may run counter to the clinical rationality of Juvenal Urbino: but
Florentino Ariza is, in a gentle sort of way, rather laughable and
hardly a genuinely subversive alternative to the doctor. Indeed, if
the novel does exalt disorder and rebellion, it also shows the value
of fidelity and stability. Whereas Juvenal Urbino always insisted on
travelling to Europe, Florentino Ariza and Fermina Daza find their
love on a journey in Colombia, along the River Magdalena, in a
boat made in Colombia. But the difference is not so great. The boat
is called *Nueva Fidelidad*. Its predecessor (which was not built in
local shipyards and can therefore be associated with Juvenal
Urbino) was called *Fidelidad*. There has been no revolutionary
transition or iconoclastic break here. The only break of any sort
comes at the end when the couple escape from reality, as the ship's
captain agrees to declare the vessel in a state of quarantine, so that
the couple can be alone together. In other words, their charming
love affair does what the characters of *Cien años de soledad* have
been criticised for doing: they abandon historical time for mythical
time as they drift almost aimlessly along the River Magdalena
aboard the now atemporal world of the *Nueva Fidelidad*, as it flies
its false yellow flag for an unreal quarantine. Could it be that the
publicly progressive socialist author has a secret longing or nostalgia for stability and tradition?

Interestingly enough, this is the only novel of those mentioned
here which does not obviously attempt to subvert the popular genre
it revolves around. Yet in not so doing it perhaps reveals the true
face of the modern Latin American novel: a sophisticated confec-
tion for a well-read liberal public. And indeed that yellow flag, flap-
ping falsely in the wind, is itself a kind of image of the new novel,
as it invites us to read into it a significance which it does not ultimately have. Julio Méndez, the fictional counterpart of José
Donoso, in his novel *El jardin de al lado* refers to 'el mítico nombre
de *boom*', while Donoso himself wrote at the beginning of the
decade of the 1970s that 'el *boom* ha sido un juego'.[20] But, in many
ways, the Boom is more real than the new novel. The Boom did

take place and helped promote an awareness of something called the Latin American new novel. It is that 'new novel' which may be something of a myth or game. The Latin American new novel is a novel which is really rather old, which is based on a rejection of an only notional or imagined conventional realism and whose novelty and fascination lie in an impossible combination of Americanist referentiality and literary self-referentiality. When Antonio Skármeta says that 'la literatura del boom ha hecho más por cubrir que descubrir',[21] he is perhaps exposing the untenability of the new novel, as exemplified by the Boom, at least at the level of ideas. Its coherence, in this sense, is largely an invention of literary criticism. The new novel resists reduction to any cohesive system. Therein lies its strength as literature and its weakness as ideology.

What follows is an attempt to explore some of these areas of strength and weakness. The notion of 'politics' will be employed in a broad sense (that is, not just concerning matters of government and the state but also the broader arena of power and personal or sexual politics). The term 'popular' will refer mainly to mass culture but also to subjects like accessibility and social class. Differing degrees of conflict and reconciliation will be identified or, at least, posited. And, it should be stressed that the focus will be on the articulation of such problems within fiction itself rather than on the dynamics of popular culture as something other than the literary.[22] Adopting a conceptual rather than strictly chronological layout, the two major figures influential in changing the direction of the new novel will be considered first. Puig will be used to illustrate some of the central contradictions outlined above, while Cabrera Infante will then be availed of to develop further some of the theoretical issues concerning the post-Boom (and the related matter of postmodernism), which are actually more open to difference and dispute than has so far been suggested – in particular, the vexed question of what actually constitutes the 'popular'. Three previously 'canonised' authors of the Boom whose later work manifests the influence of the shift towards the popular will then be examined. First Vargas Llosa, whose *La tía Julia y el escribidor* is often linked by critics to the work of Puig and Cabrera Infante, but who, albeit in a not terribly politically correct way, can be seen to resolve the conflicting demands of the High and the Low, and then Fuentes whose *La cabeza de la hidra* may not. The third established author is Donoso: his *La misteriosa desaparición de la marquesita*

*de Loria* – a less cumbersome or overt effort at reconciling politics
and play than *Casa de campo* – also manages a degree of success,
but while avoiding the arguably limited 'political' perspective of
Vargas Llosa (though within what some might perceive as a more
limited literary project). Following on from this discussion of the
major players, the seventh chapter will offer a view of the post-
Boom proper – and, in a less critical vein, propose some reasons for
its possible inconsistencies – by looking closely at one of the new
names to emerge from it, Mexico's Gustavo Sainz and his *La
princesa del Palacio de Hierro*. Finally, the book will close with a
pair of chapters on two women novelists who represent two
contrasting approaches to the issues raised in this discussion. In the
chosen novel by the Brazilian Clarice Lispector, the dilemma of the
intellectual writer struggling with the conscience's urge to counte-
nance the popular (in the sense here also of the 'popular' classes) is
the theme, while the demonstrably popular (in the sense of
eminently accessible) *La casa de los espíritus* by Isabel Allende will
be seen as one of the best attempts – controversially, perhaps, given
its assumed conservatism in the eyes of some academics – to
combine politics with the popular as it effectively seeks to demystify the new novel of the Boom. The pattern described, then, will
not ultimately be a hopeless one of irreconcilable opposites but one
of potential meaningful resolution.

## Notes

[1]Steven Boldy, 'Julio Cortázar: *Rayuela*', in Philip Swanson (ed.),
*Landmarks in Modern Latin American Fiction*, Routledge, London and
New York, 1990, p. 118. After each initial reference, all subsequent unambiguous references will be incorporated into the main body of the text,
except when in a new chapter, where the full reference will be repeated.

[2]For a fuller account of this point of approach to the new novel, see my
'Introduction: Background to the Boom', in *Landmarks in Modern Latin
American Fiction*, pp. 1–26. It should also be acknowledged that, though
the term Latin American is used throughout, both the aforementioned and
the present chapter concentrate on the specifically Spanish American manifestations of the Latin American new novel. The eighth chapter of this
book will, however, deal with a Brazilian author.

[3]Benito Pérez Galdós, *Obras completas*, Aguilar, Madrid, 1961, vol. v,
p. 1612.

[4]Carlos J. Alonso, *The Spanish American Regional Novel*, Cambridge University Press, Cambridge, 1990, p. 164.

[5]Peter R. Beardsell, '*Don Segundo Sombra* and *Machismo*', *Forum for Modern Language Studies*, XVII, 1981, pp. 302–11.

[6]Gerald Martin, Review of Philip Swanson, *José Donoso: The 'Boom' and Beyond*, Liverpool: Francis Cairns, 1988, in *Bulletin of Latin American Research*, VIII, no. 1, 1989, p. 130.

[7]D.L. Shaw, 'Concerning the Interpretation of *Cien años de soledad*', *Ibero-Amerikanisches Archiv*, III, no. 4, 1977, p. 322.

[8]D.L. Shaw, *Nueva narrativa hispanoamericana*, Cátedra, Madrid, 1981, p. 218.

[9]Quoted by Jean Franco in *Spanish American Literature Since Independence*, Ernest Benn, London, 1973, p. 219.

[10]See Roberto González Echevarría, *Alejo Carpentier: The Pilgrim at Home*, Cornell University Press, Ithaca and London, 1977, pp. 127–78.

[11]W. H. Gass, 'The First Seven Pages of the Boom', *Latin American Literary Review*, XXIX, 1987, pp. 33–56.

[12]José Promis Ojeda, 'La desintegración del orden en la novela de José Donoso', in Antonio Cornejo Polar (ed.), *José Donoso: La destrucción de un mundo*, Fernando García Cambeiro, Buenos Aires, 1975, p. 31.

[13]Interview with Z. Nelly Martínez, *Hispamérica*, XXI, 1978, p. 53.

[14]For a fuller account of the disintegration of the Boom and the emergence of the post-Boom, see my 'Conclusion: After the Boom', in *Landmarks in Modern Latin American Fiction*, pp. 222-45.

[15]Gabriel García Márquez, *Cien años de soledad*, 50th ed., Sudamericana, Buenos Aires, 1978, p. 338.

[16]Edwin Williamson, 'Magical Realism and the Theme of Incest in *One Hundred Years of Solitude*', in Bernard McGuirk and Richard Cardwell (eds.), *Gabriel García Márquez: New Readings*, Cambridge University Press, Cambridge, 1987, p. 46. See also, in the same volume, Gerald Martin, 'On "Magical" and Social Realism in García Márquez', pp. 95–116. For a further elaboration of the conflicting levels of *Cien años de soledad*, see my *Cómo leer a Gabriel García Márquez*, Júcar, Madrid, 1991.

[17] Robin Fiddian, 'Carlos Fuentes: *La muerte de Artemio Cruz*', in my *Landmarks in Modern Latin American Fiction*, p. 98.

[18]Seminar with José Donoso, University of Edinburgh, 1987.

[19]Robin Fiddian, 'A Prospective Post-script: Apropos of *Love in the Times* [sic] *of Cholera*', in McGuirk and Cardwell, pp. 191-205; Stephen Minta, *Gabriel García Márquez: Writer of Colombia*, Jonathan Cape, London, 1987.

[20]José Donoso, *El jardín de al lado*, Seix Barral, Barcelona, 1981, p. 44; *Historia personal del 'boom'*, Anagrama, Barcelona, 1972, p. 124.

[21]Verónica Cortínez, 'Polifonía: entrevista a Isabel Allende y Antonio Skármeta', *Revista Chilena de Literatura*, XXXII, 1988, p. 80.

[22]For a discussion of nonliterary popular culture or the relationship between it and supposedly élite literary cultural forms, see, for example: John Beverley, *Against Literature*, University of Minnesota Press, Minneapolis and London, 1993, and William Rowe and Vivian Schelling, *Memory and Modernity: Popular Culture in Latin America*, Verso, London and New York, 1991. Both these works will be commented upon in the third chapter of the present study.

# Chapter 2

# Manuel Puig and *El beso de la mujer araña*: Sailing away on a boat to nowhere

The Cuban novelist Severo Sarduy has described Manuel Puig's landmark second novel, *Boquitas pintadas*, simultaneously as a 'folletín casi perfecto' and 'el doble irrisorio del folletín'[1] – a serious-minded re-evaluation of the novelette form which nonetheless mocks that form. Sarduy's remarks alert us immediately to the essentially ambivalent and problematic nature of Puig's work. Hence also, the titles of Pamela Bacarisse's two books on Puig are the contradictory-sounding *The Necessary Dream* and *Impossible Choices*, referring to dreams which, though illusory, are somehow necessary and choices which, though impossible to make, simply must be made.[2] Indeed, behind Bacarisse's conclusion on Puig, that his head and his heart are at odds, there may be an even deeper suspicion that Puig's novels point simultaneously in all sorts of opposing and self-thwarting directions. This may be taken by some as an indication of the characteristic ambiguity of the Latin American new novel, whose genesis is intimately connected with a loss of faith in the supposedly simplistic, black-and-white perceptions of reality that underlay the fiction of so-called traditional realism. But equally Puig's texts can be seen simply as ones which consistently deconstruct any ideology or sentiment they appear to be expounding or expressing, texts which attempt to lead somewhere but always end up going nowhere. This is particularly evident in *El beso de la mujer araña* (1976), a work whose multiple facets generate a process of constant self-assertion and self-cancellation, a process which is reflected also, as a matter of fact, in the film version (Héctor Babenco's *Kiss of the Spider Woman*) where there is a fundamental instability between the relationship of its own elements and its relationship to the model on which it is based. In what follows, the film version (a striking embodiment of what is revealed and concealed in Puig's more 'subtle' text) will be used to illuminate our reading of the novel.[3]

The most obvious source of ambiguity is to be found in the links between the two protagonists, Luis Alberto Molina and Valentín Arregui Paz, who share a prison-cell in a Latin American jail. The strikingly contrasting nature of their offences (the former has sexually 'corrupted' an under-age boy, while the latter is a political activist) has been easily resolved by critics. Two basic arguments are usually put forward. First, both men are, on a sexual and political level respectively, nonconformists and victims of oppression; their coming-together as friends and lovers illustrates the necessarily interconnected nature of both levels of repression and shows, as the author's footnotes in the novel seem to suggest, that any effective political rebellion needs to take account of the sexual revolution. However, the second thematic justification for their relationship contradicts the first: both are also seen as evaders of reality and victims of illusions – that of the ideal of love and beauty in the case of Molina and that of the transformation of the world through political action in the case of Valentín. Admittedly, their closeness means that their characters and values both rub off on each other. But is Molina's death during an attempt to pass on a message to his friend's political associates an example of his politicisation or is he just acting like the 'heroína de una película' (285)? Does it matter that Valentín's ideological dogmatism and asceticism have been tempered by his friend's warmth and humanity, if he has led Molina to his death while he himself remains in jail, possibly to die? Is, then, change possible or just a pipe-dream?

This thematic uncertainty is compounded by the intensely ambiguous nature of the characters themselves, more especially Molina. Generally, Molina is regarded as a naive, largely sympathetic character whose kindness and generosity have an ameliorating effect on Valentín's somewhat testy and self-centred personality. But is Molina so naive, so uneducated? In the film version William Hurt portrays him, above all in the early stages, as a knowing, in some ways dominating gay 'type', more camp than feminine. He sounds sarcastic rather than ignorant, when he cheekily tells his cell-mate, 'I detest politics but I'm mad about the leading man.' When Valentín later says that, 'Fantasies are no escape', Molina retorts: 'If you've got the keys to that door, I will gladly follow. Otherwise

I will escape in my own way' – a comment echoed later by his defiant, 'I will cry about whatever I want to!' And in the novel too he is shown to be not unintelligent. His descriptions of film plots are quite stylish and his language and ideas do not always correspond to those of a humble window-dresser. Astonishingly, for example, he is familiar with Pascal:

> — Sí, pero hay razones del corazón que la razón no entiende. Y eso lo dijo un filósofo francés muy de los mejores. Así que te embromé. Y creo que hasta me acuerdo el nombre: Pascal. ¡Chupate esa mandarina! (263)

The clash between the informed tone and the childish tone here is almost incongruous. Moreover, for a man whose favourite films are *Dracula*, *The Wolf Man* and *I Walked with a Zombie* (163), he is surprisingly *au fait* with the opera. He knows Bizet's *Carmen* (72) and earlier reveals a knowledge of *Rigoletto* which Valentín lacks:

> — … y si querés te sigo la película, y si no querés, paciencia, me la cuento yo a mí mismo en voz baja, y saluti tanti, arrivederci, Sparafucile.
> — ¿Quién es Sparafucile?
> — No sabés nada de ópera, es el traidor de *Rigoletto*. (25)

This last quote also hints at another of the ambiguities in Molina's make-up. Despite his good side, Molina is betraying Valentín by spying on him on behalf of the Warden. Though Molina never reveals his companion's secrets and actually foils the plan to weaken Valentín physically and later agrees to pass on a message for him, he still deceives his friend. This idea is conveyed clearly in the film via the punctuation of a scene in which Valentín elaborates on his comment to Molina, 'you're so kind', by a series of flashbacks to the interview with the Warden from which Molina has just returned. And in the novel, Molina's inner thoughts give the game away when we read: '*las enfermeras del turno del día, bromas y sonrisas con pacientes buenos que obedecen todo y comen y duermen pero si se sanan se van para siempre*' (192). If Molina looks after Valentín and nurses him back to health, it is because he is what the activist might call 'una madre castradora' (143). Thus there is a sinister aspect to the image of Molina as 'la mujer araña, que atrapa a los hombres en su tela' (265): true, he has 'saved' Valentín – 'la mujer-araña me señaló con el dedo un camino en la

selva, y ahora no sé por dónde empezar a comer tantas cosas que
me encontré' (286) – but he has done so via guile and seduction.
There is a final twist, though, for the effeminate 'heroína', having
become a kind of *femme fatale*, causes his own seduction and his
own death. But even so, having said all that, there is no denying
that Molina is still very much a likeable character.

Already, then, it is becoming apparent that it is, to say the least,
difficult to pin down *El beso de la mujer araña* to any global interpretation. Things become yet more problematic when we switch
our attention to modes of narrative. One of the most notable
features of the novel is its hybridisation of different types of narrative or levels of discourse. The text is assembled from a pot-pourri
of movie narratives, songs, letters, documents, dialogues, interior
monologues and footnotes. The film also reflects this hybridisation:
the popular romantic thriller is contained within the framework of
a seemingly serious, 'arty' film, a basically American film based on
an Argentinean novel but made by a Brazilian director, with
William Hurt using an obviously American accent alongside Raúl
Julia's Spanish-American accent, both against a background of
Portuguese, as the repeated PAVILHÃO IV sign reminds us (not to
mention the Brazilian actress Sonia Braga playing Marta with a
Brazilian accent, the Spider Woman in silence, and the half-French
half-German Leni Lamaison with an amazing French accent). In a
novel and a film largely concerned with the narration of movies, it
seems obvious, then, that a central interest is the actual construction of discourse, that both novel and film are self-referential in that
ultimately they are reflections on their own creation. In this sense
the two 'texts'[4] problematise the whole issue of narrative or
discourse and their relation to reality.

Of course, self-referentiality does not foreclose the possibility of
a link with an external referent. Given the novel (and film's) political theme, questions of authority and power are raised via the
exploration of the hierarchical structure of discourse. On its most
straightforward (or so it seems) level, this manifests itself in the
opposition of 'popular' narrative and 'serious' narrative. An intriguing feature of the audience reaction to *Kiss of the Spider Woman*
is that they tend to laugh at the film within it – the popular romantic thriller narrated by Molina and made in the style of Hollywood
B-movies of the thirties or forties (though in fact it is a German
Nazi propaganda film, given the title *Destino* in one of the novel's

footnotes). Indeed, in the film of the novel, *Destino* is clearly presented as an exaggerated parody of this genre of popular black-and-white films. Leni, the heroine, pouts divinely at the camera during her first appearance; she is almost a caricature of the typical glamorous French chanteuse; her incredibly over-the-top French accent delivers lines like, 'How could you fall in love with an enemy of France?'; she dramatically clutches her breast and goes faint as the handsome German officer Werner's 'eyes begin to burn into her soul'; and eventually dies in her lover's arms – to the accompaniment of suitable music – having made a noble sacrifice on his behalf and her country's behalf. Meanwhile, the – in *Destino*'s terms – nasty Jews (described as 'weird smugglers') and Resistance workers (represented by a 'hulking club-foot and his half-deaf flunky') are always introduced by menacing music and, in the case of the latter, are blacker-than-black villains. One scene which is particularly parodic is that in which Leni's young friend, Michèle, is run down by the revenge-hungry club-foot and his sidekick after the villain has declared in a mock-French accent: 'Her time is up!' Here there is over-dramatic music and an over-long close-up of the screaming girl frozen into immobility and with hands aloft as the car takes an unnecessarily long time to hit her.

It is fairly plain, then, that the 'arty' film *Kiss of the Spider Woman* wishes to mock the more 'popular' type of movie represented by *Destino*. But this position is, once again, highly problematic. In the novel, as in the film, there is doubtless an implied criticism of the hegemony of Hollywood values and their equivalents: they encourage conformism to stereotyped models and unrealistic escapism (it is significant in this regard that Puig's first novel is entitled *La traición de Rita Hayworth*, i.e., film betrays by purveying false or untrue values). At the same time, though, it is undeniable that Molina's film narrations are extremely enjoyable in their own right. In the novel, the account of *Destino* is glossed by lengthy footnotes which clearly reveal its status as Nazi propaganda; but in Chapter 4 the footnote is confined to the centre of the chapter so as not to spoil the momentum of the thrilling climax to the story which displaces the knowing footnote in the last part of the chapter. The point is that Puig is really re-evaluating popular movies here. As he himself has said:

> Creo que siempre ha habido una especie de despotismo de los géneros culturales respetados con relación a los géneros menores. Yo

pretendo realizar algo muy fácil de seguir para el gran público y, al
mismo tiempo, hecho con cierto rigor. Creo que son muy válidos
ciertos recursos del teatro popular y de la novela popular. El cuidado
de la intriga, el interés anecdótico, el golpe de escena, me parecen
muy legítimos. Lo que me parece inmoral es el aburrimiento.[5]

So, if popular culture aids the submissiveness of the less educated
masses, the educated bourgeoisie are victims of their own snobbery
towards popular art; if popular culture is repressive in one sense, it
can be liberating in another. Again the novel is pulling in two directions simultaneously, though clearly the element of caricature is not
so apparent here as it is in the film version.

But the film version has its own difficulties on this topic. *Kiss of
the Spider Woman* clearly sets itself up as an 'arty' film, worlds
apart from cheap, conventional, mainstream entertainment. This is
the effect of the opening sequence, where a long tracking-shot
around a dark, dank room (the cell) climaxes with a splash of
bright colour in the form of Molina's blue gown and red head-dress
(actually a towel). The striking, perplexing and obviously cineastic
nature of this shot is set against the offscreen and then onscreen
diegetic sound of Molina's narration of the trivial-sounding popular film *Destino*. This technique, then, seems to assert the superiority of Héctor Babenco's film over popular B-movies. The film's link
with popular movies becomes even more apparent when we
compare the 'inner film' (*Destino*) with the 'outer film' (the story of
Molina and Valentín) – in essentially the same way as occurs in the
novel. Graphic editing repeatedly establishes a parallel between
Molina and the star Leni. Meanwhile, the 'bad guys' from the
French Resistance are echoed in the 'outer film' in the shape of the
Warden and his assistant (there seems to be a connection between
the smoking, evil-eyed club-foot and the moustache-fingering,
slant-eyed cripple, the Warden). But just as Leni, despite the pres-
sure from the Resistance, agrees to help the cause of her lover
Werner, so too does Molina avoid action on the prison authorities'
behalf and works instead for the cause of his lover Valentín. Werner
convinces Leni of the righteousness of the German crusade by
showing her an anti-semitic film which purportedly exposes the
cruelty and greed of the Jews. This episode follows a scene in which
the couple dine together, framed by a scene in the 'outer film' in
which Molina and Valentín have just enjoyed a wonderful meal
together. Both couples at this point are growing together in love

and confidence, and therefore Molina's words on the 'inner film' here could equally apply to his own situation vis-à-vis Valentín. He says: 'Leni … begins to see things through Werner's eyes. From that moment on Leni understood Werner's mission – to liberate humanity from injustice and domination.' And so Leni now 'promises to help ensnare his [Werner's] enemies.' She goes on a mission for her lover but is killed, as Molina will be in similar circumstances later. Finally, as she dies Werner seems to hear one of her songs, just as Valentín will 'see', in his delirium following Molina's death, what looks like one of his companion's films.

However, the most interesting aspect of the 'inner'/'outer' parallel has yet to come. The ending of the 'inner film' is over-dramatic, over-sentimental and distinctly corny – but the ending of the 'outer film' is really a modern re-working of similar movie conventions. The contemporary-sounding dramatic music and the slow zoom-shot when Molina is making his telephone call to Valentín's cell of political activists are standard features of modern Hollywood thrillers. Standard thriller-music returns when Molina attempts to make contact with the cell accompanied by equally standard editing techniques as the action cuts regularly from Molina to his pursuers in the crowd. The point is that the audience is being engaged on the level of a popular film, on an equivalent level to the corny ending of *Destino* – yet the audience does not laugh here. In *Kiss of the Spider Woman*, then, the audience is encouraged to laugh at the conventions of popular cinema, but at the same time is induced to enjoy them and be absorbed by them. So, in effect, the members of the audience are being made to laugh at themselves: they are forced to recognise their own prejudices and reassess the nature and value of so-called high-brow and low-brow culture. Nonetheless, the problem still remains of how one squares the film's political dimension, which carries an implicit critique of the movie industry's subtle contribution to social conditioning and the maintenance of established values, with its 'popular' dimension, which re-enacts the forms which assert the very conservatism the film attacks.

The 'serious-versus-popular' dichotomy raises once more, of course, the vexed question of referentiality. The 'popular' implies mass conformism which is challenged by the probing experiments of modern 'serious' art; or, from an opposite viewpoint, the 'serious' implies an official bourgeois culture which scorns and prevents interaction with the tastes of the 'popular' masses. Both sides of the equation seem to cancel each other out, the implication being that – ultimately – literature or film or art have nothing to say to us. It is, as it were, the form of narrative that matters and not the content. Hence the interchangeability of the two stories 'Leni/Werner-versus-Resistance' and 'Molina/Valentín-versus-Authorities' and the way *Destino* in the novel is enjoyable in its own right regardless of its politics (which can easily be substituted anyway by a different set of political norms).

Both novel and film contain numerous allusions to the form-over-content argument. Molina points to the irrelevance of a film's political content when in reference to *Cat People* (1942, directed by Jacques Tourneur and produced by Val Lewton) he comments to Valentín that: 'a vos te gustó la colega arquitecta, ¿qué tiene de guerrillera ésa?' (23). Moreover, an awareness of the Nazi aspect of *Destino* is irrelevant to one's possible enjoyment of it: 'me ofendés porque te ... te creés que no ... no me doy cuenta que es de propaganda na ... nazi, pero si a mí me gusta es porque está bien hecha, aparte de eso es una obra de arte' (63). In other words, film is film and fiction is fiction, and this is the level on which audiences or readers react:

> — ¿Vos sabés lo que eran los maquís?
> — Sí, ya sé que eran los patriotas, pero en la película no. Vos dejame seguir. Entonces ... ¿qué era lo que seguía?
> — Yo no te entiendo.
> — Es que la película era divina, y para mí la película es lo que me importa ... (85-6)

In a parallel way, the two texts contrast literary criticism and literary appreciation. In the film, Molina tells Valentín 'I don't analyse my films: it just ruins the emotion', but when, in the novel, he asks Valentín for a snap reaction, the latter replies: 'No sé, tendría que analizarlo ...' (77). So, in a sense, Valentín, who constantly comments on and interprets Molina's films, represents the literary critic who attempts to divine meanings and impose interpretations. Thus Valentín makes a psychoanalytical reading of the RKO chiller *Cat People* in which the heroine Irena's fear of turning into a panther woman on being kissed is explained in terms of her frigidity and sexual paranoia (21–36) – an interpretation which is later ridiculed when her psychoanalyst (with whom Valentín is said to identify) is torn apart by the woman after his kiss does indeed transform her into a panther woman. A similar example is when Valentín's socio-psychological reading of the film, based on the protagonist's preservation of his apartment's decor as his mother had it, is exploded by Molina's revelation that he simply invented the fact that it used to be his mother's home and that 'a lo mejor él lo alquila amueblado' (24). The fundamental problem is that Valentín is always seeking an explanation in reality, seeing Irena as 'una psicópata asesina' instead of simply accepting that she is nothing more than 'una mujer pantera' (45). He cannot accept that – in William Hurt's words as Molina – a movie is 'just a movie'.

So, fiction should not be read as referring to any external reality, the texts suggest, and appreciation is more authentic than analysis. But at the same time both texts (and especially the novel) encourage a critical reading or literary interpretation. Valentín tries to promote a political consciousness to check Molina's unthinking 'art-for-art's-sake' attitude and, as we have seen, the simultaneously trivial and pernicious movie *Destino* is mocked in the novel's film version. What is more, the existence of academic-style footnotes in the novel, offering a psychoanalytical and ultimately sociopolitical perspective on the main text, seems designed to prompt serious critical reflection on the novel's ideas and implications. Indeed while Molina and Valentín's dialogue on *Destino* suggests that form is more important than content, the footnote on it – by exposing a Nazi propaganda document on the film – stresses that content *is* important. Valentín's argument that 'quien no actúa políticamente es [un ladrón] porque tiene un falso concepto de la responsabilidad' (108) may be more valid after all.

In fact, the two texts do much to emphasise the inevitably political effects of narrative or discourse. Leni, falling under Werner's spell, reacts emotionally to the Wagnerian music playing at his home: 'this music is magical … I feel like I'm floating on air' – a clear reference, given the Nazi context, to the dangerously influential nature of art. In the movie's second 'inner film' the lonely, tearful Spider Woman on her desert island is watching over a shipwrecked man, who is actually Valentín, at a point when in the 'outer film' Valentín is starting to fall for the tearful Molina. Clearly Molina is the Spider Woman (she is played by Sonia Braga who also plays Leni, with whom Molina is closely identified) who has trapped or seduced Valentín on his own desert island (the cell) via his film stories, his food and his care. The narration of this film (pertinent but wholly of Molina's invention) clinches the seduction and is another example of the highly influential (and possibly dangerous?) nature of art. In fact the entire process of film narration is a form of seduction by Molina of Valentín, as the already noted sexual sub-theme of *Cat People* may hint. Narrative is by nature seductive and influential.

What is beginning to emerge now is a link between narrative, sexuality, ideology and power. In a novel or film about sexual and political domination, the actual narrative forms employed are images or representations of social and political hierarchies and the exercise of power. For instance, at one end of the scale we have the popular movies and songs of the powerless masses (especially women), and at the other end the official or authoritarian world of reports and footnotes – with the experimental metatext of the novel (or film) as a whole functioning as a serious, challenging alternative to the status quo. This would be an attractive explanation of the texts' inclusion of disparate narrative forms, were it not for the pervasive ambiguity with which each narrative level is imbued. Once more, the texts' political thrust is neutralised by their own inconsistencies, as an examination of each narrative form will show.

The contradictory nature of popular narratives (repressive and liberating) has already been thoroughly explored. What is interesting in the novel is the way Molina's lively narrations of popular films are constantly set against dialogue (dialogue later mixed in with interior monologue or stream-of-consciousness, for want of better terms). This reminds us of the (earlier) novels of Vargas Llosa and the quest for autonomous narrative. A basic aim of the new novel in Latin America was to encourage readers to overcome their traditional passivity by removing the guiding figure of the omniscient narrator and replacing him with a kind of self-propelled narrative which the reader would have to interpret actively for him- or herself. What the novel is doing, then, is projecting the role of a narrator (via Molina's film narratives) and simultaneously rejecting that role by enclosing those narratives within a framework of autonomous narrative. Using the words of Milagros Ezquerro, there is a downgrading of 'une narration "didactique" où le narrateur cherche à imposer *sa* vision au lecteur/auditeur en oblitérant, par l'accumulation de précisions et de détails, la liberté d'imaginer et d'interpréter' in favour of 'une narration "anti-didactique" où le narrateur efface sa propre vision, éludant toute description d'un espace simplement allusif, d'un espace "en blanc" que le lecteur peut à son gré imaginer et interpréter.'[6] *El beso de la mujer araña* thus becomes a species of show-piece 'new novel' which demonstrates the advantages of that genre's techniques over those of old-style traditional realism. This links also with the political theme of authority and power: Molina's narrative is authoritarian and repressive, since it forces upon the reader or listener its own point of view, while Puig's narrative (the novel as a whole) is more progressive in that it liberates the reader and allows him or her the freedom to form their own interpretation. There is considerable truth in all this, but – alas – again the full picture is not quite so simple.

First, though, the novel (and the film) clearly do expose the limitations of omniscient narration, in particular realism. At one stage, a discrepancy emerges between *Cat People*, a film Molina has seen *in reality*, and his narration of it. This provokes irritation in Valentín:

> — Entonces me estás inventando la mitad de la película.
> — No, yo no invento, te lo juro, pero hay cosas que para redondeártelas, que las veas como las estoy viendo yo, bueno, de algún modo te las tengo que explicar. (24-5)

This dialogue is echoed in the film version:

> 'How can you remember all this crap? You must be making it up.'
> 'No, I'm not ... It's ... Well, I embroider a little, so that you can see it the way I do.'

The point is that the neutrality of the realist narrator is merely an illusion, for the narrator inevitably steers the reader towards his own point of view. There are, for instance, numerous examples of Molina inadvertently interpreting the narrative rather than just expounding it. How could Molina possibly *know* of the following thoughts of film characters, having simply seen their actions on the screen:

> Entonces Leni se queda sola y piensa si ella podría querer a un invasor de su patria, y se queda pensando ... (58)

> Las palabras de él la hacen medio estremecerse, todo un presagio la envuelve, y tiene como la certeza de que en su vida sucederán cosas muy importantes, y casi seguramente con un fin trágico. (62)

Ella se muere de miedo pero consigue disimular. (81) (How does he spot her fear, one wonders, if she manages to conceal it?)

… y más abajo hay fotos, fotos de él y otra mujer, ¿sería la primera esposa?, a la chica le parece reconocerla, le parece haberla visto antes, de veras está segura de haber visto esa cara antes, en alguna parte, ¿pero dónde? (177)

The narrator here is not transcribing what he knows of reality but projecting his own assumptions on to it.

There is, of course, a possible explanation for this. Films do give the viewer clues to characters' thoughts or feelings via gestures, facial expressions, non-diegetic mood music and so on. However, things are not so straightforward, because the film we are reading about or seeing is *not* the real film but merely Molina's recollection of it. The exaggerated quality of the filmed version of *Destino* is due to its status as an equivalent of the narrated film of the novel: that is, it is a visual manifestation of a memory, not the real thing. But this reintroduces the thorny problem of realistic representation. *Destino* is clearly a black-and-white film – but there are constant hints of colour (the curtain behind Leni in the night-club, for instance, is red). Memory distorts, interprets and adds to reality: the narrator (literally) colours the picture of reality and presents a subjective rather than objective view.

Related to this is that when Molina is recounting to himself the story of *The Enchanted Cottage* (1949, directed by John Cromwell) or telling Valentín the story of *I Walked with a Zombie* (1943, directed by Jacques Tourneur), his own thoughts interact with the film narratives:

… *Una cicatriz desde la punta de la frente que corta una ceja, corta un párpado, tajea la nariz y se hunde en el cachete del lado contrario, una tachadura encima de una cara, una mirada torva, mirada de malo, estaba leyendo un libro de filosofía y porque le hice una pregunta me echó una mirada torva, qué feo que alguien te echa una mirada torva, ¿qué es peor, que te echen una mirada torva, o que no te miren nunca?, mamá no me echó una mirada torva, me condenaron a ocho años por meterme con un menor de edad pero mamá no me echó una mirada torva …* (109–10) (There is a switch in topic here from the protagonist of the film to Valentín.)

Ella no sabe qué hacer, y se le ofrece para secarle la espalda, no sabe
cómo entretenerlo, distraerlo, *la pobre enfermera, no tiene suerte, le*
*dan al enfermo más grave y no sabe qué hacer para que esa noche no*
*muera o la mate, más fuerte que nunca el peligro al contagio* porque
él ya va a empezar a vestirse ... (177) (A switch here from the heroine and her husband to Molina and Valentín.)

The point is that the narrator cannot keep himself out of his narrative, and – for realist texts -this means that the narrative itself must
be unreliable. Hence the regular emphasis on mistakes and failing
memory in the novel. Molina's narratives are peppered with
phrases like 'pero me olvidé de contarte que ...' (73), '¡ah!, me
olvidaba decirte' (82), 'porque yo no te dije que ...' (86), 'ah, pero
me olvidaba algo importante' (172) or 'el otro le pide que lo acom-
pañe, pero no, esperá, es el mismo jefe que lo convida a un trago
...' (231) – all convey a sense of the insecure foundations or shift-
ing sands of the narratives. A good example comes when Molina
tells Valentín that Leni is shown a photograph of 'un criminal
bárbaro' (97–8), while the official document in the footnote states
quite clearly that she spotted him during the projection of a film
(94). Thus the relationship between Molina's 'text' and its external
referent is shown to be highly suspect.

There is an obvious political dimension to all of this: tyrannical
popular culture can impose false or hypocritical values on an unsus-
pecting public. Molina's references to 'trucos del cine' (80), and the
unnoticed effects of 'la música casi imperceptible y muy dulce que
no se sabe de donde proviene' (112), underline the manipulative
powers of the mass media. But, of course, Molina is a reader (or,
more literally, a viewer) as well as a narrator. His misreading of the
films he has seen suggests that it is the reader who makes the text
rather than the narrator (or author). His version of *I Walked with*
*a Zombie* is markedly different from the original. It is interesting
too that he describes the zombies walking 'con los brazos estirados'
(179) – a commonly-held cultural assumption about zombies – , but
in the real film they do not walk that way. Readers' assumptions
colour narratives, therefore, just as much as narrators'. This
subverts the notion of the guiding or conditioning narrator of traditional narrative. Indeed the popular films narrated in the novel are
open to multiple interpretations and even recreations. Molina and
Valentín each create their own reading of *Cat People*:

— Es todo imaginación tuya.
— Si vos también ponés de tu cosecha, ¿por qué no yo? (29)

They later disagree on the ending of the Mexican-style romantic film about the journalist and the singer (Puig's invention), Molina concluding it is a 'final ... enigmático' (263). The very nature of 'reading' means that traditional realism or popular films can be just as problematic as any other artistic form.

Nonetheless, set against the supposedly 'traditional' and 'limited' form of the film narratives is the supposedly more 'modern' and 'sophisticated' autonomous narrative of the novel as a whole. Certainly, the use of dialogue and what can be roughly – if not altogether accurately – termed interior monologue does, on the surface, dispense with the role of the conventional narrator. Politically, this is a 'freer' form (though at the same time limiting in that, through problematisation, it dilutes the impact of any political 'message' and is possibly self-defeating, since it is used for scenes which are arguably less engaging than the film narratives they complement). But does it work anyway as autonomous narrative? The sheer range of narrative devices employed may actually raise awareness of a hidden narrator. In the film, for example, the already-mentioned conscious juxtapositioning of Molina's conversation with Valentín and the flashbacks to his interview with the Warden draws attention to the editing process and reveals the presence of an offscreen director. In the novel meanwhile the interior monologue passages (used for internal thoughts, dreams, delirium and so on) have a similar effect. While there is some narrative and thematic justification for them (insofar as they provide an additional perspective on the characters and hint at their evolution towards each other's position), they are not terribly convincing. Surely Molina's thoughts on *The Enchanted Cottage* are too stylised when he says to himself, for instance: 'El pianista ciego, rodeado por sus invitados, los ojos casi sin pupila no ven lo que tienen delante, es decir las apariencias: ven otras cosas, las que realmente cuentan' (104)? The rhythmic quality and the repetitive pattern of the *mujer / muchacho / madre / padre / muchacha* passages of Chapters 6 and 7 also expose a high degree of authorial patterning. Finally, the interaction of the characters' thoughts and dialogues in Chapters 9 and 10 is obtrusive, as they appear for the first time quite late into the novel: they are presumably there to underline the developing relationship of the two men and prepare us for its consummation, so that Puig is seen to be introducing them simply because he *needs* to. In any case, they are unconvincing, as the following interchange shows:

> Y colorín, colorado, este cuento se ha terminado. ¿Te gustó? *el paciente más grave del pabellón ya está fuera de peligro, la enfermera velará toda la noche sobre su sueño tranquilo*
> — Sí, mucho. *el rico duerme tranquilo si le da su oro al pobre*
> (216–7)

Leaving their bizarrerie to one side, the rigorous parallelism of thought pattern in two different people destroys any impression of narrative autonomy and brings to mind a machinating author behind the scenes.

Other favourite devices of Puig's for creating the illusion of authorial withdrawal are the use, as in *Boquitas pintadas*, of letters, reports, songs and so on. But Oliveira Filho points out that the report format of Chapter 8, where the speakers are designated DIRECTOR, SUBOFICIAL and PROCESADO, has the opposite effect:

> Aqui, a ocorrência da indicação cênica de quem fala expõe a presença de um narrador-editor que as coloca. Na ânsia de se despersonalizar diante de sua narrativa, esse narrador-editor, contraditoriamente, mais aparece como um agente extradiegético e, de uma forma estranha, dotado de uma acintosa forma de onisciência que se queria evitar.[7]

Moreover, these formats all raise, once again, the question of the treacherous nature of discourse. The reports (especially given their authors) suggest official discourse, authority and power.[8] However, the reports are also pervaded by uncertainty. The transcript of the Warden's telephone conversation displays an inability to interpret Molina's actions and contains the phrase 'no sé cómo explicarme' (249). Similarly, there is confusion over the perfectly straightforward meaning of Molina's gay linguistic games in which female names are adopted and what is presumably Hedy Lemarr's name is transcribed as 'Jedi(?)' (272). Finally, in the film the report ends up by assuming that Molina had been planning to escape with the activists, that he had agreed to be shot and that he had been more heavily involved with the 'Movement' than they had suspected – none of which is strictly or necessarily true. This is, of course, all a reflection of officialdom's inability to comprehend or tolerate vitality or ambiguity, but does hint too at the problems of authenticity in discourse and of interpretation.

Letters and songs have a similar effect. The letter is written in code (138-39) and in this sense is symbolic of literature which is a kind of coded version of reality. Lilia Dapaz Strout has noted in this respect that:

> El arte de Puig es el de la traición, la traición a sí mismo. *El beso de la mujer araña* es una trampa, un ejercicio diabólico de impostura y decepción. Dice una cosa pero significa otra, como la carta de la compañera de célula de Valentín, que es una metáfora de toda la novela ...[9]

At the same time the letter comes from a 'popular' source (Valentín's uneducated girlfriend in the Movement) and is linked to the bolero sung by Molina, for 'la carta ... dice lo mismo que el bolero' (140) (which is, in fact, called *Mi carta* [137]). So, the popular bolero has relevance to Valentín's situation and the letter from a 'popular' background has a hidden meaning: the value and potential complexity of popular culture is thereby alluded to. But earlier on we learn that the songs in *Destino* were not translated into Spanish:

> — ... Y canta.
> — ¿Qué dice?
> — Andá a saber ..., porque no traducían las canciones. (80)

We are back in the realm of contradiction again, for this implies that the form of the songs is more important than their content, thus minimising their relevance to reality.

The most notorious level of discourse in the novel, though, is probably the footnotes. There are two topics treated in them: one is an extract from a studio publicity document concerning *Destino*; the other is a survey of various theoretical works on homosexuality. Footnotes imply informed academic insight, the truth even, and are therefore a form of authoritative discourse. The fact that the *Destino* footnote comes from the Nazi propaganda service stresses the authority factor. But there is a dual aspect to this authority, both political and literary. The ideal of the super-race hinted at in the footnote relates to the idea of perfection in narrative: and, like the German people, readers long for and are taken in by the unambiguous security of absolute realism (represented by the truth of footnotes and doubt-free Nazi doctrine). The young Germans are described in terms of a 'trazo rectilíneo' and 'negro y blanco' (90), suggesting symmetry and certainty, while Werner's eyes 'están puestos en la Verdad' (94); and consequently 'el pueblo reconoce lo que es auténtico y se aferra a ello' (93–4). This all applies to the prevalence of realist narrative and not just Nazism. If, as the footnote says, 'cumple al arte ser la expresión (del) espíritu de nuestra época' (90), then the favoured code of realism (given the Nazi parallel) is an official culture which is dangerously authoritarian. It is significant that the footnote refers to 'la *virilidad* del trazo rectilíneo' (90, my italics) and states that 'no hay lugar para la mujer política en el mundo ideológico del Nacional Socialismo' (98): a dominant, fossilised masculine code is seen to suppress a marginal but subversive feminine code. Linking this to art, German art is 'tan puro e inspirado, mientras en el resto de Europa se ha impuesto un arte por demás frívolo y efímero, ... un arte meramente decorativo y abstracto destinado a perecer como las prescindibles modas femeninas' (90): yet these are allusions to the other levels of the novel (feminism, homosexuality, popular culture and experimentalism) which subvert the official discourse of the footnote. Indeed the interpretative stance of the footnote's account of *Destino* is no less subjective than Molina's and, at times, the exaggeration and manipulation is blatant. What is more, the fact that the document is, in any case, a mere invention of Puig's reduces its authoritarian realism to irreality: it is no more 'real' than Molina's unreliable narratives.

However, having problematised the nature of the footnote, the text finds itself in all sorts of difficulties when it comes to the footnotes on homosexuality. These are, in essence, anti-authoritarian (on a sociopolitical and literary level). The first note rejects any physical, biological hereditary factor in homosexuality and in later notes attention is redirected to public perceptions of homosexuality: given that the notes begin in the middle of a film on political authority which provokes a discussion of sexual roles, this could be taken as a critique of omniscience or narrative authority, of the notion of the all-powerful 'creating' author – a shift, as it were, from author power to reader power. The danger of authoritarian discourse is hinted at by theorist Altman's observation that 'mucho de lo que se consideraba normal e instintivo ... es en cambio aprendido' (170) and the footnotes, as a whole, form an argument in favour of sexual and social liberation. This is reflected in Marcuse's

favouring of 'una erotización de la entera personalidad' as opposed
to a culture which is against 'el uso del cuerpo como mero objeto,
medio e instrumento de placer' (170–1). In this sense, Puig's text
echoes Sarduy's view of language and sexuality, as a 'juego cuya
finalidad está en sí mismo y cuyo propósito no es la conducción de
un mensaje ..., sino su desperdicio en función del placer'[10] – revolutionary in that its non-utilitarianism and assertion of the pleasure
principle are in direct confrontation with cherished bourgeois
values such as restraint and productivity.

But this is where the problems begin. Puig clearly does wish the
footnotes to communicate something, to be 'useful' – yet he challenges authority by utilising an essentially authoritarian form. To
convince us of the need for change, he actually exploits the scientific credentials of the footnote form in order to expose weaknesses
represented by that institutionalised form. In Chapter 8 the footnote is set against the official report of Molina's interview with the
Warden. On one level, the footnote on free love is a challenge to the
Warden's rigid and conservative morality, but its form is actually
analogous to that of the official report. Moreover, the notes remind
us that homosexual practice can become 'una forma de represión
tan grande como la heterosexualidad exclusiva' (155), alerting us
to the dangers of inverted authoritarianism. Indeed, the 'hidden'
author here is not really all that hidden and appears as a subtle
guiding figure in his own right. The gimmick of the invented Danish
doctor Anneli Taube to conclude the argument is a blatant manipulation of the available theoretical material (just as the exaggerated
tone of the *Destino* footnote is a cue for the reader to disagree with
it) and the very introduction of footnotes to prepare us for the
sexual consummation of Molina and Valentín's 'love' is a barely
covert plea for acceptance and understanding,[11] a narrative clarification not all that different from Molina's embellishments of his
film narratives. The footnotes may even remind us of narrative
unreliability: some seem arbitrary in terms of their *immediate* (not
overall) relation to the text (e.g. 102, 133, 141) and are given in a
segmented, piecemeal manner which hints at human beings' partial
grasp of reality based on limited information. Their content similarly touches on ambiguity and 'la mutabilidad esencial de la naturaleza humana' (155). And in the end that content has little to offer.
The Marcusian alternative is utopian and idealistic, while Anneli
Taube's offering is no more than a 'happy medium'.[12]

However, both texts (novel and film) also beg the question: is there really any content here at all, any relation to external reality, if the texts are ultimately self-referential? Much has been made of the parallels between the characters' real lives and their screen counterparts. But at one stage Molina alludes to his and Valentín's own situation as if it really were a movie, calling it *El misterio de la celda siete*. This calls attention to the fact that the characters are not real but merely fictional creations, as in a movie. In fact, not only is the texts' presentation of films suspect, their presentation of reality is too. In the film version, characters' memories of reality are presented realistically, unlike Molina's recollection of the fictional film *Destino*, which is hazy, distorted and stylised. This induces us to accept the memories as 'truth'. But when Molina describes his waiter-friend Gabriel ('His white tunic, the way he moved, his sad smile – everything seemed so perfect, like in the movies'), there is a considerable discrepancy between what we hear and what we see (the scene *looks* rather prosaic and ordinary). Which is the reality? And is the film being consistent in its reflection of it?

More importantly though, there is a high degree of intertextuality between the film narratives themselves and between them and the fictional reality of Molina and Valentín. A blind pianist appears in the Mexican film (229) – is it more than a coincidence that a blind pianist is the narrator in *The Enchanted Cottage*? The bolero in the Mexican film (230) is also reminiscent of the bolero discussed by Molina and Valentín. Furthermore, Molina -quite impossibly – remembers exactly all the words of all the songs in the Mexican film. Does all this not suggest that not only are Molina's films fictions but that he himself is a fiction too? In the film *Kiss of the Spider Woman* the interaction between films and fictional reality is even more disturbing. Valentín crops up as the shipwrecked man in the Spider Woman film (though, as we have seen, this film may be purely Molina's invention). But more bizarrely the singer in the gay night-club visited by Molina towards the end of the film following his release from prison sings the song *Je me moque de l'amour*, which is actually a jazzed-up version of the song sung by Leni earlier on in *Destino*. Is external reality in the film therefore any more 'real' than *Destino*? Moreover, Sonia Braga plays not only Leni and the Spider Woman, but also – crucially – Marta. The same woman appears in Molina's memory or invention of films as appears in the real life outside jail of Valentín, something to which

Molina has had no access. Thus doubt is cast on the realism and the reality of that part of the text we are encouraged to believe is most real and most important.

The central problem of Puig's text (and Babenco's reading or version of it) is that in encouraging their own application to reality they cloud and confuse the nature of that application and ultimately finish up by cancelling it out altogether. The last words of the novel are 'este sueño es corto pero es feliz' (287) and Gustavo Pellón has already noted that this more or less sums up the ideological depth of the work.[13] And, in the film, as Valentín sails off into the distance with the beautiful Sonia Braga, we too suspect that what we have just been watching is in the end not much more than a short but happy dream.

## Notes

[1] Severo Sarduy, 'Notas a las notas a las notas ... a propósitio de Manuel Puig', *Revista Iberoamericana*, XXXVII, 1971, pp. 555–67.

[2] Pamela Bacarisse, *The Necessary Dream: A Study of the Novels of Manuel Puig*, University of Wales Press, Cardiff, 1988; *Impossible Choices: The Implications of the Cultural References in the Novels of Manuel Puig*, University of Wales Press, Cardiff, 1993.

[3] All references are to Manuel Puig, *El beso de la mujer araña*, 2nd ed., Seix Barral, Barcelona, 1981, and *Kiss of the Spider Woman* (1984), directed by Héctor Babenco, starring William Hurt and Raúl Julia, with Sonia Braga. There is also a theatrical version of *El beso de la mujer araña* included in Manuel Puig, *Bajo un manto de estrellas*, Seix Barral, Barcelona, 1983, and more recently, a highly successful musical, considerations of which are outside the scope of this chapter.

[4] It seems reasonable to use the term 'text' for film as well as prose: we can speak of film narrative in a similar way to the term narrative prose or fiction. Indeed, an important guide to film art is James Monaco's aptly titled *How to Read a Film*, Oxford University Press, New York, 1977. Film terms employed in this essay are those used in David Bordwell and Kristin Thompson, *Film Art: An Introduction*, Addison-Wesley Publishing Co., Reading/Menlo Park/London/Amsterdam/Don Mills/Sydney, 1980.

[5] Elizabeth Pérez Luna, 'Con Manuel Puig en Nueva York', *Hombre de Mundo*, III, 8, 1978, pp. 69–71 and 104–7. The reference is to p. 104.

[6] Milagros Ezquerro, *Essai d'analyse de 'El beso de la mujer araña' de Manuel Puig*, Institut d'études hispaniques et hispano-americaines,

Université de Toulouse-Le-Mirail, Toulouse, 1981, p. 20.

[7]Odil José de Oliveira Filho, 'A voz do narrador em *O beijo da mulher araña*', *Revista de Letras*, XXIV, 1984, p. 56.

[8]The report form is not confined to the novel. It occurs in the film and is given added weight by a change of narrative voice and style (from Molina to report-writer), the introduction of non-diegetic typewriter sounds, and deep space and deep focus to suggest the distance between the representative of authority (the agent or agents) and the representative of the ordinary individual (Molina).

[9]Lilia Dapaz Strout, 'Más allá del principio del placer del texto: Pascal, Puig y la pasión de la escritura: "El misterio de la celda siete"', *Hispanic Journal*, LI, 1983, p. 87.

[10]Severo Sarduy, 'El barroco y el neobarroco' in César Fernández Moreno (ed.), *América Latina en su literatura*, Siglo XXI, Mexico, 1972, p. 182.

[11]It has been frequently accepted that a central function of the footnotes is to pave the way for and justify the protagonists' love-making. See Juan Manuel García Ramos, *La narrativa de Manuel Puig (Por una crítica en libertad)*, Secretariado de Publicaciones de la Universidad de La Laguna, La Laguna, 1982, p. 385.

[12]Bacarisse, *The Necessary Dream*, p. 115. On utopianism see Elías Miguel Muñoz, 'La utopía sexual en *El beso de la mujer araña* de Manuel Puig', *Alba de América*, July–Dec. 1984, pp. 49–60. Paul Julian Smith reads the footnotes in a different way, appearing to argue that they are deliberately ironised, though he makes no mention of the significance of Anneli Taube. Nonetheless, he concludes that the text 'cedes to a political purpose, which is no less potent for being unstable', while at the same time asserting: 'what we cannot do is claim instability as a goal in itself, as an essential instrument of emancipation'. See Paul Julian Smith, *The Body Hispanic*, Oxford University Press, Oxford, 1989, pp. 193–204. With regard to the relationship between text and footnotes, Smith refers to Lucille Kerr, *Suspended Fictions: Reading Novels by Manuel Puig*, University of Illinois Press, Urbana and Chicago, 1987.

[13]Gustavo Pellón, 'Manuel Puig's Contradictory Strategy: Kitsch Para-digms *versus* Paradigmatic Structure in *El beso de la mujer araña* and *Pubis angelical*', *Symposium*, XXXVII, 1983, pp. 186–201. The reference is to p. 199.

# Chapter 3

# Guillermo Cabrera Infante and
*Tres tristes tigres*: Infantile paralysis?

In a review of a collection of essays on modern Latin American fiction edited by John King, Donald Shaw complains of the way the book ends with an interview conducted by Jason Wilson and revolving around 'Cabrera Infante's inconsequential puns'.[1] Indeed Cabrera Infante criticism has repeatedly placed emphasis on the Cuban author's tendency to play around with what Fuentes has called Cabrera's very own 'Spunish language'.[2] Cabrera Infante himself has often drawn attention to a seeming lack of seriousness in his work, both by his own practice, in interviews, essays and prologues, and by his own specific comments on *Tres tristes tigres*. 'Me gustaría', he has said, 'que el libro se tomara como una gran broma escrita ... Preferiría yo que todos consideren al libro solamente una broma que dura cerca de 500 páginas.'[3] Such a sense of playfulness and humour, usually coupled with an engagement – as is also the case with Cabrera Infante – with popular or mass culture is often seen as a key feature of the Latin American post-Boom (an issue to be discussed in more detail in the chapter on Gustavo Sainz); and Cabrera Infante – though with something of a delayed reaction, for *Tres tristes tigres* was first published as far back as 1965 – has to be seen, along with Puig, as one of the major influences for change in the new novel from the late sixties onwards. Again, Cabrera himself, in the interview referred to by Shaw, declares that: 'I don't see that I have much in common with the so-called Boom ... I've always felt more comfortable with Severo Sarduy and Manuel Puig' (316). The question here, of course (and this is a question that also has to be addressed with regard to the post-Boom as a whole), is the alleged 'inconsequentiality' of humour and play, especially in the work of a formerly pro-revolutionary and now exiled Cuban. This in turn relates to questions of Popular culture and High culture, with the terms' overtones of revolutionary or, at least, social consciousness versus bourgeois individualism. Needless to say, criticism is divided on the subject, fragmenting along lines that perhaps say as much about the agenda of the critical establishment (old and new) as about the literary object of its attentions.

First of all, despite Cabrera Infante's remarks quoted above, *Tres tristes tigres* can be read as an actively political text. For a start, there is no shortage of (extra-literary) anti-Castro statements by the author. For instance, in a bitter-sounding essay, 'The Invisible Exile', Cabrera, who lives in London, comments: 'I must wear warmer clothes in my exiledom by the sea than in the tropics, where I was born, where I chose exile rather than become a pawn in a monstrous game of chess in which only one man can play king.'[4] Moreover, although he has asserted, in the interview in King's book again, that the 'genesis of a book' is merely 'the urge to publish' (306), there does appear to be something of a political dimension to the genesis of *Tres tristes tigres*. According to Seymour Menton's account, for example, the 1964 version of what is now *Tres tristes tigres*, *Vista del amanecer en el trópico*, represented a denunciation of the decadent Batista regime of the late 1950s but was subsequently morally repudiated. The second version, cutting or diluting the sociopolitical emphasis, was inspired by and intended as a continuation of the short film about the Havana night life of the fifties, *P.M.*, made by Cabrera Infante's brother Sabá and censured and confiscated by the revolutionary government. Thus it might be claimed that *Tres tristes tigres* began life as a critique of Batista and then evolved into a critique of Castro.

The social or political dimension might be perceived at both the level of content and of style and form. Though the novel is usually seen as a kind of nostalgic elegy for a bygone age, there are a number of unflattering tangential contextual references to the political situation and a number of motifs suggesting a decadent world: the aimlessness of the male characters, the false, corrupted nature of female characters like Livia and Mirtila, the self-prostitution resulting from a disadvantaged economic provenance or, in the case of Eribó, racial status, casual violence, the saturation of society with North American values, the favourable official treatment given to Mr Campbell over the unfortunate local who is unjustly accused of stealing his (purchased, Cuban) walking-stick, the success of the

commercially packaged glamour-girl Cuba Venegas with her backing
band versus the death of the obese and impoverished Estrella who
relies solely on the natural beauty and authenticity of her singing
voice. In fact many of the 'adventures' end on a tragic or melan-
cholic note, as does the novel as a whole. Isabel Alvarez-Borland
goes so far as to assert that 'se vuelve ... el libro, de apariencia tan
frívola, en un documento sociológico de una época en la que una
generación de provincianos se ven empujados por su pobreza hacia
la metrópolis, y una vez allí se ven obligados a comprometer su
integridad para sobrevivir al ambiente corruptor.'[5] Yet if the Batista
regime is crumbling by the end of the novel, there may not be much
yielding to a more favourable view of what follows. Victorino Polo
García has noted ways in which the text ridicules Castro and claims
that Arsenio Cué is mocked for his decision to join Fidel in the
*sierra*.[6] The quip that 'el español al revés es ruso' is an ironic
commentary on the revolution and the running story of what are
probably Laura's psychiatric sessions (set after the main 'action' of
the novel) may be taken as a reference to, as it were, the unconscious
of Cuban society, with the madwoman's monologue that forms the
epilogue – where political oppression is sharply alluded to ('Que
viene el mono con un cuchillo y me registra' [451]) – functioning as
a powerful extension of this image of victimisation and crisis.[7]

It is William L. Siemens who most explicitly makes the connection between this commentary on the Cuban Revolution and the
novel's technique. Turning playfulness into politicking, he attempts
to show that 'the book is highly political in offering a written text
characterised by radical multivalence as an alternative to such an
authoritative voice' (107). The subversive humour and word play
for which the novel is largely famous represent an irreverent threat
to authority (and, the implication is here, authoritarianism), achieved
formally via the 'rupture ... of a signifier or string of signifiers
expressive of an authoritative system' (113). Thus, for example, the
seven versions given of the death of Leon Trotsky as narrated, it is
joked, by seven Cuban authors dramatises a Derridean sense of the
perpetual deferment of meaning and perception. Indeed the entire
structuring of the novel around the concerns of language, orality,
memory and translation (of which more later) merely confirms the
centrality of the notion of 'Traduttore, traditore' and the impossibility of authoritative representation. The liberation of the sign, the
freedom of play and open association, all this is Cabrera Infante's

own Cuban revolution, implicitly challenging the Castrist assumption of fixed power and authority. Is this, then, the real reason why *Tres tristes tigres* is, in Cabrera Infante's appropriately playful words, a '*liber non grato* in Cuba' (Wilson, 307)?

In a similar way to that discussed in relation to Puig, there are a lot of problems with this sort of approach. The fact that Siemens is identifying a 'technique' which might normally be claimed by the Left actually to critique the Left really suggests the arbitrariness of linguistic play. In any case (and this is a familiar inconsistency), if the free play of words means that 'nothing to which they may refer is to be trusted' (116), then surely none of this can refer to the material reality of Cuban society anyway. Julio Ortega appears to fall into the same pattern. Celebrating the openness of the text (which is nothing but the spectacle of its own composition), its freedom through 'verbalness' and its independence of any reality other than that shaped by words, he, nonetheless talks of allegory, declares one character 'the mask of the author himself' and even seems to interpret the novel.[8] Even if one were to accept the correlation between linguistic or literary rebellion and social or political rebellion, this would make for a somewhat uninspiring model for action. It is difficult to imagine many rallying to Souza's call for an appreciation of the potentiality of language as 'the key to a method of building a new society' (85).

The reservations expressed above form part of a larger debate about popular culture and its relationship to the idea of postmodernism. Texts like *Tres tristes tigres* offer the opportunity of a Bakhtinian heyday for critics eager to celebrate the subversive potential of carnivalisation, a point which will be developed further later. William Rowe and Vivian Schelling, who tend to associate the term popular culture with the 'popular' classes, claim that pitting the low against the high is limited as a social or political strategy: 'This type of attitude, in its familiar forms of social messianism – the notion of the world upside down, and the cult of Carnival as subversion – has become extremely common in cultural studies. Such reversals of categories end up as utopian gestures (or alibis, in fact) on the part of the intellectual, who is obviously on the side of the angels – or rather, in this case, the devil, the low, the marginalised.'[9] The debate, then, is about elaborating effective means of resisting cultural hegemony. The problem is that while much First World criticism identifies postmodernism with play and heterogeneity, leftist critics seeking the recuperation of an alternative Third World perspective, see this as a cunning ploy to reinsert a culturally hegemonic vision. John Beverley summarises the debate in his *Against Literature*, drawing on Jameson, Neil Larsen, Roberto González Echevarría, George Yúdice and others.[10] Jameson's notion of First World postmodernism as 'the crisis and mutation of the forms of ideological legitimation of advanced capitalist consumer societies' (Beverley, 112) finds its correlate in the Latin American Boom with its tendency towards hybridisation, transculturation and 'play'. However, given that postmodernism inevitably involves a questioning of concepts of the 'great author' and the 'great work' (central to the Boom), it might more appropriately be associated with the post-Boom, the Boom really being a 'Latin American equivalent of Anglo-European high modernism' (Beverley, 112). The fluidity of the distinction between Boom and post-Boom explored in this book is somewhat at odds with Beverley and co.'s separation of Paz, Cortázar, Fuentes and Vargas Llosa on the one hand and Puig, Nicaraguan workshop poetry and *testimonio* on the other. Combining the two views, two differing broad conceptions of the post-Boom and its relation to popular culture emerge. One is associated with the incorporation of the popular into a programme of play, the other, linking the idea of the 'popular' more with the idea of the 'subaltern', is Yúdice's 'múltiples respuestas / propuestas estético-ideológicas locales ante, frente y dentro de la transnacionalización' (Yúdice, 108). Yúdice, then, as glossed by Beverley, essentially sees the linking of the Boom with postmodernism as a ruse which facilitates colonisation by transnational logic, whereas a post-Boom splintering into various trends replaces an individualised subject with a collective subject and therefore sets up a series of popular-culture-based counter-hegemonic projects (Beverley, 110). From this point of view *Tres tristes tigres* would probably have to be seen as a high culture commodity posing with a popular mask and without any truly revolutionary consciousness. Larsen, however, does posit the notion of a Latin American 'left postmodernism', though this in turn becomes a 'spontaneist myth' which postulates marginality as spontaneously subversive by its very nature, something which seems 'to give up the principle of revolution as a scientifically grounded activity, as a praxis with a rational foundation' (Larsen 6–90). Larsen, of course, is talking about *testimonio* and the celebration of alterity, amongst other things, but his remarks are equally applicable to the other trend discussed here which is that of seeing decentring through play as inherently subversive in political terms. Beverley indeed, in his reading of post-modern theorists, makes the point that 'by virtue of postmodernism's very critique of essentialism there is no necessary connection between it and the left' and proposes '*deprivileging* literature itself as a dominant cultural mode' (Beverley, 121–2). Though the focus of the present study is not the particular reading of the post-Boom, the popular and the postmodern highlighted in this paragraph, the preceding observations are clearly of relevance in calling attention to the limitations of texts like *Tres tristes tigres* as political works and, more significantly in the case of Cabrera Infante, of critical methods which seek to politicise ludic fiction.

A paper by Mark Millington, specifically referring to Cabrera Infante, attempts to consolidate the idea of carnivalisation with political commentary in a cultural studies context.[11] Although he criticises *Tres tristes tigres* as limited because of its machismo and heavy reliance on European and North American cultural referents, Millington does appear to express approval of a culturally positive form of play here. Concentrating on the section 'Los visitantes', he links tourism with the notion of North American cultural imperialism to develop the story (or stories) of the Campbells' Cuban vacation into an image of the corruption of Cuban identity through the desire to attract foreign capital and the consequent absorption of northern values. The story of Mr Campbell's walking stick in which he forcibly appropriates, with the unquestioning connivance of the local authorities, something which does not belong to him is seen to parallel official US conduct towards Cuba up to 1958 and 'indica que la presencia de los Campbell no produce un encuentro entre las culturas, sino que tal presencia es destructiva para la isla y su integridad.' Having said that, Millington goes on to show how the text seeks to express cultural independence of North America. The four versions of the story – Mr Campbell's, Mrs Campbell's corrected version, and the two conflicting translations – oppose the North American urge towards authority and monologic control with the subversive dialogic strategy of Cabrera Infante's novel. 'Los visitantes', Millington suggests, 'desplaza el monólogo norte-americano y así tipifica el ímpetu recreativo de una cultura resistente y dialógica.' The novel, based on textuality and intertextuality, mixes and matches and re-mixes and re-matches a whole range of quotations, misquotations, tongue-twisters, games, stories, parodies, translations and native and foreign, classical and modern cultural references to generate a polyphonic discourse that resists any easy cultural synthesis. This last point is important, for what Millington is really saying is that cultural identity is not simply a question of intrinsic qualities or essences because culture is necessarily a process of adaptation, transformation and translation, in the same way that *Tres tristes tigres* brings out a process of passage through novel, anti-novel and, then, the further problematisation of that binary distinction. *Tres tristes tigres* is not just timeless 'carnival' but a cultural product and, hence, Millington concludes by criticising the tendency of much Anglo-European criticism to suck writers like Cabrera Infante into the normalising ambit of western theories with the resulting effect of deculturalisation.

Millington's approach seems to combine the desire to read playful texts politically with avoiding their circumscription into a normative focus. However, it is not clear that this is always possible. When is carnival an imposed western theory and when is it an example of meaningful cultural transformation? Can a text be both open and actively political? Can it be 'saying something' while it is completely open-ended? Where does one draw the line between a vibrant Cuban dialogic discourse and a colonised Cuban discourse that is saturated by foreign influence? How vibrant can such a discourse be judged anyway in an evocation of the Batista period? And how far do 'cultural' readings account for cultural transformations within the author? How far is an author like Cabrera Infante an individual and how far is he a representative of a particular culture? Why are new theories based on cultural context any more valid than approaches which situate texts in an international literary context? Do they privilege the views of critics over authors? Do they assume that some critics, even those not from or not based in Latin America, have more of a right to speak for the subcontinent than others? What does 'Latin America' mean anyway?

Whatever the favoured answers to such questions, the fact remains that Cabrera Infante himself (though some theorists would dismiss the validity of his position, arguing that all discourse is political) has repeatedly insisted that *Tres tristes tigres* is basically a large-scale joke and that, for instance, 'la literatura debe exclusivamente tener que ver con la literatura. Cualquier otra preocupación es totalmente extraliteraria y, por tanto, desde mi punto de vista actual, condenada al fracaso.'[12] María Elvira Sagarzazu's claim (in the same book that contains the Siemens essay quoted above) that 'much ink and time have been wasted in trying to explain the success of the modern Latin-American novel while side-stepping a key factor, namely that its force originates in its commitment to reality'[13] is, at best, an oversimplification. It is largely play that brought Latin American literature to international attention even if the allure of (socio)politics aided its promotion. Like social or political readings, exclusively 'literary' ones are not without their difficulties, but certainly much of the 'freedom' of *Tres tristes tigres* comes from a realisation that while literature may be, in some (partial and problematic) ways a reflection (though never a copy) of reality, it is above all else literature – and, unlike reality, anything can happen in literature.

The sort of play indulged in in *Tres tristes tigres* is usually said to be associated with Menippean satire and the carnivalesque.[14] Interestingly, Ardis L. Nelson tells us that, 'differing from our usual conception of satire, in which man's vices or follies are held up to ridicule with a decidedly moral or didactic purpose, Menippean satire is light-hearted and has no such moralistic end' (xxiii). This opens up the field of play and, moving on to carnival, Stephanie Merrim says that 'it is well known that the structure of a carnivalesque work is characterised by an extraordinary freedom of composition which manifests itself in a multi-generic or collage texture' ('Secret Idiom', 97). Given Bakhtin's work on the *menippea* and carnival, it is easy to see how critics go on to read Cabrera Infante's fiction in terms of a festive, uninhibited dialogic imagination. The best body of work seeking to describe the patterning and functioning of this imagination is Merrim's. Her starting point is that the ludic represents a kind of opposite or anti-world of the 'real' world. Hence the backdrop against which all else happens is the dark world of night life, seemingly timeless, artificial, utopian, an autonomous, alternative world to diurnal reality. From here it is but a short step to see this as a linguistic world in which a dialogic language can create an alternative to the monologic imposition of conventional reality. If, following Kristeva's reading of Bakhtin, the number one represents the Logos and monologic discourse and the numerical term 0-2 (i.e. not one but the space between zero and two) dialogic practice, then the linguistic freedom implied by the palindrome can be taken as an illustration of this alternative world. The palindrome is a symbol of both play and perfection (a word

like 'ojo' can be playfully reversed yet retain a beautiful symmetry).
Bustrófedon extends this to palindromic numbers:

> y lamentando de paso él (*sic*) que Adán no se llamara en español Adá
> (¿se llamará así en catalá? me preguntó) porque entonces no sola-
> mente sería el primer hombre sino el hombre perfecto y declarando
> el oro el más precioso de los metales escritos y al ala el gran invento
> de Dédalo el artífice y el número 101 sea alabado porque era, es
> como el 88 (loado sea) un número total, redondo, idéntico a sí mismo
> la e-ternidad no lo cambia y como quiera que uno lo mira es siem-
> pre él (*sic*) mismo, otro uno, aunque decía que el perfecto-perfecto
> era el 69 (para alegría de Rine) que es el número absoluto ... (214)

The phrase 'otro uno' here suggests that ideal space between zero
and two, an alternative reality or identity. Thus linguistic play is
both a liberation from a stultifying logocentrism and also the incep-
tion of a perfect alternative order.[15]

The basis of linguistic play is what John M. Lipski has called
paradigmatic overlapping.[16] Specifically this is a form of wordplay
in which a paradigm is added to a series of syntagmatic qualifiers, as
in:

> y nosotros en el más acá muertos de risa en la orilla del mantel, con este
> pregonero increíble, el heraldo, Bustrófeno, éste, gritando, Bustro-
> fenónemo chico eres un Bustrófonbraun, gritando bustrórriba
> marina, gritando, Bustifón, Bustrosimún, Busmonzón, gritando, Viento
> Bustrófenomenal, gritando a diestro y siniestro y ambidiestro. (208)

For Merrim, on a wider plane, this allows for a metaphoric, rather
than metonymic, discourse which generates a constant pattern of
repetition and change. For instance, the various versions of the
same events in 'Los visitantes' or 'La muerte de Trotsky' follow the
same pattern structurally, generating what Merrim calls 'an excess
of signifiers for one signified' ('Secret Idiom', 108). The same is true
of the climactic display of wordplay, the 'Bachata', whose context
is both the circling of the Malecón and a spree of activities. In turn,
correction and translation in 'Los visitantes', generational and
other differences between writers in 'La muerte de Trotsky' and the
displacement of the orderly music of Bach for the 'Bachata' all
suggest the pattern of the novel as a whole which is itself the repetition and change of both remembered reality and previous novel-
istic tradition.

Two things, however, are striking about this kind of play and tend to make suspect its innocence: one is the presence of an order or pattern; the other is the matter of 'translation'. These notions may seem mutually exclusive, in that translation implies a perpetual displacement of the source and deferment of meaning, problematising order (except insofar as the pattern of displacement and deferment could be seen as an order in itself). It is a curiosity of much Cabrera Infante criticism (not unfamiliar in criticism of Latin American literature) that it often begins asserting the playfulness and irreducibility of the Cuban's works but then goes on to indicate, nonetheless, a serious intention and a coherent (if alternative) structure.[17] Merrim sees *Tres tristes tigres* as enjoying 'a cohesive language' with its own 'rules and grammar' ('Secret Idiom', 96). Yet, despite the author's protestations of unbridled playfulness, one might be tempted to see the search for a language or order as the quest (or implied quest) of the novel itself (that is, not just of the critics). The novel is, after all, supposedly an 'experimento ecológico' designed, according to the author's 'advertencia', to 'reconstruct' the past and recreate the 'idioma secreto' of the nightlife scene in Havana in the 1950s. And the central characters Silvestre, Cué, Códac, Eribó and Bustrófedon are all reflections of the author and artists in search of some kind of objective or goal. But the characters' quests largely fail (they are 'tristes tigres' or 'trapped tigers') and the 'experimento ecológico' does too, given the novel's mutative linguistic basis (the 'tres' in the tongue-twister of the title does not appear to capture the past accurately) which stresses the treachery of memory and translation.

Treachery or, at least, betrayal can be traced as an obvious theme in the novel. Nelson charts it well – the web of lies and deception in 'Seseribó', the untrustworthiness of most women characters, Cué's disloyalty to his country and traditions, the self-betrayal and narrative delusions of Cué and Silvestre. The theme peaks, of course, at the end with Silvestre's announcement of marriage to his friend Cué's former love, Laura. But perhaps more interesting is the possible self-betrayal of Bustrófedon, the inspiration of the other characters and of the very wordplay around which the novel revolves. Talking of Bustrófedon's palindromes, Cué asks: '¿No te parece significativo que no acertara con el mejor, el más difícil y más fácil, con el temible? *Yo soy*' (358). Is there a void at the heart of all these word games? Possibly. The 'advertencia' tells us that the book is oral in quality and an attempt to capture spoken Cuban (as opposed to mere Spanish). Yet clearly the text betrays this expectation: often it makes no attempt to capture Cuban dialects and notable parts consist of typographical novelties such as blank, black or inverted pages, words written in circles, geometric shapes.[18] The same point could be made about Nelson's interesting description of the novel's musical structure. Even Merrim's view of the centring of the 'discourse on the actual physical properties of the sign – its plastic and musical dimensions' ('Secret Idiom', 107) is limited, as this would mean the book having no discernible pockets of meaning at all (which is plainly not the case). All of which is leading us more closely to the question of betrayal in translation from one form or medium to another. That this idea underlies the whole book is suggested by its centrality in the prologue when the MC who introduces the 'show' (not just the show at the Tropicana but the 'show' of wordplay that will constitute the entire text) offers a false 'translation' of 'the tropics' in the shape of the glitzy spectacle in the club and mixes languages in a series of sometimes close, sometimes inaccurate, sometimes misleading linguistic translations. Of the cases of translation that follow in the main body of the text, that of 'Los visitantes' is the most striking. The Spanish translations inevitably change the story. Rine Leal's, as the surname implies, is literal but appalling. Silvestre's (a translation of a translation) is correct yet has none of the flavour of the original. Moreover, Mrs Campbell has 'translated' Mr Campbell's 'translation' of 'reality' via her 'corrections'. In any case, she herself is ultimately revealed to be a 'translation' when she is unmasked (?) as a fictional authorial projection. 'Traduttore, traditore' indeed.

Again, though, nothing is so straightforward. In a complex argument, Merrim tries to make the case that, given the impossibility of the 'ecological' task of translating and preserving fifties Havana nightlife, language itself is therefore brought to the fore (in the form of wordplay) and can thus no longer be accused of betraying reality as it is now operating autonomously, only in relation to itself. Not only is this a rather tortuous conceit, it is also undone by the pattern – which she herself acknowledges – of the crumbling validity of linguistic play in the face of an encroaching real world. Linguistic games and nightlife, in both a local and more universal context, are really methods of evasion which eventually reach breaking point: the 'Bachata' is both the culmination of the characters' desperate shilly-shally as well as the moment of its destruction as friends betray each other and are about enter into 'real' life, while the golden (?) age of the nightlife is going to end anyway for the regime is about to fall. Indeed the whole nightlife scene, with its associated charms of potential erotic adventure and heroic self-realisation with glamorous women mediated through the model of Hollywood films, becomes – in a way reminiscent of Cortázar's 'El otro cielo' – a false and ultimately doomed means of escape from the drudgery of an empty life.[19] Eribó, driven by a disadvantaged background, has sold out to a humdrum job with Solaún ('me hallaba refugiado en esa tierra de nadie, en el foso que era mi oficio del siglo XX: ni artista ni técnico ni obrero ni lumpen ni puta: un híbrido, una cruza, un engendro, un parturiunt montes ... nascetur ridiculus mus' [48]) and takes refuge in nocturnal clubland, especially in rhythm or music, but even there fails in a relationship with the upscale Vivian Smith Corona Alvarez del Real. Códac also turns to the night for reasons of elusion, looking for authenticity in the voice of Estrella or, later, Las Capellas, but Estrella dies and he simply drinks. The story is similar for Silvestre and Cué, the climax to their story being the 'Bachata' where, struggling against the idea of 'time', a fast car, word games and showing off to women substitute real fulfilment. Both eventually abandon the nightlife scene – yet Laura's psychiatric sessions do not paint a positive picture of Silvestre's subsequent married life either. What is more, these failures are all artists (musician, photographer, writer and actor) suggesting the frustration of the creative impulse of the novel as a whole. Even the two characters who seem most to represent artistic authenticity, Bustrófedon and Estrella, die – and die rather ordinary deaths at that, conquered by time and mediocrity. In fact the main body of the 'narrative', such as it is, concludes with Laura as a psychiatric patient and the epilogue ends the novel with the ravings of a madwoman. Despite all the claims made for the novel's ludic jollity, the overall vision seems to be deeply pessimistic.

If *Tres tristes tigres* is playful, then, such play is seen, it might be argued, as a pitiful evasion of reality. This is one of the oddities of much ludic or popular/mass-culture-informed fiction from Latin America: the dependency for literary appeal on the very thing it appears to subvert or criticise. And this brings us back to politics once more. For if play is not taken as a sign of active political engagement or is said to be existing for its own sake, then this itself can be judged 'political' in the sense that it can be thought to suggest a reactionary or irresponsible political position. This appears to be the view, for instance, of M.-Pierrette Malcuzynski.[20] Noting that there is no necessary connection between the carnivalesque and a subversive ideology, Malcuzynski posits no connection between 'the presupposed subversive specificity of (the novel's) artistic praxis and *Tres tristes tigres*' conservative ideology' (34). Like Merrim, she sees a transmutational system as the novel's core, but puts special emphasis on the reductive transformation of object into language as the essence of the game. The Havana nightlife, which is the 'object' to be captured in the novel, is incarnated in Estrella. Her style is converted into verbal form by Bustrófedon and she even becomes a linguistic or literary jewel when she, following some extensive play on words representing her, is transformed into a star- ('estrella') shaped anagram based on the association with the diva of the words 'Dávida ávida: vida' (42). She is like, then, the searched-for Queen's jewel in *The Three Musketeers*, with the three 'tigers' (who, like the musketeers, are really four) rallying to Bustrófedon's play on 'All for one and one for all' (207). Given that these artistic musketeers are often barely distinguishable and linked to Bustrófedon, they can all be taken as reflections of the author (linked to them anyway by his inscription as GCI in the text) in his quest to transform 'object' into language. For Malcuzynski, this leads to 'a hermetically closed work with the *illusion* of "ouverture"' (43). Indeed she argues that, rather than generating polyphonic co-existence, the transformational process, seemingly designed to avoid paralysis, becomes a form of pointless paralysis in itself and is even based on a pattern of repeated domination of one voice over another. Finally, she criticises Cabrera Infante for flaunting the signs of openness and innovation in a covert refusal to subvert ideologically the reality portrayed (pre-revolutionary Cuba) and for indulging in 'a wilfull ... and a subtle diversion tactic which orients the critic towards aesthetic problematics' (51).

So, the circle has been completed from Siemens' claim that play is a kind of political statement to Malcuzynski's claim that play is a political betrayal. This highlights a fundamental feature of much contemporary criticism, the assumption that 'good' literature is somehow connected with political engagement or, at least, that political engagement is what 'matters' in literature. Increasingly too, the 'political' has come to be associated with the incorporation of popular culture. Apart from the nightlife scene, the most striking element from popular culture in *Tres tristes tigres* is the inclusion of popular movies. Nelson, Merrim and especially Kenneth E. Hall, amongst others, have all studied filmic connections in the novel, cataloguing a whole range of references and parallels, thematic and technical.[21] An interesting characteristic of these studies is that the connections they identify are largely formal correspondences with film techniques and specific films and even Merrim, who takes a more interpretative approach, has little to say on *Tres tristes tigres* in comparison to *El beso de la mujer araña*. The reason is perhaps that there is little reflection in the novel on the sociopolitical implications of mass cultural (particularly North American) influences on society. In fact, twice Silvestre recounts a real, witnessed scene of bloody violence before going to the cinema, yet the real scene pales compared to the more vivid 'reality' of the movie he sees (41–2, 436–7). There seems to be virtually none of the 'reflective distance … from the cinematic image' that Rowe and Schelling say they see in Puig's novels (217). They go on to maintain that 'what is important is that it (i.e. cinematic fetishism) is displayed, critically, as an area of mystification and potential demystification within which Puig's characters actively negotiate' (217). But who wants to experience critical distance and demystification when they go to the movies? Do not most people go for precisely the opposite reason? Expecting an author to critique popular movies in a certain way is the same as demanding that he display certain political attitudes. The absence of such a critique or such attitudes may be politically revealing, but they do not make anyone a 'bad' author.

The one criticism that might be made of Cabrera Infante is concerning his own self-portrayal as an assailant of high culture. In *La Habana para un infante difunto* he says that 'nada me complace más que … lo vulgar' and that 'en cuanto a la expresión de vulgaridad en la literatura y en el arte, creo que si soy un adicto al cine es por su vulgaridad viva.'[22] Yet, as Nelson has pointed out ('Cine', 397–8), in Cabrera Infante's film book *Un oficio del siglo xx: G. Caín 1956–60*, the only film he relates directly to the novel is Michelangelo Antonioni's *L'avventura* – that is, a high-culture film. And this says something about *Tres tristes tigres*. It may be playful and deal with nightclubs and movies, but it is not a piece of popular culture. It is a complex, difficult novel which owes as much to Borges as it does to the 'popular'. But does it, like some other comparable works, also play politics with the popular? That, as has been discussed, is a moot point. Perhaps one should simply accept the author's own evaluation, that it is simply an intricate, multiplex joke. Cabrera Infante clearly thinks he is very funny. We may think he just makes 'inconsequential puns', but should we criticise him for not writing the book we think he should have or, perhaps worse, pretend that he has?

## Notes

[1] 'Guillermo Cabrera Infante: An Interview in a Summer Manner with Jason Wilson', in *Modern Latin American Fiction*, ed. John King, Faber and Faber, London, 1987, pp. 305-25. The review is by D. L. Shaw in *Modern Language Review*, LXXXIV, 1989, p. 510.

[2] Carlos Fuentes, *La nueva novela hispanoamericana*, Joaquín Mortiz, Mexico City, 1969, p. 31.

[3] Rita Guibert, 'Guillermo Cabrera Infante: conversación sobre *Tres tristes tigres*', in Julio Ortega, *et al.*, *Guillermo Cabrera Infante*, Fundamentos, Madrid, 1974, p. 20.

[4] Guillermo Cabrera Infante, 'The Invisible Exile', in *Literature in Exile*, ed. John Glad, Duke University Press, Durham and London, 1990, p. 34.

[5] Isabel Alvarez-Borland, 'Identidad cíclica de *Tres tristes tigres*', *Revista Iberoamericana*, LVII, 1991, p. 232.

[6] Victorino Polo García, 'De *Tres tristes tigres* a *La Habana para un infante difunto*, un espejo para el camino', *Revista Iberoamericana*, LVIII, 1992, p. 563.

[7] Guillermo Cabrera Infante, *Tres tristes tigres*, Seix Barral, Barcelona, 1965, p. 360. See: William L. Siemens, *Worlds Reborn: The Hero in the Modern Spanish American Novel*, West Virginia University Press, Morgantown, 1984, p. 156; Raymond D. Souza, *Major Cuban Novelists: Innovation and Tradition*, University of Missouri Press, Columbia and London, 1976, p. 82; Alvarez-Borland, p. 232. All other references to Siemens will be to 'Guillermo Cabrera Infante and the Divergence of Revolutions: Political versus Textual', in *Literature and Revolution*, ed. David Bevan, Rodopi, Amsterdam and Atlanta, 1989, pp. 107–19.

[8] Julio Ortega, *Poetics of Change: The New Spanish American Narrative*, University of Texas Press, Austin, 1984.

[9] William Rowe and Vivian Schelling, *Memory and Modernity: Popular Culture in Latin America*, Verso, London and New York, 1991, p. 193.

[10] John Beverley, *Against Literature*, University of Minnesota Press,

Minneapolis and London, 1993. See Beverley for references to Jameson, Larsen, González Echevarría and Yúdice. The quotation from George Yúdice is from '¿Puede hablarse de postmodernidad en América Latina?', *Revista de crítica literaria latinoamericana*, XXIX, 1989, p. 108.

[11]Mark I. Millington, 'Voces múltiples en Cabrera Infante', paper given at the *Primer congreso anglo-hispano*, Huelva, 1992. I am grateful to the author for supplying me with a copy of his manuscript.

[12]Emir Rodríguez Monegal, *El arte de narrar*, Monte Avila, Caracas, n.d., p. 65.

[13]María Elvira Sagarzazu, 'New Concerns for the Novel: A Latin American Viewpoint', in Bevan, p. 164.

[14]Ardis L. Nelson, *Cabrera Infante in the Menippean Tradition*, Juan de la Cuesta, Newark, 1983; Stephanie Merrim, 'A Secret Idiom: The Grammar and Role of Language in *Tres tristes tigres*', *Latin American Literary Review*, VIII, 1980, pp. 96–117 and '*Tres tristes tigres*: antimundo, antilenguaje, antinovela', *Texto crítico*, XI 1985, pp. 133–52. All references, unless otherwise indicated, will be to these works.

[15]See Merrim, 'Antimundo', pp. 141–4. The theoretical references are to: Mikhail Bakhtin, *Problems of Dostoevsky's Poetics*, Ardis, Ann Arbor, 1973 and *Rabelais and his World*, MIT Press, Cambridge, 1968; Julia Kristeva, 'Le mot, le dialogue et le roman', in *Semiotiké*, Seuil, Paris, 1969.

[16]John M. Lipski, 'Paradigmatic Overlapping in *Tres tristes tigres*', *Dispositio*, I, 1976, pp. 33–43.

[17]Patterns of order or structure other than those discussed here have been identified. See, for example, Alvarez-Borland and Josefina Ludmer, '*Tres tristes tigres*: órdenes literarios y jerarquías sociales', *Revista Iberoamericana*, XLV, 1979, pp. 493–512.

[18]M. Victoria García Serrano makes this point in 'Un pre-texto problemático: la advertencia de *Tres tristes tigres*', *Hispanófila*, XXXIV, 1991, p. 90.

[19]See Alvarez-Borland for a thorough account of this aspect of the nightlife scene.

[20]M.-Pierrette Malcuzynski, '*Tres tristes tigres*, or the Treacherous Play on Carnival', *Ideologies and Literature*, III, 1981, pp. 33–56.

[21]Ardis L. Nelson, '*Tres tristes tigres* y el cine', *Kentucky Romance Quarterly*, XXIX, 1982, pp. 391–404; Stephanie Merrim, 'Through the Film Darkly: Grade "B" Movies and Dreamwork in *Tres tristes tigres* and *El beso de la mujer araña*', *Modern Language Studies*, XV, 1985, pp. 300–12; Kenneth E. Hall, *Guillermo Cabrera Infante and the Cinema*, Juan de la Cuesta, Newark, 1989.

[22]Guillermo Cabrera Infante, *La Habana para un infante difunto*, Seix Barral, Barcelona, 1979, p. 530.

# Chapter 4

# Mario Vargas Llosa and *La tía Julia y el escribidor*: Freedom, authority and textual control

The success of Manuel Puig and, to some degree, Guillermo Cabrera Infante, and their significance in the emergence and development of a post-Boom can perhaps be seen or detected in the changes in style, tone, and content that characterise the literary production of established authors of the Boom like Mario Vargas Llosa, Carlos Fuentes and José Donoso in the ten years or so after the end of the 1960s. In the case of Vargas Llosa, for example, there is a pronounced shift towards play and accessibility in works like *Pantaleón y las visitadoras* (1973) and *La tía Julia y el escribidor* (1977) in a way which echoes features such as the humourous use of written documents, the inclusion of popular narratives and references to movies, music, nightlife and youth culture, features typical of *Boquitas pintadas*, *El beso de la mujer araña* and *Tres tristes tigres*. In particular, there are obvious points of comparison between *La tía Julia y el escribidor* and *El beso de la mujer araña*[1] with their similar interests in the relationship of 'High' and 'Low' culture and their framing of mass media narratives in the context of an apparently more sophisticated novel form. One might therefore expect to see a parallel concern with the links between popular culture and social or political issues in both writers. However, at this level, the connections between the two authors become more obscure. In drawing attention to the clear convergences of interest in Puig and Vargas Llosa, Gerald Martin, for instance, nonetheless asserts that the latter 'does not in fact here give any implied critique of the mass media upon helpless individual consciousness, as Puig invariably does'.[2] And indeed a casual or maybe even close reading of *La tía Julia y el escribidor* may not yield much strong evidence of any real social or political intention. Yet the difference between the two is not so unproblematic. As the second chapter attempted to suggest, Puig's sociopolitical stance and his attitude to the mass media is more ambivalent (or confused) than Martin admits.[3] As for Vargas Llosa, the main body of his work – and, with this, Martin would agree – is deeply engaged in social, political and historical questions. It would thus seem rather peculiar for a major piece like *La tía Julia y el escribidor* to exclude such matters altogether. The key (and, for many, upsetting) issue in Vargas Llosa is not so much the presence of 'politics' as the question of political perspective. Many critics, Martin among them, have focused, usually disapprovingly, on the marked shift from Left to Right in the Peruvian's authorial and more manifestly public postures. What this implies also is a movement from ideological commitment (or at least engagement, for the early Vargas Llosa is not all that politically coherent anyway) to profound scepticism. *La tía Julia y el escribidor* (coming after *Pantaleón y las visitadoras*, a comic satire on the military mentality at the time of the reformist Velasco regime and which initiated the aforementioned change in tone and betrayed a lack of identification with the characters and situations portrayed) may be taken, then, as a representation or dramatisation of that sense of ideological break. The political significance of the novel may therefore be precisely that it is not a political novel. An acceptance of this starting point may reveal the novel to have a good deal of coherence as a work of literature. The problems begin to emerge when the novel is considered in the more expansive context of the author's wider literary corpus and extra-literary political life. The question is whether the bitter debate regarding Vargas Llosa's political trajectory should be sidelined by the obviously 'literary' nature of this work or whether it should inevitably colour our reading of it.

A first point to be made is that a number of critics, presumably less inclined than some others to indulge in Vargas Llosa bashing, do see a continuity between the 1977 work and its more clearly socially-conscious predecessors. Dick Gerdes recycles Vargas Llosa's theory of the 'elemento añadido', but is less clear on what the target of the novel's 'criticism' is (apart from bad writing).[4] Sara Castro-Klarén claims that 'the plots of the novel are charged with social issues that Vargas Llosa had been exploring before *Aunt Julia and the Scriptwriter*', but does not say much about what those social issues are here.[5] If such approaches remind us of the difficulty of reading this as a social novel, other commentators, like Rita Gnutzmann and Marvin A. Lewis find a bit more meat to support their view.[6] They see the novel as a kind of inverse *Conversación en la Catedral*, Vargas Llosa's caustic attack on the Odría regime. The very absence of political detail, the seemingly casual references to 'el General', and the Mexican visitor's attack on 'las dictaduras militares (en el Perú padecíamos una, encabezada por un tal Odría)'[7] imply that the novel's adoption of the point of view of the values and attitudes of the Peruvian middle classes in the 1950s constitutes a critique of the same. Moreover, there is a good deal of indirect allusion to Peru's endemic pattern of social stratification. The dualism of High and Low culture which defines the novel's structure underlines this. The snobbish Radio Panamericana contrasts with the plebeian Radio Central as does the smug world of Marito's family with the many sordid tales of Pedro Camacho's soap operas. Indeed the middle-class romance of Marito and Julia is presented in counterpoint to the larger social canvas provided by Camacho's stories. The map he uses to provide a setting for his stories underscores, in a rather crude way, the city's rigid social divisions and recalls the inclusion of a city map in the early editions of *La ciudad y los perros* (in which the young cadets functioned as a microcosm of the city and state). The owners, bosses, artists, writers, office workers and general skivvies at the radio stations, meantime, are presented clearly in terms of the hierarchical relationships between them. What is more, the two stations can be seen as having a manipulative cultural function: the upscale one assisting the imposition of outside standards by its diet of US pop music and movie news, the downscale one promoting the acculturation of rural immigrants via popular shows and Latin or indigenous music. The central importance of radio soap operas in the novel, originally imported from pre-revolutionary Cuba, might also be taken as an indictment of an escapist, frivolous and sterile cultural situation.

These last points, of course, raise the question of whether *La tía Julia y el escribidor* does, in fact, like Puig's novels (up to a point), seek to expose the negative role played by the mass media in cultural conditioning. That this is the case is, in part, the argument of Ellen McCracken.[8] However, she is at her most persuasive in her critique of the mass media in terms of ownership and commodification of culture rather than in its formation of ideology. The part-owner, Genaro Jr., humourously dubbed the 'empresario progresista' and more interested in 'los negocios que [en] los honores' (18), is the stereotypical populist modern businessman, happy to lower himself to any level for the sake of making fast money (as reflected in his willingness to carry the heavy typewriter for his new 'investment' Pedro Camacho [27]). Judging radio serials by circulation figures and market-research surveys, he buys them not according to their quality but their weight. His values are brought out symbolically when he hands over the work things of Marito, who works in the newsroom, to an accountant and a writer of soap operas (26). The prevalence of commercial values and the centrality of mass appeal are encoded in the depersonalisation of Pedro Camacho who is routinely referred to as a machine and 'fenómeno radiofónico' or characterised with the phrase: 'no es un hombre sino una industria' (16, 17). Yet, despite the focus on the mass market at the supply end, there is little to suggest, in the novel, that the demand is shaped or controlled. Some may feel that the parallel between the affair of Marito and Julia and the content of soap opera romances (of which more later) implies a form of social conditioning; and McCracken attempts to portray Julia as a victim of mass media ideology because she analyses her relationship with Marito as if it were a radio- (or, better, movie-) drama: 'En el mejor de los casos, lo nuestro duraría tres, tal vez unos cuatro años, es decir hasta que encuentres a la mocosita que será la mamá de tus hijos. Entonces me botarás y tendré que seducir a otro caballero. Y aparece la palabra fin' (206). However, the novel does not emphasise any of this and, indeed, the characters seem very aware of the melodramatic nature of their relationship and playfully indulge themselves in comparisons. In any case, though Julia is a fan of popular movies and listens to the 'radioteatros', she displays a good deal of independence, is often shown to have more wisdom and common sense than the young intellectual Varguitas and, importantly, had never even heard of Pedro Camacho before despite his supposedly huge fame in her native Bolivia. Indeed many readers may well conclude that Julia (who, of course, in real life published a rejoinder to Vargas Llosa in the form of the book *Lo que Varguitas no dijo*) is more a victim of a self-centred husband than of mass media ideology.

In fact, the entire pattern of social commentary in the novel is really rather watered down or so indirect as to lack much sting. Thus Lewis' claim that the novel 'render[s] a critical evaluation of

Peruvian reality not dissimilar to what was achieved in his earlier social realist novels' (140) seems somewhat dubious. The so-called criticisms are few and far between, nearly always indirect and certainly lack the backing or force of any strong or clear narratorial perspective. The alleged villains of any social critique scenario are curiously sympathetic and entertaining: the effusive entrepreneur Genaro Jr., the eccentric writer of soap operas Pedro Camacho (more manipulated than manipulator and most definitely not in control of his audience by the latter stages of the novel), even Rebagliati the colourful and vulgar director of the scandal sheet *Extra*. And, of course, if the novel were a critique of the evils of hierarchy and middle-class values then that critique would obviously have to include the protagonist (and, by extension, the author) Marito/Varguitas (the representation of Mario Vargas Llosa). The author, one can safely assume, does not wish to do a hatchet-job on himself and hence the emphasis of the book is not so much 'society' as the more personal arena of Vargas Llosa's own life and career. The social theme is, in other words, subordinate to the twin themes of love and writing. The very cover of the book, with the author's name and the novel's dualistic title, draws attention to this: it will be about the author's personal relationship to both matters, not a vast social landscape.

This apparently simple conclusion points to what is really a rather complex question or set of questions. The separation of the personal and the political is itself a thorny issue, especially in the light of contemporary theory which often basically boils down to the idea that the personal is always political and no discourse can be divorced from ideology. Related to this is the issue of a real person seemingly writing about himself in what appears to be a work of fiction. The question arises then of the relationship between Mario Vargas Llosa and Marito/Mario/Varguitas,[9] between author and protagonist and, of course, between autobiography and fiction. All of this in turn relates to a central concern of Vargas Llosa's 'theoretical' or literary critical writings: the relationship between reality, on the one hand, and, on the other, realism or even play (Martin has already noted the evolution in Vargas Llosa from a sober, if complex, realism that distinguished him from other successful Latin American writers to a kind of playful parody more typical of the new novel as a whole [209–10]). This is not the place to trawl once more through Vargas Llosa's theory of writing.[10]

Suffice it to say that it has always been based on a difficult combination of the objective and the subjective, be it on the external level of presenting a fuller, more 'objective' picture of reality by developing a technique of juxtaposition and employment of intermediaries ('vasos comunicantes', 'saltos temporales' and 'cajas chinas') to remind us of the potential subjectivity of its construction, or on the internal level of the author's 'subjective' recreation or, rather, transformation in fiction of 'objective' reality. Linked with this is his notion that 'un hombre escribe novelas por una parte para rescatar y por la otra para exorcizar experiencias ya extintas, que lo obsesionan y torturan. Quiere liberarse de ellas y al mismo tiempo recobrarlas ...'[11] What Vargas Llosa wants, then, is both to create fiction out of reality and turn reality into fiction. In essence, this is a desire to define order and cancel difference in an otherwise overwhelmingly complex or even chaotic world. The evolution from the labyrinthine structural forms of his earlier works towards the more rigid symmetry of *La tía Julia y el escribidor*, coupled with the neutralisation of both the youthful uncertainty of the love-struck Marito and the rampaging 'fantasmas' of Pedro Camacho by the framing of the novel from the controlling perspective of a mature and successful husband and author may suggest that the driving force behind the text is to combine all these multiple and interpenetrating elements and reduce them to a single principle of coherence.

To begin with, the main structural principle of the novel is the dualistic alternation of the stories of 'la tía Julia' and 'el escribidor', that is, of reality and fiction – insofar as the story of Vargas Llosa's relationship with Julia Urquidi Illanes is ostensibly documented from reality while the stories of Pedro Camacho would appear to be fictional creations. Yet at the same time the real-life story of the relationship of the author and his first wife becomes here a fictional version (the story of Marito and la tía Julia) while Camacho's unreal stories are based on reality (the story of the real author of soap operas Raúl Salmón) and in some ways reflect a wider portrait of social reality than the relatively enclosed world of the two lovers. Moreover, the two levels parallel and interact with each other to such a degree that the supposedly real story takes on the qualities of fiction while the apparently fictional stories begin to look more like what is supposed to be reality. Reality becomes fiction, then, and fiction becomes reality.

The interpenetration of so-called reality and fiction in the novel can now be examined more closely. Plotting links constantly underline the connection between the odd chapters and the even chapters (dealing respectively with the life of Marito and versions of the scripts of Pedro Camacho). For example, the first chapter ends with the arrival of Pedro Camacho at the radio station and the removal of Marito's typewriter. The second (which the reader may not yet be aware is one of Camacho's stories) tells the tale of the discovery by Dr Alberto de Quinteros, following his niece's fainting fit at her wedding, that she is pregnant by her brother. The third begins: 'Volví a ver a Pedro Camacho pocos días después del incidente' (55). Initially the reader probably thinks that the word 'incidente' refers to what happened at the wedding before it becomes clear that it refers to what happened over the typewriter. Thus the two plot levels are locked together and continue in this way until the end as the increasingly frenzied tone of Camacho's 'radioteatros' is matched by the rapid increase in action in the story of Marito as he desperately seeks to overcome the practical obstacles to his marriage to Julia. Even within the odd-numbered chapters the structural connection between Marito's relationships to Julia and Camacho (both Bolivian, incidentally) is repeatedly stressed. For instance, near the beginning: 'Recuerdo muy bien el día que me habló del fenómeno radiofónico porque ese mismo día, a la hora de almuerzo, vi a la tía Julia por primera vez' (16). From now on the two relationships are seen to develop in counterpoint to each other in the odd-numbered chapters. Moreover, many of the elements in the soap operas are clearly taken from things the reader learns about Camacho's own life in the sections narrated by Mario: rats, the strange run-down pensión, peculiar dietary obsessions, a dislike of motorised transport, a problematic relationship with Argentina and so on.

However, these points of contact go well beyond the structural to the extent that there is a suggestion that the two levels are so intimately connected that they are somehow the same as each other. The relationship of Marito and Julia, both romantic and scandalous, is itself like a soap opera – in fact, 'cabalito para un radioteatro de Pedro Camacho' (112). So much so indeed that the story of their efforts to marry, with all its repetitions and suspenseful breaks, is written virtually as if it were itself a serial. But Camacho's stories also echo their relationship, based as they are on convention-versus-desire, scandalous love affairs, the trials and tribulations of romance and the conflict between age and youth. In particular, the stories focus repeatedly on the themes of family and incest, a reflection of the centrality of kinship in the odd chapters (where almost everyone, including the Archbishop of Lima, seems to be Varguitas' relative and the protagonist ends up marrying first his aunt[12] and then his cousin).

This feeling that reality is like a fiction (or that fiction is actually quite close to reality) is added to by the presentation of almost all of the other characters who come into Marito's life. The actors who play the characters in the soap operas are nothing like what they seem to be to the listeners:

> actrices y actores declinantes, hambrientos, desastrados, cuyas voces juveniles, acariciadoras, cristalinas, diferían terriblemente de sus caras viejas, sus bocas amargas y sus ojos cansados... . Y, en efecto, qué decepción se hubieran llevado esas amas de casa que se enternecían con la voz de Luciano Pando si hubieran visto su cuerpo contrahecho y su mirada estrábica, y qué decepción los jubilados a quienes el candencioso rumor de Josefina Sánchez despertaba recuerdos, si hubieran conocido su papada, sus bigotes, sus orejas aleteantes, sus várices. (13)

Similarly the status and image of Pedro Camacho and Lucho Gatica are contradicted by their appalling appearance (23, 106). Appearance is not reality. Or perhaps reality is only appearance. For the seemingly real appearance of these (and other) characters is very unreal in that they are portrayed as caricatures; that is, fictional creations. Examples abound: the tiny, weird Pedro Camacho (described as a 'caricatura' [26] and as 'caricatural' [163]), the gigantic, larger-than-life Genaro-hijo (together with his father Genaro-papá), the diminutive and terrified women's hero Lucho Gatica, the incredibly scruffy and greasy Luciano Pando, the ageing Josefina Sánchez with her dyed-blonde hair, her double chin and her varicose veins, the bizarrely talented sound-effects man, Batán, with his porcupine hairstyle, the wacky Pascual with his love of disaster stories, the illiterate odd-job man and nominal news editor Gran Pablito with his funny walk and amazing wheezing ('era uno de esos personajes pintorescos e indefinibles que atrae o fabrica el ambiente de la radio' [115]), the large-bellied, big-toothed black fisherman-cum-mayor from Tambo de Mora, and so on.

The most important of these caricaturesque figures is, of course,

Pedro Camacho. Yet not only is he a caricature of himself but also perhaps of Marito (or Vargas Llosa). The increasingly weird narratives of the even-numbered chapters with their strange, obsessed characters, dark sexual fantasies, anti-Argentine tirades and cataclysmic tendencies are a grotesque parody of the progressively more peculiar Camacho we meet in the odd chapters. Equally both Camachos are a parody of the novelist. The highly disciplined workaholic Camacho is not a million miles away from the picture of the dedicated artist who structures his work with meticulous care that Vargas Llosa has sometimes painted of himself.[13] The map purchased by Camacho to help with his writing recalls, as has been mentioned, a feature of *La ciudad y los perros*. The idea of the obsessive Camacho working out his obsessions in his writings is reminiscent of Vargas Llosa's theory of writing as an exorcism of personal 'demonios'. The style and content of Camacho's soap operas is not so different from those of Vargas Llosa's own work either. The increasingly labyrinthine nature of the soaps and the swapping of characters from one story to another makes one think of the structural complexity and experimentation of the Peruvian novelist. Class difference, sweeping portraits of society, social limitations, the desire for social mobility, the conflict of free will and responsibility, corruption, sexual deviation, violence and obsessive behaviour (all features of the radio dramas) are also key elements in Vargas Llosa's own fiction. And Camacho's dramas contain elements from the work of Varguitas and Vargas Llosa. The soap about Elianita relates to Marito's *cuento* 'La tía Eliana' and the drama of the Jehovah's Witness who intends to cut off his penis that is only used 'para hacer pipí' is a clear echo of the young man's story on the impotent senator. Meantime Camacho's character Sergeant Lituma is the ubiquitous Lituma of a number of works by Vargas Llosa. In their discussions on the nature of realism, the difference that seems to emerge between Marito and Camacho is that the former uses experience of the real world while the latter uses only secondary sources such as maps and books. But in his description of his literary apprenticeship Marito is constantly writing stories based only on what he has heard from other people, and written moreover, in an attempted copy of the style of other authors such as Borges, Hugo, Maupassant, Bernard Shaw, Somerset Maugham, Hemingway and so forth. His job as a news editor and, at the end, as an editor of soap operas is a further image of this plagiaristic use of other people's material and tinkering with other people's style. And, finally, the 'real' experiences of Marito are presented, as Rosemary Geisdorfer Feal amongst others has shown, within the pattern of a model which is itself decidedly fictional: namely the picaresque. What all this seems to suggest is that the distinction between the two levels in the novel is not at all clear and that each therefore may be as real or as fictional as the other.

A tempting conclusion to be drawn from the above, particularly in the light of the sharp change from the style and tone of Vargas Llosa's earlier work mentioned before, is that *La tía Julia y el escribidor* marks the abandonment of social realism in favour of the sort of play that has made the Latin American novel (and this novel) so popular on the international market. This would be a case once more, then, of a novel playing with the idea that fiction is only fiction. This would cancel any social dimension to the novel and any application to reality. The novel would simply be about itself. In a sense, this is true. As critics have repeatedly noted it is essentially a novel about writing. It begins with an epigraph from Salvador Elizondo's *El Grafógrafo* on writing about writing and ends with a kind of epilogue where the mature author is now in a position to start writing the story which the reader is about to finish. Thus, for Sharon Magnarelli, the text presents itself as a preparation for the writing of itself, with the *énoncé* ending where the *énonciation* begins.[14] But perhaps more than a novel about writing it is a novel about a writer. No amount of contemporary theory can completely eliminate the 'common-sense' feeling that this is some kind of autobiography and therefore some kind of reflection of (or wish to reflect) reality. Nonetheless, such an autobiographical reading would be seriously compromised by the tendency to blur the distinction between Varguitas/Vargas Llosa and Pedro Camacho which inclines to suggest that the novelist is not much different from a crazy author of potboilers who ultimately self-destructs and fails in his 'artistic' enterprise. Indeed a whole series of authority figures and controllers of truth (clear equivalents to the figure of the omniscient author) have their certainty, authority and control undermined in Camacho's dramas: the doctor by the revelations about his niece and nephew, the policeman by the mysterious black prisoner, the judge by the libidinous young girl and totally contradictory sets of evidence, the powerful businessman and father by the rebellion of his wife and children. If this is not enough, the cataclysmic outcome of the stories implies that they are all killed off. Narratorial and authorial control is thus undermined. However, the whole problem seems to disappear if one accepts the somewhat obvious contention that the author of the entire text is Mario Vargas Llosa. In fact, the establishment of the narrative perspective of the mature author in the final chapter reminds us that this is, to be sure, the case. The subversive potential of Camacho's narratives is neutralised by the reality that they are written by Vargas Llosa who is himself inscribed in the novel as its own narrative perspective. Any subversive element of play is in turn neutralised by that same assertion of powerful authorial control. Thus the author is allowed to have his cake and eat it. Free reign is given to all kinds of games and associative excess, yet any threat of disruption or chaos is effectively eliminated by the ingenious clarification of central control by the novel's ending.

A key strategy in *La tía Julia y el escribidor* is not so much the alternation of perspective of author and scriptwriter as the systematic erection of the power of the former over the latter. A number of critics have made use of Roland Barthes' distinction between 'écrivain' and 'écrivant': 'l'écrivain accomplit une fonction, l'écrivant une activité'.[15] Vargas Llosa is the 'writer', while Camacho is merely a 'scribbler'. If the text presents the mature author as the creator of the entire narrative, then it is problematic to see the novel baldly in terms of the superiority of the odd chapters over the even ones. It is more a question of the 'writer''s appropriation and transformation of the tools of the 'scribbler'. Before re-examining the relationship of both sets of chapters from this viewpoint, it can first be shown that this pattern of growing power displacement exists at the level of the basic plot (that is, in the continuous narrative of Varguitas/Vargas Llosa). Essentially, the novel is about the triumph of the serious writer Vargas Llosa seen in connection with the collapse of a species of rival, the popular writer Pedro Camacho. Carlos J. Alonso's perceptive account of this process – one of a number – begins by emphasising the importance of *récit* over *histoire* in the even-numbered chapters, suggesting that their meaning is therefore Camacho's own personality and the deterioration of his creative powers.[16] This process, though, is seen in counterpoint to the story of Varguitas/Vargas Llosa's coming to maturity as a novelist or, in Alonso's words, his 'rise to a position of discursive authority' (50). It is of note that the novel begins with Camacho taking over Varguitas' typewriter yet more or less ends with Varguitas taking over Camacho's job. This reversal of fortunes is supported by a structural reversal, namely a break in the rigourous pattern of alternating chapters so that the voice in the final chapter (which should have been 'Camacho') is now appropriated by Varguitas returning triumphantly to Lima in the form of the mature author Vargas Llosa. The juxtaposition of images in Marito's words to Julia in the previous chapter is telling:

> Hablamos de lo que haríamos cuando volviéramos a reunirnos, cómo ella me ayudaría en mi trabajo y cómo, de una manera u otra, tarde o temprano, llegaríamos un día a París a vivir en esa buhardilla donde yo me volvería, por fin, un escritor. Le conté la historia de su compatriota Pedro Camacho, que estaba ahora en una clínica, rodeado de locos, volviéndose loco él mismo sin duda ... (420)

The success of the one is always seen closely in relation to the failure of the other.

Of course, what this plotting feature is really saying is that Varguitas/Vargas Llosa is really a better writer than Camacho and that serious writing is better than popular writing. Marito implies to Julia that (unlike him, presumably) Camacho is not an intellectual and is not part of the current of 'serious' literature: 'Pedro Camacho es un intelectual entre comillas. ¿Te fijaste que no hay un solo libro en su cuarto? Me ha explicado que no lee para que no le influyan el estilo' (165). Linking up with Marito's frequently expressed disdain for popular movies the further suggestion here is that popular forms like film and radio are somehow inferior to 'literature' (which he writes). Also, when it is said of one of Camacho's characters that 'su obligación era cuantitativa, no cualitativa' (171), the idea is that 'literature' is better than mass culture. This difference in quality is also suggested by the way Camacho tosses off his stories while Varguitas allows his to mature thoroughly: 'Para un parto de trillazos, con cesárea y todo, sólo necesita cinco minutos, qué más quiere. Yo me he demorado tres semanas para un cuento de tres muchachos que levitan aprovechando la presión de los aviones' (233). The very novel we are reading is testimony to the positive results of Varguitas' method while the ephemeral tales of Camacho are forgotten as he is reduced to the lowly and anonymous position of gofer in a declining sensationalist rag. Finally, on the occasions that Marito compares

Camacho's slips with the techniques of experimental fiction (282, 290), the author is really focusing attention on the originality of his own work for he and the reader know only too well that, in the case of Camacho, it is no more than a question of the most awful errors and loss of authorial control.

It would now seem then that Vargas Llosa differs from Puig in two respects. Not only is there little criticism of the ideological effects of mass culture, there is little attempt to re-evaluate it culturally either. There is only one real reflection by Marito on the possible falseness of the dichotomy between High and Low in the novel: '¿Por qué esos personajes que se servían de la literatura como adorno o pretexto iban a ser más escritores que Pedro Camacho, quien *sólo* vivía para escribir? ¿Porque ellos habían leído (o, al menos, sabían que deberían haber leído) a Proust, a Faulkner, a Joyce, y Pedro Camacho era poco más que un analfabeto?' (236). This is pretty feeble stuff and may seem like false modesty in the context of the novel's apparent assertion of the preferability of the Vargas Llosa model over the Camacho model. As a matter of fact, the novel often seems to go out of its way to devalue popular culture. Not only is it suggested that mass or popular culture is narrow, superficial and lacking in ambiguity ('advertí que las cosas que le interesaban [a Pedro Camacho] más se referían a los extremos: millonarios y mendigos, blancos y negros, santos y criminales' [65]), but it is also clearly beneath Marito who, despite his interest in Camacho the man, never actually listens, it would appear, to *any* of his soap operas, because presumably he has more worthwhile things to do. Moreover, while it is true that the embryonic intellectual Marito is sometimes treated with mild irony (which can be dismissed anyway since his faults were merely a function of his youthful enthusiasm and he has now transformed himself into the mature author who is the real narrator of this novel), there is nothing mild about the irony reserved for the writer, actors and crew who put together the soap operas. They may be remembered with some affection by the mature and successful author, who does not have to mix with them any more, but, as the brief account of their caricaturesque descriptions suggested earlier, they are consistently ridiculed in a mocking, even cruel way (to be sure, they are almost like a subspecies, referred to at one stage as 'la fauna radioteatral' [13]). It is interesting that the caricatures mentioned above are all socially inferior to Mario. So if the interpenetration of Camacho's stories and that of Marito and Julia hint that Marito's life is a kind of soap, the social difference also sets him apart from that mass cultural world. Though his family are avid consumers of Camacho's 'radioteatros', it is made clear right from the start that Radio Central has a 'vocación multitudinaria, plebeya' (12). And Marito himself, hot on the heels of an implied criticism (a very gentle and indirect criticism at that) of his family's snobbishness towards the Chinese grocer who married tía Eliana, is seen coaching tía Julia in the whys and wherefores of *huachafería*: 'yo le explicaba lo que era huachafo, lo que no se podía decir ni hacer y había establecido una censura inquisitorial en sus lecturas, prohibiéndole todos sus autores favoritos, que empezaban por Frank Yerby y terminaban con Corín Tellado' (276). Related to this is a haughtiness towards autochthonous, national or Latin American culture. Low culture is nearly always Latin American and High culture foreign. So Radio Central caters to aboriginal tastes and is therefore vulgar (12–3), tío Pancracio is made to look absurd because of his fascination with 'la música criolla' (20) and Marito laments having to see a popular movie which 'para colmo era mexicana' (20). Meanwhile one of Marito's most stimulating evenings involves seeing Arthur Miller's technically adventurous play *Death of a Salesman* and drinking whisky in a nightclub with an 'existentialist' decor, 'cierta aureola de bohemia intelectual' which 'daba la ilusión de estar en una cave de Saint Germain des Près' (238). His literary influences are all, needless to say, foreign, with the exception of Borges who can hardly be considered very *americanista*. The narrative perspective, in other words, is that of a bourgeois intellectual. Far from critiquing middle-class values by silencing all others, the novel may well be inscribing those values as the viewpoint which informs its construction.

Notions of distance and control are thus central to the authoring process dramatised in the novel. An important theme in this respect is that of sanity and insanity. Madness is a theme of a number of Camacho's stories and, from the very first one, the presentation of Richard as a positive model because he is, among other things, 'sano' (33) suggests that health and mental health are norms which would be undermined by deviation. Hence Richard's subsequent abnormal behaviour worries the doctor because it brings to mind the fact that 'en la familia Quinteros había abundantes neuróticos' (36). In the main narrative, Camacho is the neurotic while Marito leads a 'normal' life, and Camacho goes mad and is destroyed while Marito evolves into a 'sano' and successful author. This question of sanity and order spills into the organisation of the novel at the level of style and structure. Camacho's narratives, which are supposedly simplistic, become ludicrously complex and tortuous, but Varguitas' narrative, which is more reflective and which one might expect to be more psychologically and socially elaborate, is, in fact, presented with stylistic simplicity and structural clarity. The author is in control (sane). The scriptwriter is not (insane). Low culture is a mess and only High art should be taken seriously.

The idea of distance between author and scriptwriter is crucial because it ties the 'escribidor' (and what he represents) to the other pole of the novel's dualistic title, la tía Julia. An important factor linking the two poles is age. Both the figures linked in the title are opposed to the real protagonist (Marito) in that they are older than him. However, in the final chapter or epilogue, both figures from the title have lost their status in the text: Julia has been divorced and Camacho has lost his stardom. On the other hand, the young naive lover and literary apprentice has become the older famous author Mario Vargas Llosa: he has displaced the two other older figures as the central older figure of the novel. This is also a triumph of the serious over the popular because Julia is not only linked to Camacho through nationality and plotting parallels but also through her identification with popular culture. Tía Julia is 'terriblemente aliteraria', seems unimpressed by Marito's *cuentos*, likes pulp fiction and melodramatic movies from Argentina and Mexico, and becomes a fan of Pedro Camacho's soap operas (e.g., 110–1). Marito likes serious literature, writes 'literary' stories, hates popular Latin American movies and does not listen to radio soap operas. And he regularly censures Julia for her tastes. Of course, there are a number of scenes where Marito's intellectual or artistic posturing is gently mocked by Julia's common sense or his own assumption of romantic or melodramatic gestures. Nonetheless, the irony is only light and, in any case, the mature perspective revealed in the epilogue and informing the entire narrative distances the contemporary author from his youthful past and even draws credit to himself for recognising his previous limitations. Indeed the mild satire of youth and the expressions of respect towards Julia and Camacho may well be seen by some as part of a pattern of (aforementioned) false modesty which is designed to secure respect for the position of the mature author. Emblematic of this perhaps is the seemingly gracious dedication ('A Julia Urquidi Illanes, a quien tanto debemos yo y esta novela'). Despite this apparent disclaimer, it is known that the book did in fact upset both Julia Urquidi Illanes and Raúl Salmón, prompting both a lawsuit and a published alternative version.

Whatever the facts of the matter, the account of the author's coming to maturity and his relationship with the two title figures is presented in the text as a kind of winning of a victory. Again the question of age is important. If tía Julia is to be seen always in connection to Pedro Camacho then Marito's relationship to her must also be seen as representative of the process of literary maturation. The idea of Marito's youth and distance from the now well-known novelist is embedded in the very opening words of the text: 'En ese tiempo remoto, yo era muy joven ...' (11). In the young man's first meeting with Julia she treats him like a child ('la verdad ... es que pareces todavía una guagua') and uses the diminutive address *Marito* which makes him feel like a schoolboy in short pants (16–7). Following his initial negative reaction to her their subsequent relationship becomes something of a battle of the ages as well as the sexes, with each vying for control and Marito coming out on top. Scenes involving tíos Pancracio and Lucho illustrate this. The ageing Pancracio with his pretensions to a (ghastly) youthful appearance as he tries to woo Julia is ridiculed for his boring tastes, and when Julia announces that she prefers to go out with Marito rather than him, he concedes: 'Paso a la juventud' (21). Julia though wounds the younger man with the phrase, 'No te preocupes por la plata, Marito. Yo te invito' (21), and Marito subsequently tries to insist on paying. At Lucho's fiftieth birthday celebration Marito asserts his manhood by planting a kiss on Julia and telling the woman who previously spoke to him 'dictatorialmente' (63) that: 'Te prohíbo que me vuelvas a llamar Marito' (75). After the kiss, 'la tía Julia se puso a hacer bromas al tío Lucho sobre los cincuenta años' (75), the triumph of youth thus being underscored. The theme runs throughout the novel, the advantage see-sawing back and forth between the two, but in the latter stages it is Marito who is in control, standing up for himself, taking charge and protecting Julia and organising the clandestine wedding. All of this may seem to be an account of Marito's preparation for adulthood and marriage. Yet, after they are married and united together, the final chapter does not show us their relationship or tell us much about it. Instead we meet the mature, successful author who is actually divorced from tía Julia (and even more metaphorically on top since he has married his younger cousin Patricia). The suggestion is that (symbolically at least) Julia has been a mechanism to promote his coming of age as a writer. Earlier Javier had warned Marito that 'por casarte no llegarás nunca a ser un escritor' (323), though Varguitas later inverts this by claiming that 'casarme no me impediría llegar a ser algún día un escritor' (360). Not only is Varguitas right, but the relationship with Julia has become an emblem of his success as a writer in actually providing him with material for the very novel by the great writer Mario Vargas Llosa that we are reading.[17]

That Julia's symbolic importance in the novel is her role in promoting the literary career of Vargas Llosa is given added weight by the parallel importance of the age motif in the presentation of Pedro Camacho. Age and sexual tension between age groups are obsessively documented in Camacho's stories. In the first one, Dr Alberto de Quinteros, who is in his fifties, feels compelled to frequent a gym 'como si el hecho de verse desnudos y de sudar juntos los nivelara en una fraternidad donde desaparecían las diferencias de edad ...' (31). It soon transpires that all the stories stress that their protagonists are in their fifties, 'la flor de la edad'. Marito's deduction is that 'el escriba boliviano tenía cincuenta años y que lo aterraba la vejez' (73). The collapse of the scriptwriter marks the triumph of youth (Marito) and paves the way for the usurping of his position by the figure who is really enjoying 'la flor de la edad', the famous mature author of the epilogue, Mario Vargas Llosa.

The inscription of the narratorial and authorial voice at the novel's close underscores an important point about *La tía Julia y el escribidor*, particularly insofar as it relates to the treatment of popular culture. And that is that the author of Pedro Camacho's soap operas must not be Pedro Camacho but Mario Vargas Llosa, both the real author and the author figure that is inscribed in the final chapter. The associations noted earlier between the two narrative levels do not therefore have to suggest that the story of Marito is just as fictional as the stories of Camacho. It is only fictional in the sense that it is a reflection in fictional form of a period in the life of the real author Mario Vargas Llosa. It is pretty obvious anyway that the stories cannot be Camacho's, and not just because they include figures from Marito's and Vargas Llosa's own works. For a start, there is the simple fact that they are not written in dialogue but in a highly descriptive style that makes it clear that they are merely written versions of possible radio scripts. The fact that the pattern of errors and disintegration occurs not within episodes from the same story but gets worse from story to story indicates also that this is a re-creation of the feel of the progress of Camacho's dramas rather than a literal re-enactment of them. There are many things it is difficult to imagine being captured successfully on the radio, such as the apprehension of a mute black man, the sight of his scars, a young girl's description of her alleged rape via a series of physical gestures accompanied by the repeated use of the unillu-minating phrase 'así', or the incomprehensible argot of a shanty town priest. The language too becomes increasingly heavy with imagery, again signalling a divorce from the radio medium. And the content is pretty unlikely for prime-time mass-media soap opera too: the constant diet of rape, sexual extravagance and violence, and stories of a self-emasculating Jehovah's Witness or a fanatical devotee of rat-catching, or a pathological hater of children, or an obsessive, alcohol-soaked soccer referee. Indeed the progressive complexity of the stories, their increasingly suggestive narrative style and the highly original nature of their content should lead us to an important realisation about them: that they are not, in fact, particularly 'popular' at all. This is, perhaps, the crucial point. This novel differs significantly from certain other texts by Latin American authors using popular culture in that it does not attempt to give voice to the popular, let alone to the masses, but clearly seeks to appropriate popular culture for its own ends, namely the creation of a sophisticated entertainment for a literate reading public.

Finally, to conclude this consideration of *La tía Julia y el escribidor*, it is necessary to return once more to the connection between popular culture and politics that was raised in the opening remarks to this chapter. The positing of a powerful, controlling author figure can imply two very different things – depending partly on whether we choose to read the novel within terms of Vargas Llosa's wider body of published production and his public political status or simply within its own terms. It could be seen as sending out an extremely negative political message. A dominant middle-class (and patriarchal) ideology is asserted that effectively banishes alternatives to silence or irrelevance. During one of his recording sessions, Pedro Camacho 'hablaba gesticulando y empinándose, con la voz fanática del hombre que está en posesión de una verdad urgente y tiene que propagarla, compartirla, imponerla' (123). The implication is that Pedro Camacho is a victim of his own fanaticism. Should one choose to read this as something more than a colourful portrait of a comic character, one might be tempted to link this to what has been a growing concern of Vargas Llosa's work and politics since the 1970s, that is, what he sees as a dangerous tendency towards sectional fanaticism, particularly on the Left. This first surfaced strongly in the depiction of a madly driven military mentality in *Pantaleón y las visitadoras* and continued through to his account of the Canudos rebellion in turn-of-the-century Brazil, inspired by the spiritual fanaticism of Antônio Conselheiro, in *La guerra del fin del mundo*, the exploration of revolutionary political fanaticism in *Historia de Mayta* or of fanatical indigenism in *El hablador*, and his reservations towards the Sandinistas in Nicaragua, or his outspoken stance on Sendero Luminoso in Peru. Speaking of *El hablador*, for instance, William Rowe claims that

> what is clearly shown by this text, whose author is placed in Florence, symbol of the perfection of European high culture and centre from which all marginalities look the same, is that Vargas Llosa cannot conceive of simultaneous and opposing sets of signs, that is, of a heterogeneous culture, but only of an alienated discourse as the sole way in which the Other can speak within the nation, leaving us the only option an eventual integration or disappearance of the Other into a single national discourse ...[18]

Though dealing with a somewhat different topic, *La tía Julia y el escribidor* might not unreasonably be read as inscribing, in formal terms, such a view.

However, there is little in *La tía Julia y el escribidor* itself to suggest that Camacho is much of a social or political symbol and the novel as a whole does not have a great deal to say, directly at least, about politics or even society as such. As for its inscription of the authority of a bourgeois intellectual author, this may simply suggest that a middle-class author has written, for a middle-class readership, what is no more than a work of literature, which is in any case mainly about the writing of literature. This simple contention is not unproblematic, of course, particularly in the light of some of the insights of modern critical theory. Alonso, for example, concludes his article by calling into question 'the pertinence of any proposal that takes as its deluded point of departure the dissociation of rhetoric from ideology' (57). The contemporary critical commonplace that all discourse is inevitably ideological is difficult to argue with. At the same time an insistence on this point reduces it to something of an irrelevancy, since if all utterances are motivated by ideology then they are just as similar or different as they were before we realised they were so motivated. To claim to adopt a disinterested political position may be as ideologically determined a statement as to claim to be politically motivated, but they still reflect two politically differentiated positions and one is still more likely to be more overtly political than the other. Martin puts it somewhat differently when he describes Vargas Llosa's theory of writing as 'a defensive strategy to give his essentially liberal imagination freedom to manoeuvre in a literary context dominated by socialist perspectives' (206). Precisely so. The writer can choose to write about what he wants (or thinks he wants). In this sense, *La tía Julia y el escribidor* may simply be a middle-class novel. And in this sense too, there may well be no real conflict here between Vargas Llosa's literary position and his public position. Whereas in some of the writers discussed in this book there seems to be a certain contradiction between public persona and literary persona, Vargas Llosa – who has always been scrupulously honest and courageous in expressing his changing political outlook in an intellectual environment in which such views are often unfashionable – has pretty consistently changed literary tack as he has political tack. His political evolution may not be an especially palatable spectacle for many observers, but in writing a non-political novel which simultaneously embodies his own sociocultural status he has created a remarkably coherent literary work which is nonetheless born of that political evolution.

## Notes

[1]See, for example, Duarte Mimoso-Ruiz, 'Aspects des "media" dans *El beso de la mujer araña* de Manuel Puig (1976) et *La tía Julia y el escribidor* de Mario Vargas Llosa (1977)', *Les Langues Néo-latines*, LXXVI, 1982, pp. 29–47; and Daniel R. Reedy, 'Del beso de la mujer araña al de la tía Julia: estructura y dinámica interior', *Revista Iberoamericana*, XLVII, 1981, pp. 109–16.

[2]Gerald Martin, 'Mario Vargas Llosa: Errant Knight of the Liberal Imagination', in *Modern Latin American Fiction*, ed. John King, Faber and Faber, London, 1987, p. 221. Subsequent references to Martin in the main body of the present chapter will be to this essay.

[3]For a fuller picture of Martin's views on Puig, see his *Journeys Through the Labyrinth: Latin American Fiction in the Twentieth Century*, Verso, London and New York, 1989.

[4]Dick Gerdes, *Mario Vargas Llosa*, Twayne, Boston, 1985, pp. 143–4.

[5]Sara Castro-Klarén, *Understanding Mario Vargas Llosa*, University of South Carolina Press, Columbia, 1990, p. 16.

[6]Rita Gnutzmann, *Cómo leer a Mario Vargas Llosa*, Júcar, Madrid, 1992; Marvin A. Lewis, *From Lima to Leticia: The Peruvian Novels of Mario Vargas Llosa*, University Press of America, Lanham and London, 1983.

[7]Mario Vargas Llosa, *La tía Julia y el escribidor*, Seix Barral, Barcelona, 1977.

[8]Ellen McCracken, 'Vargas Llosa's *La tía Julia y el escribidor*: The New Novel and the Mass Media', *Ideologies and Literature*, III, 1980, pp. 54–69.

[9]The various names given to the protagonist will be used more or less freely in this essay.

[10]For thorough but succinct surveys of this, see Castro-Klarén and Rosemary Geisdorfer Feal, *Novel Lives: The Fictional Autobiographies of Guillermo Cabrera Infante and Mario Vargas Llosa*, University of North Carolina Press, Chapel Hill, 1986.

[11]Ricardo Cano Gaviria, *El buitre y el ave fénix: conversaciones con Mario Vargas Llosa*, Anagrama, Barcelona, 1972, p. 16.

[12]Though called an aunt, Julia is only the sister of Marito's uncle's wife.

[13]See, for example, the portrait of the novelist in José Luis Martín, *La narrativa de Vargas Llosa*, Gredos, Madrid, 1974.

[14]Sharon Magnarelli, 'The Diseases of Love and Discourse: *La tía Julia y el escribidor* and *María*', *Hispanic Review*, LIV, 1986, p. 199.

[15]From Roland Barthes, *Essais critiques*, Seuil, Paris, 1964. Quoted by Maité Bernard in 'Verdad y mentira del escribidor en *La tía Julia y el escribidor* de Mario Vargas Llosa', *Tropos*, XVII, 1991, p. 36. See also José Miguel Oviedo, '*La tía Julia y el escribidor*, or the Coded Self-portrait', in *Mario Vargas Llosa: A Collection of Critical Essays*, eds. Charles Rossman and Alan Warren Friedman, University of Texas, Austin and London, 1978, pp. 166–81.

[16]Carlos J. Alonso, '*La tía Julia y el escribidor*: The Writing Subject's Fantasy of Empowerment', *PMLA*, CVI, 1991, pp. 46–59.

[17]Magnarelli and Alonso bring out two other possible aspects of Varguitas/Vargas Llosa's linking of Julia with writing. Magnarelli discusses the theme of love-as-a-disease and sees in writing a metaphoric cure for love, in that writing exorcises the absent object of desire by making it present. Alonso's tortuous Freudian analysis has Marito defeating the threat (his father) to his Oedipal relationship with the mother-figure Julia in a way which parallels his supplanting of his other precursor Pedro Camacho: the fantasy is taken a stage further by the marriage to cousin Patricia, the offspring of which will merely repeat the name of the father, thereby cancelling the threat of the son's ever overtaking his progenitor. Both readings are ingeniously worked, though perhaps a little far-fetched.

[18]William Rowe, 'Liberalism and Authority: The Case of Mario Vargas Llosa', in *On Edge: The Crisis of Contemporary Latin American Culture*, eds. George Yúdice, Jean Franco and Juan Flores, University of Minnesota Press, Minneapolis and London, 1992, p. 61.

# Chapter 5

# Carlos Fuentes and *La cabeza de la hidra*: Spies like us

There is a moment in John Landis' 1985 comedy movie *Spies Like Us* when two politically manipulated and duped bungling American agents, played by Chevy Chase and Dan Aykroyd, improbably embroiled in an international spy intrigue, find themselves in a tent in an Afghan rebel camp where they are suddenly interrupted by the surprising intrusion of a golf ball followed closely by well-known veteran comedian and amateur golfer Bob Hope politely asking, 'Mind if I play through?'. Whereas such a ploy might be dismissed as a piece of wacky, anarchic and empty comedy typical of North American shows or films featuring the likes of Chase or Aykroyd, one suspects that if something similar occurred in a piece of literature penned by a 'serious' author it would be considered an intriguing and thought-provoking instance of intertextual play drawing attention to the complex interrelationship of fiction and reality.[1] This brief comparison highlights, once more, the problematic nature of the relationship between the serious and the popular in much contemporary fiction and the meaningfulness or significance of that relationship, especially in a novel such as the one about to be discussed (on a similar theme to Landis' film) which, as Wendy B. Faris has already pointed out, inverts the more common process of incorporating popular elements into a 'serious' framework by introducing serious issues into an apparently popular format.[2] Yet such 'intertextuality' is absolutely central to much of Carlos Fuentes' work. In particular, Fuentes himself has made a good deal of the question of intertextuality within and in relation to that famous model for the playful adventure genre, *Don Quijote*. Cervantes, he has remarked, 'brought into existence the modern world by having Don Quixote leave his secure village ... and take to the open roads, the roads of the unsheltered, the unknown, and the different, there to lose what he read and to gain what we, the readers, read in him'.[3] Thus does Fuentes summarise his oft-repeated argument concerning the great Spanish author's inauguration of modernity in prose fiction. In the twentieth century, in a different continent, one of Fuentes' own characters would, in his own way, retrace that uncertain journey into a venturous new world. Félix Maldonado, under a changed identity, quits his home and job to chase false trails, shadowy villains and a secret piece of sophisticated laser technology around Mexico and Texas in the 1978 pseudo-spy thriller *La cabeza de la hidra* – a typically modernist, in the sense of 'modern', or, more accurately, postmodernist *nueva novela* of the Latin American post-Boom.[4] There are, in fact, two broad notions of the 'modern' as auspicated by the *Quijote*. One is E. C. Riley's 'modern realistic novel', based on the generic distinction between 'romance' and 'novel'; the other is Fuentes' view of the 'modernidad radical de *Don Quijote*' as 'una novela de polivalencias' and 'la multiplicidad'.[5] Perhaps the differentiation to be made is not simply between realism and modernism, but also between the modern and postmodern. As Patricia Waugh has remarked in her book on metafiction: 'if post-modernism shares some of the philosophies of modernism, its formal techniques seem often to have originated from novels like *Tristam Shandy* (1760), *Don Quixote* (1604) or *Tom Jones* (1749)'.[6] However, such distinctions are notoriously porous, and it may be more useful to regard postmodernism, insofar as the term will be used in this chapter, as 'a condition of reading' rather than of production. If, to borrow Edmund J. Smyth's résumé, postmodernism is to be associated with 'any creative endeavour which exhibits some element of self-consciousness and reflexivity [, … or f]ragmentation, discontinuity, dislocation, indeterminacy, plurality, meta-fictionality, heterogeneity, intertextuality, decentring, dislocation, ludism', then one has but to think of Barthes' *S/Z* to realise that even a superficially *'lisible'* text like Balzac's *Sarrasine* can be shown to contain many of these inconsistent or multiple elements.[7] Cervantes was (indirectly and inadvertently) already anticipating this in his prologue to *Don Quijote* in telling the reader that he or she is not a relative of the protagonist 'ni su amigo, y tienes tu alma en tu cuerpo y tu libre albedrío como el más pintado… . Todo lo cual te esenta y hace libre de todo respecto y obligación, y así puedes decir de la historia todo aquello que te pareciese ..."[8] Thus, despite A. J. Close's reservations regarding the imposition on the classics of a 'potentially anachronistic frame of reference' based on 'the loud buzz emanating from the culture that surrounds *us*' (not *them*),[9] it does seem perfectly legitimate to read the *Quijote* in a 'postmodern' way. The point about *La cabeza de la hidra* is that it positively demands to be read like this: it is *written* to be read in this way. Operating at the level of production rather than consumption, though, the postmodernism of Carlos Fuentes becomes problematic and rather suspect. Pitting pleasure, play and politics against each other, the writing model of the modern text risks cancelling its own relevance while the reading model asserts the enduring value of the text more distant in time.

*La cabeza de la hidra*, then, can be seen in terms of a '"decentring" impulse' through which 'the text becomes a site of conflicting and intersecting discourses' (Smyth, 14), mixing so-called High and Low art, the 'serious' and the 'popular', 'romance' and 'novel', realist and non-realist elements, reflectionism and self-reflexivity. First, the popular spy-hero is, of course, the chivalric knight reborn in the twentieth century. And, on its basic level, the novel does function effectively as a spy thriller: 'an amusing, sometimes even an impassioned, narrative', according to Faris (167). All the usual clichés are here, and Fuentes himself admits that it is 'un "thriller" ..., una novela de intrigas, de espionaje' – but one which exchanges the conventional reactionary hero for 'un héroe del Tercer Mundo ..., el James Bond del mundo sub-desarrollado' (Lévy and Loveluck, 217). Romance, it seems, becomes realism and Jean Franco, for example, makes no bones about seeing the work as a political novel, while Lanin A. Gyurko classifies it as a 'thesis novel'.[10] The substance of the political theme is as follows. The hero, the 'agente mexicano' Félix Maldonado, is on a mission to secure a precious stone which, through the wonders of technology, contains classified information on secret Mexican oil reserves. The menace to the reserves lies in the Arab-Israeli conflict and its potential effects on the United States. The popular Mexican president Lázaro Cárdenas had nationalised the petroleum industry on 18 March 1938, supposedly the day of Félix's conception. 'Ese día, los mexicanos se miraron a la cara', it is said.[11] This is a reference to the foreign manager at the oil company where Félix's father worked, who never looked him in the face. In other words, the nationalisation is associated with the acquisition of identity and independence which is now under threat. That threat to identity is focused synechdochically on Félix Maldonado, a former specialist in oil reserves at Pemex (Petróleos Mexicanos) whose life is clearly symbolically bound up with the industry. Félix's Mexican identity is problematic to begin with: he is a Jewish convert, influenced by North American consumer culture, and is unable to relate to the indigenous population. Worse still, enemy agents arrange a mock death for him and graft on to him a false face. His escape from their clinic merely leads him deeper into the insecure world typical of the spy thriller, as he negotiates a baffling network of double- and triple-crosses. By the end a narrative switch finds him being referred to under his new name: his old identity is gone and he is reduced to the role of a mere puppet manipulated by alien forces. Just in case the moral has been missed, Fuentes tags on an epilogue which lurches back in time to the story of the traitor La Malinche, the mistress and guide of the Spanish conqueror Hernán Cortés. He links this to the surrender to the invaders of Moctezuma's gold. The inference is obvious: Mexico may be on the verge of another betrayal, a further erosion of identity and independence, if foreign powers are allowed to control the black gold of the nation's petroleum resources.

From what has been said so far, it is not difficult to see that the spy figure here is somewhat removed from the hero of chivalric romance. Indeed, at one stage, when the protagonist tilts at windmills in the form of a rather forlorn attack on a ship with a machete, he is described as 'un Quijote inverosímil' (137–8). In some ways, this is a send-up of a spy: Félix is a James Bond who burps painfully while awaiting a lover's assignment (31), who sweats and has dirty underwear (41), who repeatedly gets things wrong and ends up working mechanically for the enemy. Fuentes' text inflates the mood of uncertainty naturally – according to Ralph Harper – built into the spy story where, as opposed to the detective story, 'civilization itself is undermined'[12] and 'the spy moves in a Kafkaesque world whose laws remain unknown ..., forced continually to shift identity, donning one disguise after another' (Waugh, 84). The progressive doubts shown by Don Quijote in Part II of Cervantes' novel are echoed (in an inverse way) in Félix's snowballing loss of sense of self. This goes from lack of recognition, to loss of name, to (literal) loss of face, to complete loss of identity at the end. James Bond's traditional control and domination of women is also turned inside out. Félix's ideal woman, Sara Klein, is killed before he is ever able to possess her. The more carnal relationship with Mary Benjamin – the woman he devirginates and appears to subjugate physically in a particularly graphic and tasteless sex scene – turns out (it seems) to be an Israeli agent implicated in the murder of Sara. Most shockingly of all, his wife Ruth, the apparently submissive housewife playing the part of a faithful Penelope to Félix's Ulysses (273), is revealed to be the missing link in the entire drama, probably another Israeli agent and possibly even Sara's killer (the ironic inversion of the phallocratic order being foreshadowed in an earlier scene where Félix's admiration of his sizeable, pleasure-inducing penis is followed by the revelation that Ruth has not only engineered his conversion but also forced him to get circumcised). The 'poor little wife' is the most dangerous enemy, and the 'macho man' is a helpless pawn. In the clichéd world of spy fiction, nothing is what it seems. Here, that idea is taken to its limits. Though the commonplace (by now) that modernism is linked to epistemology and postmodernism to ontology may seem something of a sterile distinction, this is, nonetheless, an arena in which differentiation displaces analogy and in which individuality is annulled, reduced to mere contextualised performance.

More alarmingly, especially in a political novel, the question of identity relates to the idea of textuality. Phillip Koldewyn has already made a connection between loss of identity through brainwashing and colonialism in the novel.[13] Emma Kafalenos, meantime, has linked such matters to the idea of representation.[14] Félix and his wife own a reproduction of Velázquez's *Las meninas*, in which the painter famously paints himself in the act of painting. What is more, Félix actually looks like Velázquez in the painting. Interestingly, Ruth inverts the pseudo-conventional notion that 'Félix era el doble del pintor' to say instead: 'No, Velázquez es tu doble' (40). Later Félix assumes the name of Diego Velázquez and eventually, taking on a new identity, literally becomes 'Diego Velázquez'. Foucault's *Les Mots et les choses* has made it fashionable to apply *Las meninas* to issues of representation in literature. One could therefore see *La cabeza de la hidra* as about the representation of representation rather than of 'things', or, in Ricardou's terms, as exemplifying 'production' (the generation of a text from existing materials – including other art works or 'texts' and language) rather than 'reproduction' (the presentation of a previously determined idea of the world or an aspect of the self). The result of all this is, for Kafalenos, 'necessarily ... an instability in both signifier and signified' (146). The 'textuality' and uncertainty of identity is present in *La cabeza de la hidra* from the very start. The novel opens with these words: 'A las ocho de la mañana, Félix Maldonado llegó al Sanborns de la Avenida Madero, llevaba años sin poner un pie dentro del famoso Palacio de los Azulejos. Pasó de moda, como todo el viejo centro de la ciudad de México, trazado de mano propia por Hernán Cortés sobre las ruinas de la capital azteca' (11). Thus, from the very first sentence the text fixes attention on notions of time and intermixture (the modern day, the Mexican Revolution, the Spanish conquest, the Aztec empire and North America, Mexico, Spain, Indians), and throughout the novel these motifs are subtly reinforced. The central dilemma is that Félix dislikes 'el pulular desagradable de la gente de medio pelo', 'esa mezcla indecisa de gente' in 'una ciudad diseñada para señores y esclavos' (14). His yearning for identity and order is impossible in a hybrid mestizo zone of cultural mix. The implication also is that fixed meaning is no longer feasible in a context of intertextuality where intersecting periods and influences create a world of Bakhtinian heteroglossia. Even the Texas traffic-cop who complains to Félix, 'You a dago or a spick? Shouldn't let you people drive. Don't know what this country's coming to. No trueblooded Americans left', turns out to be an Irish-American (143). Hence the massive degree of intertextual allusion or quotation in the novel. The whole novel revolves around an interplay between a popular genre and serious art, reflected (partially) in the relationship of the movie buff Félix and his controller, the Shakespeare enthusiast code-named Timón de Atenas (Timon of Athens). The book is dedicated to the memory of a group of Hollywood actors (in fact, the supporting players in the film *Casablanca*) and many scenes and characters seem lifted straight from *The Maltese Falcon*. There are echoes too of Holmes and Watson, Raymond Chandler, Len Deighton, Dumas, *Alice in Wonderland*, boleros, pop songs, soaps, but also opera, painting, Japanese art cinema and sundry Elizabethan dramas – to offer but a brief list. At one stage, hot on the heels of a reference to John Le Carré, Timón re-reads *Hamlet* in the light of the adventure in which he finds himself. This is the basic postmodern, intertextual cultural position. When Quijote realises, in Part II of Cervantes' novel, that he has been 'read' by other readers, he is effectively forecasting a future age when Don Quijote will exist as part of 'culture', fabricated by readers reading through the filter of different times and different texts. As Unamuno would have known, Don Quijote or Hamlet or Sherlock Holmes are just as 'real' to us as Alexander the Great or Napoleon Bonaparte or Che Guevara. And are not the fictional Macbeth or Julius Caesar or Joan of Arc or Davy Crockett more knowable to us than their real-life counterparts? Hence the reference to Anne Frank in *La cabeza de la hidra*: 'la víctima más importante es Anna Frank, porque ... no la pudieron convertir en una simple cifra' (46–7). The question is: does the iconisation of Anne Frank sharpen her impact as a political symbol or reduce her to nothing more than a symbol, turning her into another kind of 'cifra' and undermining any attempt to comprehend and represent the outside world? Does, in the end, Cervantes' world have any more validity than Quijote's?

Despite his frequent political pronouncements and the clear historicism of his essay *Cervantes, or the Critique of Reading*, Fuentes still chooses to emphasise the fictionality of the text. For him, Don Quijote's 'integrity is annulled by the readings he is submitted to', and he becomes a 'victim of the act of reading' (*Myself With Others*, 59). Not surprisingly, Félix Maldonado is similarly problematised, both by a stylistic technique which strains the sense of realism or reality and a narrative technique which undermines the position of the narrator. Two striking stylistic features of the narrative are, on the one hand, an overload of excessively colloquial dialogue and concrete geographical references (largely to the streets of Mexico City) which create a kind of forced or phony verisimilitude, and, on the other hand, a repeated use of incongruous imagery (especially often similes) in the style of Chandler or Deighton, which foreground the text's artificiality. The imagery often seems deliberately silly, for example: 'Si en vez de corazón Félix Maldonado hubiera tenido un canguro guardado en el pecho, no habría saltado más lejos que en el momento de ver y reconocer a la misma muchacha que subió al taxi en la esquina de Gante ...' (74). Certain characters, meantime, introduce English or French expressions into their speech for no apparent reason, the narrative is strewn with seemingly arbitrary Buñuelesque details, and meaningless red herrings abound. Moreover, there are numerous instances of confusing signals or breaks between sign and referent. In the opening chapter Félix is worried that he is late for his 'desayuno político', yet dawdles outside the café before entering rapidly. Félix says that 'uno viene a estos desayunos para ser visto por los demás', yet had earlier said that 'ahora casi nadie desayunaba aquí'. In any case, his companion at the café, Bernstein, says: 'éste no es un desayuno político' (12–3). This compares with the nuns in the following chapter: they are not allowed by law to wear their habits but signify 'nun' by their short hair, lack of make-up, dark clothing, rosary beads and so on. So, the sign does not always signify what it seems supposed to (breakfast), yet significance is generated without conventional signs (nuns). The taxi ride in which Félix sees the nuns (repeated in a variant form at the end) is the most unreal element in the entire novel: a whole network of spies, counterspies, criminals and shady characters (alternately seeming to be linked and unlinked) turn up in the same cab (with the same driver) in a way which is never fully explained.

The characters in the novel, meantime, almost demand to be read as fictions. They are like players in a movie. Simón Ayub is suspiciously like Peter Lorre, Bernstein could pass for Sidney Greenstreet. Trevor does a good impersonation of Claude Rains and Conrad Veidt. Ruth speaks like Mary Astor. Félix dons a Bogart mac when he gets close to solving the mystery. Most astonishingly of all, though, is Timón's assertion that he bought his mansion from 'los herederos de un viejo millonario llamado Artemio Cruz' (231). This is, of course, the protagonist of Fuentes' own novel, *La muerte de Artemio Cruz*. Like Quijote, then, Fuentes' 'hero' has to be seen to be made up of words. To this end, he impersonates the playful narratorial stance of *Don Quijote*, albeit in the more self-conscious way typical of Unamuno in *Niebla*. Following a number of peculiar first-person intrusions, it gradually emerges that the narrator of the story is Félix's contact and chief of the spy network, Timón de Atenas. The narrative displacement effected by this revelation situates Félix as a puppet-figure in the style of Augusto Pérez, manipulated both politically and narratorially by his 'master'. Moreover, the final part of the novel – in which Félix walks out on Timón – suggests, via an ambiguous use of tenses, that the conclusion of Félix's adventure is just a *possible* version, a narrative invention of Timón, a fiction. But whereas Cide Hamete Benengeli in the *Quijote* is, in conscious terms, probably little more than a humourous reworking of a stock type from romance, Timón, in a Fuentesian reading of Cervantes, forms part of the ever-receding fictional spiral. Fond of textual re-readings and speaking in a code based on Shakespeare and Lewis Carroll, he is also a master of disguise and turns out to be the pro-Arab agent Trevor and the pro-Israeli agent Mann. Timón is himself an intertextual fiction. Despite a superficial generosity, he is tainted, like his Shakespearean namesake, by filthy lucre and cannot hide his real role as a protector of his own interests in the petroleum business, ending up as the villain even in his own heroic narrative. In fact, there are several hints that he and the other two villains, Bernstein and the mysterious Director General may be one and the same. Bernstein quotes Lewis Carroll (124) and both he and Trevor (Timón) bring to mind Sidney Greenstreet. The some-times seemingly omnipresent Director General knows all about Timón, and Timón often seems to know the Director's mind or use his words (e.g., 228–9, 276). Timón is ultimately no more individ-ual than Félix. He is a composite figure, hewn from other fictions, an example of intertextuality in motion and a pointer to the processes of construction of an only illusory identity in that slip-pery other reality in the world beyond the text.

The central dilemma in *La cabeza de la hidra*, then, is an unre-solved tension between the desire to comment on reality and a tendency to break the link between fiction and reality. This, as has been suggested, may be a central dilemma of the whole of the Latin American new novel. It brings to mind the dual structure of 'El jardín de senderos que se bifurcan' by that other ludic reader of Cervantes, Jorge Luis Borges. The puzzling World War I spy story framing the narrative is resolved at the end, but the inner tale of the Chinese labyrinth remains an enigma. A man-made order is pitted against an unknowable universe. Don Quijote's position is similar: through the chivalric filter, he attempts an unequivocal reading of an equivocal reality (like, perhaps, Félix's attempt to 'read' Mexico). But in Fuentes it is the writing which is itself problematic: with the *Quijote* it is more a question of a modern or, really, post-modern reading. Don Quijote the character thinks the narrative about him is different to that which is *known* to the reader. And Quijote's mis-reading of reality generates a specific but knowable fictional reality for the reader. This, once again, is like the irony at the root of so-called Magical Realism: the reader knows that the characters' 'magical' reality is fiction. Even the business of Benengeli's alleged unreliability is, as Close has noted, little more

than a formulaic joke with, possibly, no serious subversive intention (19). However, Fuentes' contemporary reading wants it both
ways – concrete and plural, historicist and ludic. Hence Javier
Herrero's classification of him as 'el más radical y el más conser-
vador de los críticos contemporáneos del *Quijote*': 'nos está ofre-
ciendo bajo la superficie de una ambigüedad contextual una visión
del *Quijote* tan unívoca como la que don Quijote absorbió de sus
heroicos caballeros andantes'.[15]

Fuentes clearly wants his novel to be a critical reflection of a
specific historical and political reality. 'All our history is lies', he
says in one interview, 'and if the writers do not speak the truth, it
will not be spoken'; in another he says that he has always been
'driven more than anything ... by the desire to inform in my own
culture, in my own country'.[16] Elsewhere he states explicitly of *La
cabeza de la hidra*: 'refleja muy bien el ambiente de la Ciudad de
México hoy en día. Creo que éste es el verdadero protagonista de
esta novela' (Lévy and Loveluck, 218). In the light of these remarks,
the significance of the hydra head of the title is obvious. 'Rome a
pour ma ruine une hydre trop fertile; une tête coupée en fait
renaître mille' are words from Corneille's *Cinna* (iv, 2, 45). 'Como
la hidra el petróleo renace multiplicado de una sola cabeza
cortada', says the epilogue to Fuentes' novel. The hydra head is the
central metaphor in the work's nationalist, political statement. It is
also, though, a metaphor of intertextuality, multiplicity and irreducibility: one Don Quijote will spawn an infinite mass of others.
Can Fuentes write an effective political novel in a self-conscious,
postmodernist style if, as Timón says, 'en una novela, ... las
palabras acaban siempre por construir lo contrario de sí mismas'
(240)? The usual 'postmodern' answer would be that the elevation
of 'difference' and the non-utilitarian pleasure principle of 'play' is
a radical blow to a fixed, false bourgeois 'order'. But this seeking to
make the 'useless' 'useful' is, as has already been suggested, a somewhat feeble political programme which fails to fill the void at the
heart of the consciously postmodern political text. Fuentes' novel
ultimately erases its own putative relevance. It is actually his
method of reading which offers more than his writing. It allows, for
instance, for an infinitely renewed reading of an essentially ortho-
dox straight-comic work like *Don Quijote*. The irony is that the
novel which sets out to say the least is the one with the potential to
say the most.

And so, finally, returning to the popular film alluding to high culture postures with which we opened this discussion, what conclusion should we draw? Should we assume that the 'spies like us' are, indeed, us, the viewers or readers, as well as the phoney roles played by Aykroyd and Chase, that we are all basically little more than 'roles' or textually generated identities? Or ... should we simply sit back and enjoy the movie?

## Notes

[1]Landis' movie is, in fact, 'textually' playful. Here, for example, as in other films by him, a number of other movie directors, such as Michael Apted, Martin Brest, Costa Gavras, Terry Gilliam, Ray Harryhausen and Frank Oz, crop up in a variety of roles.

[2]Wendy B. Faris, *Carlos Fuentes*, Frederick Ungar, New York, 1983, p. 166.

[3]Carlos Fuentes, *Myself With Others*, Picador, London, 1988, p. 24.

[4]The term 'modernist' will be used here in the basically Anglo-American sense.

[5]See E. C. Riley, *Don Quixote*, Allen & Unwin, London, 1986; 'Diálogo con Carlos Fuentes', *Simposio Carlos Fuentes: Actas*, eds. Isaac Jack Lévy and Juan Loveluck, University of South Carolina Press, Columbia, n.d., p. 216.

[6]Patricia Waugh, *Metafiction*, Routledge, London and New York, 1984, pp. 23–4.

[7]See the Introduction to *Postmodernism and Contemporary Fiction*, ed. Edmund J. Smyth, Batsford, London, 1991, pp. 9-15.

[8]Miguel de Cervantes, *Don Quijote de la Mancha*, Juventud, Barcelona, 1971, p. 19.

[9]A. J. Close, *Miguel de Cervantes: Don Quixote*, Cambridge University Press, Cambridge, 1990, p. 125.

[10]Jean Franco, 'The Critique of the Pyramid and Mexican Narrative After 1968' and Lanin A. Gyurko, 'Individual and National Identity in Fuentes' *La cabeza de la hidra*', both in *Latin American Fiction Today*, ed. Rose S. Minc, Montclair State College/Hispamérica, Takoma Park, n.d., pp. 49–60, 33–48 respectively.

[11]Carlos Fuentes, *La cabeza de la hidra*, Argos Vergara, Barcelona, 1979, p. 218.

[12]Ralph Harper, *The World of the Thriller*, The Press of Case Western Reserve University, Cleveland, 1969, p. 81. Quoted by Waugh, *Metafiction*, p. 84.

[13]Phillip Koldewyn, '*La cabeza de la hidra*: residuos del colonialismo', *Mester*, XI, 1982, p. 53.

[14]Emma Kafalenos, 'The Grace and Disgrace of Literature: Carlos Fuentes' *The Hydra Head*', *Latin American Literary Review*, XV, 1987, pp. 141–58. Kafalenos quotes from: Michel Foucault, *Les Mots et les choses*, Gallimard, Paris, 1966; Jean Ricardou, *Pour une théorie du nouveau roman*, Seuil, Paris, 1971; and *Nouveau problèmes du roman*, Seuil, Paris, 1978.

[15]Javier Herrero, 'Carlos Fuentes y las lecturas modernas del *Quijote*', *Revista Iberoamericana*, XLV, 1979, pp. 559, 560.

[16]Regina Janes, 'No more interviews', *Salmagundi*, XLIII, 1979, p. 91; Jonathan Tittler, 'Carlos Fuentes', *Diacritics*, September 1980, p. 47. Both quoted in Gloria Durán, 'The Fuentes Interviews in Fact and in Fiction', *Mester*, XI, 1982, p. 19.

# Chapter 6

# José Donoso and *La misteriosa desaparición de la marquesita de Loria*: Coitus interruptus

In a newspaper article in 1982, José Donoso lamented the almost exclusive association of Latin American fiction with long, complex, experimental, 'totalising' works and asked: '¿No ha llegado un momento de ruptura para la novela latinoamericana, de cambio …?'.[1] A couple of years previously, in 1980, he had published *La misteriosa desaparición de la marquesita de Loria*, probably the most surprising departure from his very own long, complex, experimental, 'totalising' novel from the height of the Boom, *El obsceno pájaro de la noche*. Though much Donoso criticism, partly due to a compliance with the ahistorical agenda of certain schools of literary theory, stresses the continuity of his work, it is pretty plain that there is a quite dramatic change of some kind in his writing after 1970.[2] In particular, there is an apparent reduction in complexity in the shape of the utilisation of popular or conventional genres and the abandonment of tortuous narrative structures. In *Casa de campo*, for instance, which replaces the technique or gimmick of authorial effacement, typical (in part) of the Boom, with the foregrounding of a conventional narratorial or authorial figure, the narrator comments: 'en la hipócrita no-ficción de las ficciones en que el autor pretende eliminarse siguiendo reglas preestablecidas por otras novelas, o buscando fórmulas narrativas novedosas …, veo un odioso puritanismo que estoy seguro que mis lectores no encontrarán en mi escritura'.[3] Yet, as has already been proposed in the opening chapter, the narratorial/authorial stance of *Casa de campo* is, despite the relative accessibility of the text, highly problematic. This is dramatised most obviously in the encounter between the narrator-cum-author as character 'José Donoso' and Silvestre, one of his own literary creations: the author is (impossibly) on his way to his publisher's with the final manuscript of the novel under his arm, but his plans are derailed by the insistences of Silvestre, who, incidentally, bears little relation to the Silvestre of the rest of 'Donoso's' narrative. What this suggests is that there is, after all, continuity with the ideas of the earlier work, most notably the question of the relationship between art and society or reality, but that they are being treated or explored in a new or, indeed, novel way. The post-Boom Donoso can be seen, in other words, as, rather than fragmenting the notion of authority through a conspic-uously labyrinthine narrative structure, destabilising it instead via the subversion of narratorial power from within. *La misteriosa desaparición de la marquesita de Loria* can thus be seen, as with the novels by Vargas Llosa and Fuentes and other novels considered in this book, to similar and differing degrees, as a power struggle between 'author' or, as it really is in this case, narrator and the rival claims of character(s) within the text. Donoso's novel pits an implied male narrator using both the sense of closure implicit in the popular and the authority implicit in High culture to keep in check or even destroy a potentially threatening female presence who is herself associated with the popular and has her own pretensions to authority. The seemingly lightest, most titillating and least openly political Donosian post-Boom text, then, problematises the popu-lar and becomes political through the very processes of its own deceptive articulation.

As in other works by the Chilean author, *La marquesita de Loria*, as we shall from now on call it for short, is based around a false binarism which one might dub order-versus-chaos. One pole (identity, power, convention, rationality, order – often linked with masculinity and adulthood) is opposed to and threatened by the other (fragmentation, rebellion, instinct, irrationality, chaos – often linked with 'femininity' or 'femaleness' and youth or old age). The distinction is, of course, a myth and therefore the former, dreading rupture and contamination, seeks to impose itself on and therefore create the illusion of separation from the latter. The familiar and/or popular tone of the present text may be taken as an attempt to naturalise and thus disguise and neutralise this process. For example, the documentary style gives a comforting impression of truth and knowledge. The novel opens with this tone ('La joven marquesa viuda de Loria, nacida Blanca Arias en Managua, Nicaragua, era ...'[4]) and repeats it in the account of the marquis' death: 'Ese invierno andaba mucha difteria por Madrid: falleció dos días después del miércoles de carnaval, Francisco Javier Anacleto Quiñones, marqués de Loria, antes de cumplir los veintiún años, dejando a toda su parentela desconsolada, muy especialmente a su joven viuda – nacida Blanca Arias, hija del recordado diplomático nicaragüense ...' (40–1). The narrator seems to come across as a compiler who is effortlessly familiar with his material: 'si queremos ser rigurosos hay que precisar que ...' or 'sería demasiado tedioso describir las ocasiones en que ...' (13, 35). Yet the same casual strain with which the final chapter opens ('Todavía corre por Madrid la leyenda ...' [173]) gives the game away. The legend referred to is that of the strange grey dog with golden-grey eyes who disturbs courting couples in the Madrid park, the Retiro. The redundant adverb 'todavía' indicates a certain over-anxiety behind the narrator's jocular tone. Moreover, in designating the legend, highly ambiguously, as 'una alucinación histérica que, hay que confesar, puede no ser fruto sólo de fantasías coincidentes' (174), he appears to deny its veracity while trying to look as if he is not. Why does he introduce the story if it is only immediately to problematise it? Could it be to slur the integrity of his own protagonist, Blanca, who the reader knows thinks she has a relationship with a grey dog with golden-grey eyes which no one else seems to have seen? But why should the narrator want to discredit Blanca? Possibly because she represents a threat to the sense of order inscribed in the documentary style. Partly, this is the threat to the male of female power and sexuality, but it is also that Blanca undermines order by dissolving the binary division: synthesising Europe and Latin America, power and submission, even human and animal and male and female, she is drawn to a male dog with a female name, Luna (see 77), she is reflected in him and possibly is him (insofar as it is hinted that he may be her unconscious) or maybe becomes him at the end (when she is alleged to be devoured by a dog-like creature), and, in any case, seems to find union with the dark, unexplained 'other side' he represents (e.g. 163). In a sense, then, she brings the narrative face to face with what it would prefer to ignore or not to see. Why else is her shocking and unexplained disappearance simply passed over and displaced by the cheery epilogue of the conventional documentary narrator wrapping up the life-stories of the 'normal' characters who remain behind? The disappearance, indeed, is the crucial fulcrum of this contest. Given the documentary style, the title of the book suggests a case history, yet the words 'misteriosa' and 'desaparición' imply a problem and no solution – order threatened by chaos again. Furthermore, the two main sources of popular culture utilised here are those of erotica and detective fiction.[5] Both involve (in different ways) concealment and uncovering, their culmination being closure through disclosure (climactic fulfilment in the former, solving of the mystery in the latter). In *La marquesita de Loria* there is only closure: erotic fulfilment does not take place and the mystery of the disappearance remains unexplained. The 'official' narrative tidies things up neatly by ignoring what it would rather not see, but an implied reader might feel that what the novel is really about is what it keeps secret, what it hides, what it suppresses.

The broad outline given above can now be developed in more detail. The key issue is the significance (or lack of it) of Blanca's disappearance. The question is whether it is in some way wilful (on Blanca's part) or contrived (on the part of the narrator – or perhaps other characters acting as his surrogates). Sharon Magnarelli – in what must, nonetheless, be credited as a superbly constructed essay – denies Blanca much agency of substance. She does not really separate her from the literary forms the novel parodies or pastiches. Adding Spanish American *modernismo* to erotic and detective fiction (Rubén Darío is referred to on a number of occasions and his 'Era un aire suave ...' is quoted playfully in the penultimate chapter and parallels aspects of the story of the novel), she claims that all three forms are predicated upon the urge to disguise an inherent absence and, by extension, the vacuity of the society they echo (102). Blanca, who is virtually synonymous with the text in Magnarelli's reading, is much the same. In a Barthesean nod to the idea of eroticism as a form of discourse, the critic gives Blanca's autoeroticism a linguistic meaning, saying that, in the novel, 'many of the linguistic constructs are devoted to the protagonist's self-admiration, as she "sees" herself , either mentally or in mirrors and pools of water, and as she "writes" herself in her internal monologues, carefully edits the script, sets the scene and then watches herself perform, both sexually and otherwise' (105). With Magnarelli's trademark linguistic parallel established, it is not long before there is talk of language ceasing to signify and becoming mere covering (117), Blanca herself, as her name suggests, representing this very state of affairs (though somewhat peculiarly, one might be forgiven for thinking, if language does not 'signify' anything). Blanca, as a kind of pseudo-narrator, narcissistically projects her own erotic desire on to others, needing to be and assuming she is being seen and lusted after by them. The closeness of her relationship with Luna epitomises this condition, for his eyes – with which she becomes utterly fascinated – are blank, like mirrors, empty reflections of her. With no identity other than the stereotypical practices and consumer items she sports, 'Blanca herself is an absence, enshrouded in signifiers which evoke not her but rather the elite society in which she moves' (107). And, moreover, that society is itself given over to burying its emptiness or 'nothingness' with layers of meaningless covering or adornment. So, for Magnarelli, Blanca's disappearance is the conclusion of the theme of absence made present. Blanca did not really disappear. Because she was never really there.

Notwithstanding the central contradiction concerning the representative or otherwise powers of language, Magnarelli marshalls considerable textual evidence which could be seen to support her argument (especially with regard to the projection of the wish to be seen and desired). Her point is reinforced by the link forged between Blanca and *modernismo* as well as with erotica and mysteries. A number of swan images crop up in relation to Blanca's life and, at one stage, echoing her earlier erotic adventure at the opera *Lohengrin* she sees herself, now widowed, in the waters of the Retiro as 'un maravilloso cisne negro entre tantos blancos' (46). The swan, of course, is the classic *modernista* image, so Blanca is again living in reflections, in literature rather than life, in a literature, moreover, that is most commonly associated with 'l'art pour l'art', style, surface, decoration – not with depth or substance. The language of the novel might even be said to mimic that of *modernismo*. There is the quotation in the penultimate chapter and Blanca's 'cuerpo fantaseoso' is at one stage said to be in an 'estado de sinestesia' (47), while Magnarelli identifies a proliferation of adjectivisation. A feature of the text is indeed the qualification of nouns by unnecessary adjectives or adjectivisation, as in, for example: 'sacó de su bolsillo un peine de carey y brillantes' (65). The qualification is, like Blanca in Magnarelli's reading, non-functional, sheer excess, mere supplement – if anything, it points to the absence or emptiness that characterises the high society in which the marchioness moves. Erotic and detective stories, the conventions of which the novel also mimics, are similarly surplus to meaningful requirements. 'All three forms of discourse are privileges of a leisured class – a class which consumes them and is portrayed within them, a class which has time, money and energy in excess of those used in "productive" or reproductive activities' (Magnarelli, 113).

Reducing *La marquesita de Loria* to 'empty signifiers' (122), Magnarelli's conclusion would seem to be that there is no significance to Blanca's disappearance, that it merely follows the internal logic of a narrative that the protagonist herself appears to dominate or even manipulate. Yet even Magnarelli acknowledges that 'Blanca is portrayed as conditioned by and a product of the social, artistic mythology which envelopes (*sic*) and surrounds her' (107). This may not seem to grant her much agency, but it opens the way for a reading that might begin to. An aspect of Blanca's 'conditioning', should one choose to read it this way, is that her 'natural' or 'authentic' Latin American self is swamped and distorted by European values (symbolised most obviously by the clothes, accessories and perfumes with European names with which she 'covers' herself). On the very first page it is said that, after her parents leave her in Madrid to return to their native Nicaragua, the marchioness

> se había convertido ya en una europea cabal, sustituyendo esos ingenuos afectos por otros y olvidando tanto las sabrosas entonaciones de su vernáculo como las licencias femeninas corrientes en el continente joven, para envolverse en el suntuoso manto de los prejuicios, rituales y dicción de su flamante rango ... – en el fondo todo había sido tan fácil como descartar un huipil en favor de una túnica de Paul Poiret. (11–2)

Lucrecio Pérez Blanco sees the novel as being about loss of an American identity: 'si Blanca, símbolo de Hispanoamérica, desaparece y no se encuentra rastro alguno suyo, es porque la descomposición no deja rastro del propio ser. El mestizaje de sangre, que pide un comportamiento coherente y distinto de quien mezcló la sangre, puesto que el nuevo ser es distinto, se destruye, se descompone por falta de coherencia'.[6] The difficulty here is that the novel can also be seen as problematising the very idea of an 'authentic' 'Latin American' identity that Pérez Blanco appears to believe in. Surely if European identity (which seems here to amount to little more than a stream of conventions, fashions and designer goods) is a construct, then so is a Latin American identity which takes for granted 'las licencias femeninas corrientes en el continente joven' or, in a later example, 'esa pasmosa vocación para las perversiones que suele darse aparejada con la ternura en las hembras del trópico' (34). Examining Blanca's enraptured look at the opera, Casilda 'no pudo sino meditar cómo algunos seres muy primitivos, por ejemplo esta linda muchacha, tienen una pureza tal que les facilita la comprensión de lo más inaccesiblemente selecto del arte' (23). Of course, the reason for Blanca's rapture is not any primitive tropical purity but the fact that she is being surreptitiously masturbated by Paquito. Given that it is later revealed that Casilda has the hots for Blanca and given the Frenchwoman's fetishistic use of the term 'primitivo' to describe the young widow's image (115), it can be seen that Blanca's native primitiveness is itself a cultural invention: it is little more than the erotic cliché (especially in the arts) of the member of a dominant group's fetishistic desire for 'difference' in the form of a 'young girl', a 'bit of rough', a 'black man' or whatever (it is worth noting, especially for Casilda, that Blanca and her family are also bound up with notions of cultural and racial inferiority). In fact, Blanca's sexual adventures, following the series format typical of erotic literature, rehearse many of the usual clichés. By the time she is faced, in the second-to-last chapter, with a ménage-à-trois involving a lesbian romp and male cross-dressing, she is 'mortalmente aburrida' (162). In the final chapter, it is after the clichéd violent encounter on the back seat of her Isotta-Fraschini with her own 'bit of rough', the chauffeur Mario, that she walks away and disappears forever. Does this not intimate some degree of consciousness and action on the marquesita's part? And does not the relieved tone of the tacked-on epilogue of the final four pages, which restores order and surveys the smug and materially satisfactory lives of the characters who survive the marchioness, also imply Blanca's challenge to and rejection of the lifestyle of the others? As Ricardo Gutiérrez-Mouat comments, referring to erotic play, though he could equally be referring to material indulgence, 'ante este aburguesamiento del carnaval erótico, a la marquesita no le queda otra solución que protagonizar el misterio de su propia desaparición'.[7] And in this respect *modernismo*, for Gutiérrez-Mouat, has a wider sociopolitical significance beyond that suggested by adjectivisation. What Darío represents is the propagation through literature of a falsely naturalised myth of Latin American identity, 'la impostación de un yo ficticio y artificial, y la apropiación

de esta impostura a través de la lengua poética' (267). Blanca, it
might be argued – in her rejection of social and sexual clichés, her
relationship with Luna and her disappearance – breaks with both
normalising social constructs and with the artistic constructs that
underpin them. In one sense she is clearly the marquesa Eulalia
from 'Era un aire suave ...', 'maligna y bella', who toys with her
lovers and 'ríe, ríe, ríe'. Yet Darío's poem ends with the lines: 'Yo el
tiempo y el día y el país ignoro; | pero sé que Eulalia ríe todavía, | ¡y
es crüel y eterna su risa de oro!'.[8] As Magnarelli has already pointed
out (115), these lines indicate that the poet sees Eulalia as nothing
but his own personal literary creation. If Donoso's novel uses the
language of Darío's *modernismo*, one might therefore be inclined to
infer that Blanca's actions in the text represent a rebellion against
her linguistic construction and fixing. Her struggle is to transcend
the restrictions that the narrative seeks to impose on her.

The relationship between protagonist and narrator raises important questions about representation. In particular, it raises questions about High and Low and about male representations of the
female or, indeed, the 'feminine'. The implied narratorial perspective of *La marquesita de Loria* can be taken as masculine. This is,
by and large (and with some notable exceptions), the usual viewpoint of erotic or detective fiction; the tone here is purportedly
authoritative and clearly masculine in, say, its comments on
women; and the real author is, of course, a man. Also the theme of
Blanca 'being seen', as well as the motifs of painting, the female
model and the male artist, all suggest the male gaze. As has already
been mentioned, the marquesita tends to perceive herself in terms
of other people's looks of desire and, on top of this, she pictures
herself as a Paul Chabas *baigneuse* and poses nude for the painter
Archibaldo Arenas. Feminist art historian Linda Nochlin comments that 'the acceptance of woman as object of the desiring male
gaze in the visual arts is so universal that for a woman to question,
or to draw attention to this fact, is to invite derision, to reveal
herself as one who does not understand the sophisticated strategies
of high culture and takes art too "literally", and is therefore unable
to respond to aesthetic discourses'.[9] For a woman to challenge the
validity of the female nude or the sexualisation of the representation
of the female, this would be 'undermined by authorized doubts, by
the need to please, to be learned, sophisticated, aesthetically astute
– in male-defined terms, of course' (Nochlin, 32). Applying the

painter-(female) nude relationship to the narrator-(female) character relationship in Donoso's novel, we can deduce that Blanca's
sexual exhibitionism and narcissism is simply her internalisation of
the implied male narrator's urge to see and portray her as sex
object. What appears to be narration from Blanca's viewpoint in
her sexual fantasies may actually often be the subtle and naturalising imposition of the dominant masculine narratorial viewpoint,
which is not as neutral, distant, detached or playfully light-hearted
as it seems. This is the Foucaultian notion that 'symbolic power is
invisible and can be exercised only with the complicity of those
who fail to recognise either that they submit to it or that they exercise it' (Nochlin, 2). Yet this is equally a pattern of power and
potential resistance. To quote Foucault:

> In effect, what defines a relationship of power is that it is a mode of
> action which does not act directly and immediately upon others.
> Instead it acts upon their actions: an action upon an action, on exist-
> ing actions or on those which may arise in the present or the future... .
> A power relationship can only be articulated on the basis of two
> elements which are indispensable if it is really to be a power rela-
> tionship: that 'the other' (the one over whom power is exercised) be
> thoroughly recognised and maintained to the very end as a person
> who acts; and that, faced with a relationship of power, a whole field
> of responses, reactions, results, and possible inventions may open
> up.[10]

Blanca, then, can acquire consciousness and contest her representation. She sees through the painter Archibaldo and leaves him; and
she abandons too the narrator's attempted imposition of an erotic
narrative by forsaking sexual high jinks, turning to Luna and disappearing.

What is beginning to emerge from behind the mask of a seemingly straightforward and amusing sophisticated pastiche of a
popular genre is a more complex picture in which the mask itself is
the very ploy activated to disguise the underlying reality of a power
battle. Essentially a battle between a male narrator and his female
protagonist, it is revealed by the (absent) presence of a further
implied narrator (or, rather, implied author) who appeals to the
insight and understanding of an implied reader. The reader is
encouraged to see between the lines, in other words, and spot the
limitations or inconsistencies of the projected narrator. The reader

is the real detective in this mystery story and the villain he or she catches in the act is none other than the male narrator himself. An obvious example is the epilogue. The official narrator tries to 'close' the narrative by adopting a chirpy tone and describing a society enjoying harmony and satisfaction. Yet the alert reader cannot fail to notice his complete avoidance of or inability to explain or discuss the nature or implications of the marchioness's disappearance. The casual final line of the text, referring to the walks taken by Archibaldo and his new wife (incidentally, Blanca's sister – perhaps a more ruly and socially appropriate version of the marquesita?) 'seguidos por Luna, su gran y fiel perro gris' (198) is another pointer for the reader to pick up. The sheer unproblematic timbre of this statement must prompt the reader to feel that the official narrator is concealing something or refusing to face something, for he is simply glossing over the fact that Luna had previously appeared (at least) to have gone off to Blanca's, been involved in her disappearance, and is possibly still – in some phantasmal manifestation – haunting the shady corners of the Retiro to this day. A clue to assist the reader in deciphering this tendency is already given earlier in the presentation of Archibaldo Arenas. As a painter of portraits, he is like the narrator as compiler or chronicler, that is one who copies or reproduces reality in his art. Yet a detail reveals that he actually falsifies reality: he paints Tere Castillo as a 'pescadora gallega' when she is in fact a high society 'andaluza' (57). The implication is that the narrator does the same sort of thing. An example is the story of the death of the marquis, Paquito. Paquito's death is caused by complications arising from a bad cold which was aggravated when, insufficiently dressed, he left a fancy-dress ball early with Blanca in poor weather conditions. But two differing explanations as to why he left are given.[11] The first, fleetingly given shortly before the documentary-style death announcement quoted earlier as if by the official narrator, is that he 'fled', 'pegado a las faldas de Blanca porque tanta algarabía le causaba desazón', too scared to tell his mother he is going (40). This is a clear image of male weakness. The second (and more memorably expressed) version, presented more from Blanca's point of view, is that his determination to confront his mother and her alleged lover fills him with strength and energy, producing a huge erection and the determination to take his wife straight home and 'violarla' (51). What this indicates at the very least is that the narrator is at some level untrustworthy. Or, worse, that he is uneasy and manipulative. If the second version is from Blanca's viewpoint, then the narrator has manufactured her internalisation of the supposedly typical female (but actually male) fantasy of powerful male sexual potency. Blanca's 'point of view' here is really a narrative manipulation so that she is made to validate what is actually a projection of the male narrator's desire for sexual security. But surely, in the narrator's own terms, the first 'official' version, rather than Blanca's, should be the truth. This version though would confirm male weakness – which seems to be the truth anyway – for Paquito is, in fact, impotent. Thus the driving force behind the narrative power struggle is actually male sexual anxiety.

Fundamentally, it is the sense of order guaranteed by faith in binary logic that is felt to be in jeopardy. Political historian Carole Pateman says women have traditionally been perceived as 'potential disrupters of masculine boundary systems of all sorts', while Elaine Showalter, quoting Toril Moi, states that 'women's social or cultural marginality seems to place them on the borderlines of the symbolic order, both the "frontier between men and chaos", and dangerously part of chaos itself, inhabitants of a mysterious and frightening wild zone outside of patriarchal culture'.[12] It follows that the more the 'presence' of woman, the greater the sense of peril in man. Hence the narrator's need in *La marquesita de Loria* to impose himself on Blanca and assert his own presence in the epilogue. His anxiety suggests two possible things: that he is threatened by Blanca's leaving him, her independence, her departure from his familiar erotic narrative into an altogether less sure world; or that he gets rid of her himself, that he makes her disappear rather than confront what she is exposing herself and therefore exposing him to. The threat of greater female presence can be related to Showalter's comments on the emergence of the so-called New Woman at the *fin-de-siècle* (a world not dissimilar from the 1920s Madrid setting of Donoso's novel and with explicit parallels in Showalter's book to the current *fin-de-siècle*). Echoing the earlier remarks here, she discusses misogyny in *fin-de-siècle* painting: 'there images of female narcissism, of the *femme fatale* and the sphinx, of women kissing their mirror images, gazing at themselves in circular baths, or engaging in autoerotic play mutate by the end of the century into savagely "gynecidal" visions of female sexuality' (10). This is all remarkably like what happens to Blanca. Her self-consciousness and solitary sexual experiments do evolve in a deadly direction: two men die after sex with her and she, on a number of occasions, mentally verbalises the fatal power of her flesh. Moreover, Showalter's New Woman was particularly worrisome because her anarchic sense of sexual independence was thought to threaten the institution of matrimony (38) and presumably the male privileges that traditionally went with it. It is interesting in this respect that Blanca's thirst for carnal knowledge, 'este enloquecedor anhelo de lo desconocido' (46), takes off after the death of her husband. The widow is a traditionally troublesome image for the male: the idea of the Merry Widow, like Blanca, financially and therefore sexually independent, sexually experienced but unconstrained. Or there is the Black Widow, bringing death and associated with dark forces, again like Blanca with her mysterious canine companion, her links with the moon and the black women of the Caribbean with their tarot cards. The widow, of course, traditionally wears a veil, as does Blanca in her mourning outfit. Veils are strongly identified with female sexuality and the male gaze. According to Showalter, the veil traditionally represented the hymen (hence the conventional link with chastity) and 'Nature' in scientific or medical discourse was often likened to a woman whose secrets would be yielded when unveiled by man. But the veiled woman also connoted mystery and her 'secrets' were linked to the riddles of birth and death. Indeed Freud's reading of the image of the veiled woman in terms of the myth of the Medusa is the background to his theory of the male castration complex. To unveil woman is to confront the genitalised head of the Medusa, the upward displacement of the *vagina dentata*. The discovery of the female sexual organs incurs simultaneously the fear of decapitation or castration. This may well explain all the talk of penises in *La marquesita de Loria* – a projection of the narrator's male anxiety on to Blanca. Hard, 'iron' rods are frequently evoked yet the truth is that don Mamerto's penis is tiny, Almanza needs a corset to keep his up and Paquito's goes flaccid at the crucial moments. As Mary Ann Doane says, in her study of *femmes fatales* and veiling in cinema, 'the phallus actually becomes important only insofar as it might be absent, it might disappear. It assumes meaning only in relation to castration'.[13]

Veils, sexuality, decapitation and castration, decadence and the idea of the *femme fatale* are elements which all combine in the story and myth of Salome (a focus of Showalter's analysis), which finds interesting echoes of itself in *La marquesita de Loria*. As Showalter reminds us, she was painted by Gustave Klimt as an elegant lady of the *Belle Epoque* who holds the severed head casually by her side – another parallel with the narratorial fear that underlies the glamorous portrait of Donoso's 1920s high-society marchioness. More intriguing still is Oscar Wilde's play *Salome*, particularly his 1893 edition accompanied by the drawings of Aubrey Beardsley. *La marquesita de Loria* is also accompanied by illustrations from old editions of *La Esfera*, which – though much less sinister and suggestive – display certain period similarities with Beardsley's. The first drawing from *Salome* depicts the moon in a somewhat sexual context and its title was changed from *The Man in the Moon* to *The Woman in the Moon*, again echoing aspects of *La marquesita de Loria*: fear and mystery represented by the moon and Luna, sexual ambiguity and the dissolution of binary divisions. A further vague connection is the linking of the moon to death and disappearance. The Page of Herodias urges Narraboth to look at the moon rather than at Salome and later laments: '... now he has killed himself... . Well, I knew that the moon was seeking a dead thing, but I knew not that it was he whom she sought. Ah! Why did I not hide him from the moon?' This makes us think both of Blanca's withdrawal from sexuality in favour of a disappearance involving Luna and the male narrator's dual fear of female sexuality and chaos. But what Salome represents above all is the enthralling and terrifying unveiling of the female self. The widow's veil of the marquesita de Loria expresses not only her disquieting blurring of boundaries (the veil is neither complete exposure nor complete concealment) but is also relieved of its connotations of chastity, modesty and unavailability: 'la joven marquesa viuda de Loria paseaba por los senderos del Retiro luciendo para ojos desconocidos ... el misterio de su luto. Pero de sus orejas se cimbraban dos lágrimas de oro facetado cuyo brillo trascendía los velos del duelo con perversos guiños impuestos por la ligereza del paso de la joven' (55). Within a few pages, the wind has lifted her veils and she is receiving copious *piropos* (59). Then she initiates her post-marital sex life and causes the death of the diminutively-endowed don Mamerto. All of this is a symbolic returning of the male gaze and part of a process of breaking with the self-image of woman as male sex object. What is more, it exposes the constructed nature of the masculine othering of women. The face behind the veil is probably normal after all. As Cixous says, 'You only have to look at the Medusa straight on to see her. And she's not deadly. She's beautiful and she's laughing'.[14] It is the fear of looking straight on that makes the marquesita disappear or at least makes the disappearance be ignored.

Effectively, what happens in *La marquesita de Loria* is that Blanca is both object and agent. She connotes what Laura Mulvey terms '*to-be-looked-at-ness*' in her seminal essay on female representation in film, 'Visual Pleasure and Narrative Cinema',[15] while at the same time marks the transition from heroine as reflection of the hero's dynamics to heroine with agency. Yet even without or before agency, so the theory goes, the male unconscious has to deal with castration anxiety (based on 'the visually ascertainable absence of the penis'), since even 'the woman as icon, displayed for the gaze and enjoyment of men, the active controllers of the look, always threatens to evoke the anxiety it originally signified' (Mulvey, 13). Mulvey sees two avenues of escape for the male unconscious, both of which would seem to correspond to strategies employed (or attempted) by the implied male narrator of *La marquesita de Loria*. One is fetishistic scopophilia, 'a complete disavowal of castration by the substitution of a fetish object or turning the represented figure itself into a fetish so that it becomes reassuring rather than dangerous' (Mulvey, 13–4). This is clearly essayed in *La marquesita de Loria* but does not seem to work. The other is voyeurism, involving 'preoccupation with the re-enactment of the original trauma (investigating the woman, demystifying her mystery), counterbalanced by the devaluation, punishment or saving of the guilty object' (Mulvey, 13). Certainly, the narrator subjects the case of the marchioness to investigation and tries to devalue her by presenting her as sex-crazed and shallow. It is important to remember that the narrator adopts a playful, ironic tone more often than a documentary approach: this, coupled with the mocking adjectivisation mentioned earlier, allows him to appear superior and deflate Blanca. Yet he fails to demystify her mystery and fails, it can be argued, to devalue her. Perhaps then he manages to punish her. *Salome* ends with Herod calling for the woman's death. In Bram Stoker's *Dracula*, another *fin-de-siècle* work with evident links to *La marquesita de Loria*, Lucy's sexualised vampiric impurity (echoes of Blanca and Luna) is corrected by men decapitating her (Freud's Medusa-related castration anxiety again) and driving a stake through her heart (the relieved flaunting of the phallus). Blanca, meantime, is destroyed by a horrific monster (so Mario claims) and the world is put right again by the epilogue.[16] Returning now to the sketches from *La Esfera*, their arrangement suggests a similar urge to punish and regain control. The drawings, which precede each chapter, all of women, all suit the period tone of the text and may be taken to parallel it closely. The first three (of eight) all correspond to the action in the chapter concerned – widowhood, a masked ball, a woman alone in her bedroom. This all suggests strong narratorial control and organisation. Yet in the third chapter, the woman portrayed appears to be looking out straight ahead. This is the only picture in which the woman's eyes are not covered or turned away. Is this a breakdown in the power of the male gaze (control) and a pointer to Blanca's self-discovery or self-assertion? It could well be, because the illustration preceding the next chapter (the fourth) – a woman in a tennis dress – indicates a crumbling of the rigidly ordered parallels since it refers to an episode which does not take place until the sixth chapter. Indeed the next three illustrations bear no clear-cut relation to the chapters at all. Narratorial command of the entirety of the text is being undermined, it seems. But the placing of the final illustration reestablishes control. It is of a woman and a sporty motor car, alluding to Blanca's final and probably fatal journey in the last chapter. And here the woman is looking away and, for the first time in the drawings, is veiled. The inference may well be that the male narrator is back in charge, female modesty is restored, the female threat will be destroyed. Not so fast, though. The veil is an ambiguous image, problematising boundaries as much as fixing them. And, in the most important illustration of them all, the one in colour, on the cover, the female figure is looking right out at the other looker, eyes wide open and clear, returning the gaze, even, given the intensity of the eyes, acting as the gazing subject rather than the gazed-at object. Maybe the protagonist does get one over on her narrator after all.

The point is that there is something of a truth to both views of the outcome of the battle, for Blanca does not score a 'triumph' in any conventional sense and the narrator does manage to restore a semblance of order. The outcome is similar to that of Donoso's early story 'Paseo' (and maybe, too, a variation on it, *Este domingo*) where an orderly but strangely uncomfortable narrator recalls the unexplained disappearance during his childhood of his aunt with a mysterious dog. The narrator's life is controlled but wanting, while the aunt's disappearance is seen as both a collapse into chaos and a glimpse of fulfilment or meaning. So what Blanca achieves is to transcend false, sterile and limiting notions of order, but that achievement – though potentially meaningful for her – is presented as dark and perturbing because it erodes the order-predicated binary logic upon which conventional narrative, society and even 'civilisation' depend. Turning now to examine this process more closely, the first thing to notice – before even considering Blanca's 'alternative' – is the unsettled nature of the narrative itself. The narrative depends in part on the illusion of documentary realism. Also, in mimicking a popular genre, it depends on the illusion of a comfortingly familiar format. Yet many narratorial interventions have a tongue-in-cheek quality about them (simple random examples would be the references to 'el banquete – si de banquete puede calificarse tan rústico ágape' or Almanza's 'retazos de fandangos absolutamente irrepetibles' [31, 155]). The language too is often exaggeratedly stylised (a good example here is the account of Blanca's erotic-cum-romantic visit to Archibaldo's studio where a short time lapse is described four times in eight pages as 'un siglo', there are three 'maravillosos' in a single paragraph and the first kiss ('dulce beso') of the encounter 'los haría – como lo aseguraban todos los novelistas – vibrar al unísono' and 'parecía haber encendido otra luz en el estudio' [122–30]). Moreover, there is a dramatic intervention towards the end in the report of the chauffeur's reaction to the disappearance: '... montó en el Isotta-Fraschini para ir a toda velocidad al puesto de policía más cercano, donde contó lo que el autor de esta historia acaba de contar en este capítulo y que está a punto de terminar' (193–4). In one sense, such interventions reinforce narrative authority, by signposting a relaxed and superior organiser or creator. At the same time though, they disrupt the mode of documentary realism, question the popular genre feel of the text, conflict often – in terms of tone – with the events narrated, and betray an anxiety over narratorial presence (the last quotation immediately preceding the narratorial imposition of the order-restoring epilogue in the face of Blanca's chaotic disappearance). The text then seems to lack the '*colle* logique' which Barthes sees as fundamental to the 'readerly' text.[17] It is this rupturing of narratorial security which allows us to read Blanca's story as that which generates the textual discomfort.[18]

The essential feature of Blanca's story is the displacement of her sexual or material quest (voiced as a quest for knowledge and fulfilment [e.g. 12, 46–7]) and linked to a desire for gratification through power (e.g. 14, 58ff) by its opposite.[19] Sexual situations from the start are juxtaposed with instances of death or the appearance of morally sterile characters like Almanza. The lengthy and delayed build-up to the highly-charged description of the eventual sexual *rencontre* with Archibaldo Arenas (which promises to be the pinnacle of satisfaction) is almost immediately undone by Blanca's sense of disappointment and virtually instant abandonment of him. This is a pivotal encounter, for Archibaldo not only represents the meaninglessness of the sexual-material quest, he also provides Luna, the key figure in the displacement of the quest. Luna, of course, may not exist as such in a conventional sense (none of her staff notices him, Archibaldo does not miss him and he is still with him at the end).[20] He is, thus, part of Blanca, the unconscious side she has learned to suppress but is now beginning to see. Either way, it is what he represents that matters. And it is the opposite to Archibaldo. The painter's lemon-grey eyes turn out to be merely black and empty (120, 166, 168); instead Blanca immerses herself in the lemon-grey eyes of 'ese perro terrible y maravilloso' in a way she never could in anyone else's (166). The eyes (which are like two moons) are linked to the black or half-caste women who read tarot cards and talked of witchcraft to Blanca as a child:[21]

> ... las mestizas de su niñez en las noches de miedo le señalaban las dos lunas idénticas en el horizonte (i.e. the moon and its reflection) para calmarla. ¿Pero por qué había producido esta hecatombe doméstica, Luna, su Luna, su perro querido a quien, ahora se daba cuenta, había echado de menos durante todo el día, sobre todo a sus ojos suspendidos en el horizonte mismo de su imaginación. (141–2)

Luna is part of a dark other side and is wreaking havoc in her world yet is what she really wants. He is an alternative to the material (he literally destroys the sumptuous but redundant elegance of her 'alcoba de raso color *fraise ecrasé*' [12] converting it into 'esa fétida ruina que la satisfacía' [170]) and the sexual (increasingly tiresome erotic incidents are juxtaposed sharply with the thrill of her return to Luna [140, 162–3, 184] and the erotic – or pornographic – cliché of the sexual encounter of woman and animal pointedly does not materialise [143]), offering her a unity or possibility of completion

– 'dos lunas que eran una sola' (106) – which she has been lacking in her life so far. The climax comes when she abandons the known world altogether by disappearing with the animal into 'la oscuridad total donde sólo podían existir los remansos lunares de los ojos de Luna' (189), seemingly devoured by a dog-like creature (193). All that remains of her are an ornate handgun, a silver clasp, a French shoe and a classy gold watch – all fetishistic images of the material and sensuous world she has left behind. There is no body. The narrator may have got rid of her.[22] But her 'absence' might also be his castration fear and her assertion of freedom from the male gaze. Blanca rejects the role that is written for her and undermines the very epistemological and ontological categories that give shape to society's script.

A final point concerning the narrator–marquesita dialectic is its relationship to that of Europe and Latin America. As has already been suggested, the post-Boom and even the postmodern in Latin America are concepts very much wrapped up with questions of intertextuality and cultural transnationalism, with two broad tendencies (sometimes different, sometimes convergent) emerging, one involving play and interaction with popular or mass culture, the other supposedly more popular-rooted and involving greater local cultural and political specificity. *La marquesita de Loria* is certainly not the latter (in the sense that, say, *testimonio* is) but it does come between two books dealing very obviously with Latin American politics (*Casa de campo* in 1978 and *El jardín de al lado* in 1981), the latter precisely dealing with the link with European perspectives. And interestingly enough, Donoso has defined the modern Latin American novel as 'being about identification, a search for national identity and for personal identity'.[23] Blanca's personal identity does have a strong continental and intercontinental dimension. Denoting and connoting her tropical provenance, her beauty is routinely described with terms like 'sus lindos brazos de criolla' (14) and her genital region is referred to with terms like 'vegetación' and 'selva' (at one stage 'su vellón casi no animal' [101]). The dangerous beauty and sexuality of the *femme fatale*, which needs to be contained, is thus identified with 'Latin Americanness'. The containment is effected by European discourse. Blanca is like a 'continente vacío' (167), to be filled with European signifiers. Displaying the complicity characteristic of the Foucaultian notion of power, she allows her identity to be remodelled via European fashions and practices and rewritten via the European-style narrator's pastiche of Spanish erotic fiction. However, while Blanca is moulded by Europe as she is by the narrative, her Latin Americanness is resistant. Even the fragrance of L'Heure Bleue cannot conceal her 'ardiente aroma de criolla' (57). And she vows to hit back at accusations of *cursilería* (96): 'ella, al fin y al cabo, era una bravía hembra del continente nuevo, del que no se avergonzaba pese a que eligiera cubrirlo con un barniz de civilización, barniz que estaba dispuesta a romper en cuanto le conviniera' (74). Part of the marquesita's challenge to narratorial authority, then, is also implicitly a challenging of eurocentrism. Again, if the narrator is implied as European or Europeanist as well as male, then the implied reader will recognise the (implied) author as Latin American. The truth is, though, that Blanca, educated as she is 'tanto por las negras del trópico como por las monjas de España' (13), is both. As is the author, who is as much part of a European and North American cultural tradition as he is of a Latin American one.[24] Indeed the entire Blanca–narrator dialectic and the issues it has raised here draw attention to the deeply intratextual and intertextual construction of the novel. 'You must acknowledge', Donoso has remarked, 'that my novels, especially the last ones, on one level are postmodern and are involved with the confusion of the telling and the told, but on another level, they preserve a sort of sociological and, somehow, political meaning' (Montenegro and Santí, 12–3). Perhaps Donoso manages to achieve this balance – in this work at least, if not necessarily in the more overtly political *Casa de campo* – because the novel neither seeks the inscription of a strong authorial voice as in *La tía Julia y el escribidor* nor particularly seeks to reconcile a clear political agenda with the problematisation of the relationship between literature and reality as in *La cabeza de la hidra*. Oddly enough, *La misteriosa desaparición de la marquesita de Loria* has received very scant critical attention. This is probably because it has been considered frivolous and superficial. Yet it is the very subtlety of the interaction between the surface and what lies behind it that makes this novel one which does manage, without undoing itself, to be European and Latin American, popular and serious, at the same time.

# Notes

[1] José Donoso, 'Dos mundos americanos', *El Mercurio (Artes y Letras)*, 14 Nov. 1982, p. 1.

[2] Sharon Magnarelli's impressive work is an obvious example of the application of a theoretical model which brings out similar 'themes' across a variety of differing works. See her *Understanding José Donoso*, University of South Carolina Press, Columbia, 1993. All references to Magnarelli in this chapter will be to her 'Disappearance Under the Cover of Language: The Case of the Marquesita de Loria' in *Studies on the Works of José Donoso*, ed. Miriam Adelstein, Edwin Mellen Press, Lewiston/ Queenston/ Lampeter, 1990, pp. 101–29. For a discussion of the evolution in Donoso's work from Boom to post-Boom, see, for example, my *José Donoso: The Boom and Beyond*, Francis Cairns, Liverpool and Wolfeboro, 1988.

[3] José Donoso, *Casa de campo*, 3rd ed., Seix Barral, Barcelona, 1980, p. 54.

[4] José Donoso, *La misteriosa desaparición de la marquesita de Loria*, Seix Barral, Barcelona, 1980, p. 11.

[5] Donoso himself describes the novel both as a take-off of Spanish erotic fiction of the 1920s and as a whodunnit in 'A Conversation between José Donoso and Marie-Lise Gazarian Gautier', in *The Creative Process in the Works of José Donoso*, ed. Guillermo I. Castillo-Feliú, Winthrop Studies on Major Modern Writers, Rock Hill, 1982, p. 15.

[6] Lucrecio Pérez Blanco, 'Acercamiento a una novela de denuncia social: *La misteriosa desaparición de la marquesita de Loria* de José Donoso', *Revista de Estudios Hispánicos*, XVI, 1982, p. 400.

[7] Ricardo Gutiérrez-Mouat, *José Donoso: impostura e impostación*, Hispamérica, Gaithersburg, 1983, p. 252.

[8] Rubén Darío, *Poesías completas*, Aguilar, Madrid, 1961, pp. 615–17.

[9] Linda Nochlin, *Women, Art, and Power and Other Essays*, Harper and Row, New York, 1988, pp. 29-30.

[10] Michel Foucault, 'The Subject and Power', in *Michel Foucault, Beyond Structuralism and Hermeneutics*, eds. Hubert L. Dreyfus and Paul Rabinow, 2nd ed., University of Chicago Press, Chicago, 1983, p. 220.

[11] Magnarelli offers a more or less opposite interpretation to the one given here, though her comments on the point of view in each version concur roughly with mine. See pp. 103–4 and pp. 124–5 n. 11.

[12] Elaine Showalter, *Sexual Anarchy: Gender and Culture at the Fin-de-Siècle*, Penguin, New York, 1990, pp. 7–8. Showalter quotes Carol Pateman from Susan Aiken *et al.*, 'Trying Transformations: Curriculum Legislation and the Problem of Resistance', *Signs*, XII, 1987, p. 261 and Toril Moi, *Sexual/Textual Politics*, Routledge, London and New York, 1985, p. 167.

My comments on the New Woman, the Veiled Woman, Salome and *Dracula* draw on Showalter. The quotation from Oscar Wilde is from Showalter, *Sexual Anarchy*, p. 155.

[13]Mary Ann Doane, *Femmes Fatales: Feminism, Film Theory, Psychoanalysis*, Routledge, New York and London, p. 45. The central fear of the disappearance of the phallus becomes a literal reality in Donoso's 'Chatanooga Choochoo' from *Tres novelitas burguesas*, another story inverting traditional notions of sexual power.

[14]Hélène Cixous, 'The Laugh of the Medusa', in *New French Feminisms*, ed. Elaine Marks and Isabelle de Courtivron, University of Massachusetts Press, Amherst, 1980, p. 255. Quoted in Showalter, *Sexual Anarchy*, p. 156.

[15]Laura Mulvey, 'Visual Pleasure and Narrative Cinema', *Screen*, XVI, 1975, p. 11.

[16]The pattern of this epilogue is inverted in an interesting way in Donoso's *El jardín de al lado*, where the narrative of an insecure male author turns out, in the final chapter, to be actually that of his wife. In a remark which may intimate male sexual insecurity, Donoso has commented that: 'Julio (the author character) se transforma en mujer... . Él busca una transformación todo el tiempo, quiere ser otro: no se da cuenta de que quiere ser *otra* en el fondo'. See my 'Una entrevista con José Donoso', *Revista Iberoamericana*, LIII, 1987, p. 997.

[17]Roland Barthes, *S/Z*, Seuil, Paris, 1970, p. 162.

[18]This sort of pattern is discussed in more detail in my 'Structure and Meaning in *La misteriosa desaparición de la marquesita de Loria*', *Bulletin of Hispanic Studies*, LXIII, 1986, pp. 247-56.

[19]The quest is both material and sexual in that both are perceived as sources of possible satisfaction and forms of power, but – more fundamentally – the latter depends on the former, since it is wealth and status which allow for unquestioned sexual freedom and adventure.

[20]Intriguingly, though, Luna does not appear to be present when Blanca visits Archibaldo's studio.

[21]It is a motif of much Donoso fiction that women, servants, the elderly, the poor, blacks or other races are associated with witchcraft or the dark side: in other words, they represent an alternative or threat to the dominant order whose sense of survival depends on the repression of that which it would prefer not to have to deal with.

[22]Given that the novel can be seen as a whodunnit, Blanca's 'killer' might well be the narrator. The fact that a shot is heard and a gun is found might, on the other hand, indicate a suicide, reinforcing perhaps the idea of Blanca's agency and choice and her rejection of society. Magnarelli

suggests a possible scenario wherein Casilda would be the killer (p. 126 n. 22), presumably framing Mario – whose prosecution she vigorously pursues (*Marquesita*, p. 194) – for the crime.

[23]Amalia Pereira, 'Interview with José Donoso', *Latin American Literary Review*, xv, 1987, p. 58.

[24]In a recent interview, Donoso admits also that his generation of writers from Latin America were exploring the 'already-made vocabulary of images' of the European and North American novel of experimentation. See Nivia Montenegro and Enrico Mario Santí, 'A Conversation with José Donoso', *New Novel Review* I, no. 2, 1994, p. 13.

# Chapter 7

# Gustavo Sainz and *La princesa del Palacio de Hierro*: Funniness, identity and the post-Boom

If there is anything approaching a consensus on what distinguishes the post-Boom from the Boom in Latin America, it would appear to have something to do with the relative accessibility of the former in reaction to (or, at least, in contrast with) the narrative complexity of the latter. In particular, as we have noted, this supposed accessibility is often related to the incorporation of humour and elements from popular culture. The 1974 novel *La princesa del Palacio de Hierro* by the Mexican Gustavo Sainz, with its foregrounding of 'pop' or youth culture, its playfully colloquial language and its apparent sense of fun, would therefore seem to be a perfect representative of the post-Boom. It betrays most of the characteristics that Antonio Skármeta has seen as typical of this new generation of writers, and Donald Shaw, following the line of Sainz's contemporary and compatriot José Agustín, even sees Sainz, rather than (as is often claimed) Manuel Puig, as the key initiator of this trend in the post-Boom.[1] However, while it may be tempting simply to see a work like *La princesa del Palacio de Hierro* as a fun-culture rites-of-passage novel, the entire question of the post-Boom's attempted incorporation of humour and pop(ular) culture is, as has been discussed, highly problematic. *La princesa del Palacio de Hierro* may prove to be similarly less straightforward than at first sight. The most basic level of criticism would already seem to suggest this. The novel (and the more general phenomenon of the *Onda* or 'Scene' with which Sainz was in the past associated) has been seen as either funny or serious, as a trivial glorification of youth culture or as a critical commentary on its underlying values.[2] Perhaps a key to this uncertainty is the question of 'funniness.' Following Susan Purdie's terminology, wherein 'joking' can be termed to refer to those occasions where the characteristic effect of 'funniness' is generated, and glossing Lacan, 'joking paradigmatically involves a discursive exchange whose distinctive operation involves the *marked* transgression of the Symbolic Law and whose effect is thereby to constitute jokers as "masters" of discourse'.[3] This idea of joking discourse operating as 'the aberrant case whose marking defines the central field' (Purdie, 158) provides a valuable inroad into the 'problem' of reading Sainz's novel. In it the unnamed protagonist (the Princess of the title) gives an account of a series of comic adventures in which she transgresses the norms of family and gender while simultaneously inserting herself within them. Moreover, her transgressive narration is possibly neutralised by an implied commentary by an implied author to an implied reader. Yet, at the same time, the appeal of the bulk of the novel to the reader must rest upon the very transgressiveness of the *princesa* and her narration. Thus writing and reading (or speaking and listening) emerge, like notions of gender and family, as means of structuring reality, while those very processes, and the relationships between them, are concurrently problematised. It has already been remarked that the shift from the modern to the postmodern is frequently seen as a shift from epistemology to ontology. In a parallel way, the slippage from Boom to post-Boom may reveal, behind all the apparent transparency of the latter, a break with the 'totalising' tendency of the Latin American 'new novel' and a surging mood of insecurity before an increasingly contingent sense of identity.

A commonplace, by now, of much contemporary critical theory is that identity is constructed rather than given. The very title of *La princesa del Palacio de Hierro* suggests this. The protagonist has no name to individualise her but simply a title or definition of her role given by her mother ('princesa' – a conventional, constructed identity) and her job (in the upscale department store, the Palacio de Hierro). Indeed the title implies, echoing as it does the poem 'Sonatina' by Rubén Darío (who is mentioned briefly at the end of the tenth chapter), that she is helplessly imprisoned in her role. Her identity is structured in particular by gender, family and, though more problematically here, class. There are countless examples of her parents pressuring her to mix in only appropriate circles and of her brother and uncle ensuring she complies to adequate standards of feminine behaviour. She works in a shop while typing her male friends' dissertations to help them get on in their careers and internalises her subservient female role to such a degree that her narrative seems to reduce women to their sexual organs, a mere object of male sexual pleasure: her friend is seen patting her 'vagina recién utilizada',[4] while she suspects one of her boyfriends of chasing 'alguna vagina calva y arrugadísima' (221). However, the role models are hypocritical and the acquired role unsatisfying. Her parents' social background is not high society, her father and uncle's money comes from dubious sources and the protective uncle is a crook and rapist. In fact, it is hinted that her parents do not even care much about her at all: they do not even notice her (accidental?) suicide attempt and she is only able to talk about her true feelings or problems to the clients in the store. Her narrative, meantime, betrays increasing signs of thinly-disguised unhappiness. Yet her relationship to both role and models is quite complex. Her raunchy narration celebrates the world of sexual adventure and infidelity, pornography, drugs and violence at the same time as it brings out her unease. In a sense, echoing the earlier remarks on joking as a discursive exchange, this is a reflection of the Lacanian notion of the acquisition of identity: 'man's [*sic*] desire finds its meaning in the desire of the other, not so much because the other holds the key to the object desired, as because the first object of desire is to be recognised by the other' (cited in Purdie, 169). This ambiguous identification with an oppressive masculinity is brought out in the first chapter. The novel opens with a confident female narrative voice introducing a character called Vestida de Hombre seen confronting a policeman – a clear image of the usurping of male authority. Yet the next page offers an equally clear image of female insecurity as the Princess mentions her turned-in feet and tells us she is the centre of attention at a nightclub to which she is sometimes denied access and never allowed to enter without her brother. She insists on her popularity in the club even though she is clearly marginal to the main story being told (the very male-centered fight in the parking lot over a set of stolen hubcaps). Indeed, in the space of a few lines she goes from being 'La Popular' or 'Miss Popularity' to 'la clásica pendeja' (9). The chapter ends with an account of a bizarre encounter in a restaurant where the Princess's tone of sexual confidence gives way to the powerful male sexuality of a manipulative maître d'. Her repulsion and rejection disguises an obvious sexual attraction, borne out by her subsequent relationships with largely similar sorts of men in the rest of the novel. And her relationship with her brother and uncle further bear out this pattern. Her abusive brother becomes a kind of best friend and mentor (78), while the cheerfully described rape of Vestida de Hombre is framed by references to her uncle, the perpetrator, as 'simpatiquísimo' and a 'muy buen tipo' (143–4). Yet, although she likes men to be 'un poquito cabrones' (81) and later feels excited at being kidnapped – 'esa sensación de impotencia y disponibilidad me hacía femenina, me lubricaba' (277) – she also yearns to be treated as she is rather than as she is seen, that is to be accepted on her own terms rather than as the object of an other (202) and later gets frustrated at her lover's anger when she wants to talk seriously or more profoundly, saying: 'es que puedo ser superrelajienta, superplaticadora, supertodo … , pero cuando trato de ser de otra manera y trato de ser un poco más seria y todo, ya nadie me conoce, nadie me entiende' (250).

Though the above examples may not reveal a fully postmodernist aesthetic in Sainz, there is certainly a difference from the modernist aesthetic of a Boom novel like, say, Fuentes' *La muerte de Artemio Cruz* (1962) where Artemio's identity seems to be either a question of moral choices or some kind of existential given. What *La princesa del Palacio de Hierro* reveals is a break with the 'totalising' tendency of many modernist novels of the Boom which, for all their fragmentation and questioning of conventional theories of reality and realism, nonetheless seek to install some kind of alternative 'viewpoint', implying some kind of wholeness of vision. This can be seen in the differential treatment of the 'city' in the two types of novel. If Shaw's article cites the view that urban contexts are a feature of the post-Boom, it is also clear that many of the major works of the Boom were urban novels and that there has, anyway, been a long tradition of Latin American urban fiction and even a trend in experimental urban writing can be traced back to Roberto Arlt (1900–1942). As J. Ann Duncan has remarked of Fuentes and as could be said too of Vargas Llosa, the urban novels of the Boom offer a kind of 'patchwork quilt' vision of society (15), whereas Sainz here gives more an image of the processes of construction of the individual within an urban setting.[5] In this sense, as with family and gender, the streets of Mexico D. F. in Sainz's novel are 'menacing, but … also adventurous' (Jones, 16). Thus the immorality of the world described by the Princess is both a burden and a means of self-affirmation. Drugs, violence, theft, casual sex and infidelity are all ways of affirming identity in the vast urban metropolis as well as emblems of the corrupting models that shape identity. Of particular interest in this respect is the relationship – noted by Julie Jones – established between the family home and the city streets. Illustrating the pull between the demand for domesticity and the will to self-expression, the family home is associated with the world of the Princess's parents and, later, her husband (that is, the acquisition of a conventional female identity), while the outside world offers her the illusion of more presence and possibility. Again, though, the latter is more complex than Jones' idea of the assertion of individuality in the face of an impersonal metropolis, for the popularity the Princess acquires in the outside world is based on her internalisation of patriarchal values while her opportunity for self-expression in the store as opposed to the family home situates her in another dependent social, economic and even gender (she later models clothes for the store) role. A further point here is that, in a novel largely about youthful adventures in the big city, the narrative perspective is that of a domesticated married woman. The Princess's husband, clearly a central presence in the grown woman's life, is defined in her narrative as an absence insofar as he is never identified and represents the only relationship with a male lover that is not described. Thus for all that her narrative may have the flavour of self-affirmation it is in fact told from a perspective of complete socialisation.

This last point leads us to the crucial (and, once more, ambiguous) role played by language in the construction of identity. Given that the narrator is an older, married woman, her narrative emerges as an attempt to recreate a lost youthful and (illusorily) freer past. Jones concludes her study with the observation that the Princess 'is left only her way with words as a means of recreating the utopian street life that once conferred on her a feeling of plenitude and vitality' (22) and, indeed, it would seem that the exuberant colloquial and highly creative language that characterises the protagonist's narrative embodies the energy, rebelliousness, freedom and excitement she sees in her former youth. In giving voice to her past, the Princess may seem to be producing a classic loss-of-innocence tale, glorifying the youth and freedom which has been inevitably overtaken by the grimly corrupt or stultifying realities of adult life. Yet, as has already been suggested, that notion of youth and freedom is – in some sense, at least – just as much of a construct as any conventional, socialised adult identity. If the Princess is seeking to recuperate that constructed past in language, the implication may well be that she is not so much recuperating it as (literally) recreating it, that is actually constructing it as much as reconstructing it. From Lacan onwards, the link can be seen between the acquisition of identity and the acquisition of language. And, of course, Lacan's concept of 'subjectivity', as opposed to mere identity, sees selfhood as acquired through interaction with others rather than in terms of the traditional humanist notion of the self as a given, autonomous essence. In this novel, then, the relationship of the individual to language may be seen in terms similar to the relationship of the individual to family, class, gender group or the city. Language in action is, in other words, also the process of the construction of identity. Or, what language constructs is, by definition, a construct. Casual references in the novel imply this: for example, to the Princess's psychiatrist who, from one session to the next, interprets his written notes on her rather than interpreting *her* directly (78) or to the porn movies where the sexual activity seen by the viewer is acted out rather than literally carried out (280). At one stage, the Princess complains that one of her boyfriends, the Monje (or Monk), only reads, studies and quotes poetry, and beseeches him instead: 'no me hables de tus versos, si quieres vívelos, asúmelos, envuélvete en ellos ...' (137). This is almost immediately followed by a quotation from Oliveiro Girondo: 'Hasta Darío no existía un idioma tan rudo y maloliente como el español' (137). So, language, in some sense, fictionalises reality and the Princess prefers to live that fiction. Indeed her own language, one might suspect, tends to fictionalise too: consider, for instance, her highly stylised description of the kiss that precedes her loss of virginity (57) or the extremely romantic tone – punctuated by cinematic references hinting at the role of popular culture in forging her vision – of the account of her romance with the handsome Italian Yiovani (or Giovanni) in the seventeenth chapter (neither situation particularly meriting the language, one might feel). One could go even further and suggest that her narrative is a lie, either in part or (who knows?) possibly in its entirety. She lets slip at one stage that she lies to the Monk, or at least withholds the truth from him (179), and, of course, she is constantly two-timing her boyfriends. A small detail possibly gives her away: her allusions to the attentions of Carlos Stamatis in the eleventh chapter do not appear to square

with her (now forgotten?) remarks on him in the fourth chapter. In
the fifteenth chapter, too, she claims to have taped the telephone
conversation with the government minister who has been harassing
her, yet the evidence does not suggest that she did so. And is it
believable that the First Lady gave her a present of a trip to Europe
as a consequence of this? And – it seems – a gas station (of which
there is no mention ever again)? Such details make other accounts
less acceptable, such as the story of the Monk's ejaculation over her
belly rather than in her vagina because he was actually penetrating
the ghost-girl who had come between them in the haunted house
where they were staying! In the light of all this, other episodes,
which may have seemed merely odd (like the restaurant scene in the
opening chapter and the related story of the waiter-cum-gangster-
cum-pimp-cum-taxi-driver Capitán Tarcisio) may now seem over-
embellished or invented. Her keenness to deny that she attempted
suicide or had an abortion (despite hints to the contrary in what are
really highly ambivalent reports) may equally now smack of falsehood. And the whole story of the affair with Giovanni may now
seem a fabrication. However, the very interesting sixteenth chapter
could be seen as providing an explanation for this tissue of possible
untruths. The chapter draws attention to its own significance by its
surprising shortness (only about a page long). Also it has a reflective flavour of sorts in that it is the only chapter to deal at all with
her current (married, domesticated) situation. As if to convince the
reader or herself that her days are full and meaningful, she
comments that her telephone never stops ringing and lists a series
of very unlikely telephone calls, concluding: 'Y así pasa el tiempo,
pasa rapidísimo, como un coche esport que corre hecho la madre
¿no es cierto?' (207–8). The suggestion is that she invents a life to
fill the void that is her own. The quotation from Girondo that
immediately follows reinforces the point. She has no joy in life and
so is spinning a fictional alternative. She has turned herself into a
fictitious character within her own fictitious narrative: 'Pero dime | –
si puedes – | ¿qué haces | allí, sentado | entre seres ficticios | que en vez
de carne y hueso | tienen letras, | acentos, | consonantes, | vocales?'
(208).

    This last quotation from Girondo, however, takes matters a
stage further. It suggests not just that the Princess's identity is a
fiction in the sense that it is a construct but also that she herself is
a fiction in that she is a character in someone else's novel. The sheer

virtuosity of her language creates the impression that her act of narration is a kind of performance, not just in the sense that it is designed to deflect attention from the underlying banality of her life, but also in the sense that it generates what is, ultimately, a work of fiction. When she refers at one stage to her boyfriend Mauricio, she comments that 'ha entrado poco en esta historia ¿verdad?' (87), inadvertently drawing attention to the fact that this is, after all, only a story. Having said that, there is yet a further dimension to the novel which encourages the view that the text's emphasis on its own fictionality is not simply a continuation of that trend in the Latin American new narrative (by this stage rather old hat anyway) which plays with the idea that fiction is only fiction as a reaction to traditional realism's alleged equation of fiction with reality. This is brought out in an anecdote told by the Monk. Korzybski does not flee when his students tell him a tiger is coming because he believes that 'the word is not the thing', but is then, unfortunately, eaten when the tiger does turn up (179). Is this a commentary on the new novel's tendency to take refuge in unreality? Certainly, it suggests that behind 'words', there is some external reality. The point about the novel's foregrounding of fictionality, then, may be to bring out the fictionality of the narrator in order to mark the presence of a separate implied author or, even, *the* author Gustavo Sainz. This brings us back to the question of humour and addresses an issue which should now be becoming quite striking: that, for a supposedly 'funny' book, it all sounds rather serious so far. What the novel does, in effect, is to erect the strong presence of an implied author who offers a critical (or, at least, complementary or different) perspective on the apparently frivolous narrative stance of his narrator–protagonist. The not especially bright or well-educated narrator provides the fun and games, while the intelligent and cultivated implied author conveys a serious reflection on them. Or the strong implied author, as creator of the narrator, is a powerful source of both humour and creative energy on the one hand and insightful reflection on them on the other.[6]

This is not at all unproblematic. The positing of an implied authorial presence may appear inevitably to devalue the Princess's narrative and the Princess herself (as autonomous forces at least) on which and on whom the novel's appeal to most readers would, one imagines, largely rest. In particular, if the implied author is figured as male, 'he' problematises his own implied commentary on the construction of female identity and the critique of the social construction of identity in general. If, in relation to the novel's use of humour, one accepts Purdie's contention that 'the capacity to joke is connected with possession of that "proper" language which commands full subjectivity, for it is that full subjectivity which patriarchy consistently denies to women and, by extension, to its other abjected groups' (128–9), then the implied author is properly powerful and the Princess as woman and, what is more, uneducated woman, is the mere target or butt of the implied author's commentary. Moreover, 'Butts', says Purdie, 'are definitionally lower than, more discursively inept ... than, and above all *different from* Teller and Audience' (129). Thus an appeal is also made to an implied reader, figured as both male and educated or intellectual. Raymond L. Williams has already remarked that the expressions of pettiness and vulgarity that characterise the Princess's narrative 'are effective strategies for fictionalising a reader who is superior to the characters' (384). The implied commentaries on identity-acquisition examined above operate in a similar way, flattering the implied reader with insights that the protagonist lacks. Indeed the language she uses is often a marker for the implied reader to 'read' her in a more knowing way, as in, for instance, her comic Hispanicised renderings such as Deiri Cuin, Nanci Güilson, Cherloc Jolms, Guachinton, Mayami, jolivud, jelou, and so on. Also, there is an implied higher narrative level aimed at a reader figured as intellectual. Gerald Martin, for instance, sees Joycean echoes, arguing that the entire novel 'may be construed as one long homage to the Molly Bloom soliloquy'.[7] And the novel contains an Acknowledgements section identifying the quotations at the end of each chapter as belonging to Oliveiro Girondo, which, for Williams, 'distance the reader and make the [*princesa*'s] somewhat frivolous anecdotes a focus of analysis' (385). Not only are other allusions mentioned here (unmarked in the main text), but there is also a reference to the illustrations accompanying the original edition, provided by 'importantes artistas contemporáneos' (285). The illustrations included in the edition cited here may be seen as providing another level of implied commentary. Noticeably, the pictures (including the cover) are (largely) of nude women, while the few male figures depicted are all clothed, reinforcing the idea of a male implied reader, for, as John Berger has noted in his *Ways of Seeing*, in painting, 'women are depicted in a quite different way from men – not because the feminine is different from the masculine – but because the "ideal" spectator is always assumed to be male and the image of women is designed to flatter him'.[8] One might even be tempted to gloss the earlier remarks on the Princess's interpretation of her female identity in terms of male models by venturing the possibility that the lusty accounts of sexuality and defloration, though narrated by a woman, are actually inscribing a conventionally construed male notion of identity.

The matter of the novel's 'funniness' can now be examined more closely. Clearly, the pattern of an energetic fun-filled narration of bawdy adventures framed by a creating and controlling implied authorial presence reflects the liberation-versus-containment debate on the notion of 'carnival'. The Bakhtinian position that carnivalesque behaviour subverts symbolic hierarchies by exposing them as arbitrary constructs rather than immutable givens can obviously be challenged by the claim that the culture based on such hierarchies, by authorising and controlling such behaviour, uses carnival as an ultimately constraining force. As Purdie says (and for 'low' in the present context, read 'female' or 'uneducated'): 'carnival, in inverting symbolic hierarchies, also reinscribes them: to create a socially low person as "King for the day" in fact assumes that a ladder of social advantage is an eternal truth, and its carnivalesque nature asserts that this embodiment of the ladder is incorrect' (126). In *La princesa del Palacio de Hierro*, the entire narrative, in which raunchy rebelliousness appears to be voiced from a perspective of the narrator's socialisation into patriarchal structures and subservience to a male implied author, expresses this dilemma. The peculiar restaurant scene in the opening chapter is emblematic of this. It is based on a play between firstly a carnivalesque 'world-upside-down' in which expected norms in a posh eatery are overturned by the ribald antics of gay men, prostitutes and young hoodlums and secondly the extraordinarily authoritarian presence of the controlling maître d'. The Princess revealingly comments at one stage that 'la situación se nos resbalaba de las manos' (18). Carnival here does not give authority to the subaltern figure but accentuates its loss or denial.

A look at the novel's humour in terms of transgressing and marking of norms, as mentioned earlier, brings out a similar picture. If the Princess's voluble language appears energetic and subversive from one point of view, from another it underscores the conventional idea (inscribed in joking discourse) that women's speech is 'inferior' in that women – especially when objectified in joking – are constructed as nagging, gossipy and as people who talk too much (Purdie, 133). Moreover, the sheer linguistic excess of the Princess's monologue and its constant appeals to its unnamed addressee points to an anxiety of positionality. In Purdie's words: 'Women's speech typically demonstrates the apprehension that they have to work harder to gain attention by using redundant exaggeration, repetition and emphasis, and by naming their hearer; and seeks continual reassurance that they *are* being attended to by using "tag questions"' (139). A parallel expression of insecurity in the Princess is her repeated references to driving, women's driving being another conventional topic of joking. The novel is full of scenes identifying men with their cars and depicting wild car chases and scenes of drunken driving. Yet the Princess is driven by men or takes taxis (the powerful maître d' is later said to become a taxi driver) because she is too scared to drive her own car and when the girls are involved in a car accident they react hysterically and rush to locate their boyfriends so that they will sort things out for them.

Yet, insofar as the Princess herself is (to a greater or lesser extent, depending on point of view) characterised as a joker, she appears to invert the usual hierarchies by having fun at the expense of men. Again though, the transgression reaffirms the norm. Her comic two-timing, for instance, ultimately creates anxiety for her. More interestingly, her joking at the expense of 'weak' men (itself an acceptable form of male joking) is inevitably founded on the idea that the desired norm is potent masculinity (rather in the way that 'feminist' jokes about 'tiny dicks' unwittingly support the implied desirability of 'big dicks'). The most obvious butt in this context is the Monk, who, as his name implies, is, unlike 'normal' men, studious, retiring, spiritual, virginal, malleable, cowardly and (though the narrative is, once more, ambivalent on this point) not conventionally good-looking. However, not only do the numerous scenes in which she takes advantage of him or makes him look foolish betray the Princess's own slavery to conventional constructions of masculinity, but there are also indications that this view is false – the Monk gets one over on her at one point (109) – and that he is really something of a positive role model for her – she falls in love with him and says that she has learned a lot from him (183). In a sense, her inability to resist the social construction of the self erases the possibility of a more authentic self.

Joking, then, is an enactment of the processes of attempted affirmation and actual acquisition of identity discussed earlier. If the Princess is herself a 'joker', what she is seeking – as with her verbal reconstruction or renegotiation of her own history – is 'the pleasure and power that all joking yields in its temporary resolution of th[e] contradiction [of identity]' (Purdie, 147). But that resolution is ephemeral and therefore does not give the lie to Lacan's view that, given the inextricable link between language and identity, identity remains contradictory because language is contradictory. The Princess is joking, therefore, simply to convince herself that her life is somehow pleasurable or meaningful or authentic. Hence, she (or, more accurately, her construction) inverts Northrop Frye's theory of 'comedy' based on the humanistic notion of the triumph of natural forces (see Purdie, 153ff). Her youthful exuberance does not correspond to the festive celebration of an innate vitality, traditionally seen as the essence of comedy ever since Frye's *Anatomy of Criticism*, precisely because she is a construct rather than an essence. This is why the novel's ending is not the conventional 'happy ending' which became the definitional characteristic of comedy from Frye onwards. Conventional resolution through marriage is not provided. Indeed, the final chapter reveals a sense of anxiety before the marriage, is based on the absence of the husband as a character rather than his presence, and ends with a dream hinting at the pernicious influence of the mother as an image of the processes of socialisation and the moulding of identity. The epilogue, finally, is a passage from *Waiting for Godot* in which Vladimir and Estragon refer to those who need to 'talk' about life more than to have lived it. Such talk is defined as 'noise'. Life is thus seen as both constructed verbally and meaningless.

The problem with much of the above is, of course, the constant slippage between narrator and implied author (and possibly real author). Who is the joker? The Princess? The implied author? Sainz? How far is the novel just joking? How far is it attempting to be serious? Is it a comment on reality? Is it a comment on the fictional construction of reality? Is it a comment on its own fictionality? There is no global resolution of these conflicting questions, yet perhaps one can glimpse something of an explanation (albeit only in part) of the problem of inconsistency identified here and in similar texts. The point is that what the present novel reveals –

consciously or unconsciously – is a radical insecurity about its own identity. And this sense of its own textuality – of the unavoidable intertextuality of narrator and implied author – inevitably incorporates both author and reader in the intertextual process. Each is in turn constructing and constructed in the process of writing and reading. Identity is thus about these processes of construction rather than about any previously given or eternal essence. This is the basic postmodern condition. It may also be the condition of the post-Boom. Implicit in the complex narrative structures of much fiction of the Boom was the possibility of a key, of making sense of the labyrinth. In much of the fiction of the post-Boom it is the very process of 'making sense' of things that constructs the labyrinth. One aspect of the shift from Boom to post-Boom, then, is the shift from product to process: a shift, in other words, from 'text' to 'textuality'.

## Notes

[1] See Donald Shaw, 'Towards a Description of the Post-Boom,' *Bulletin of Hispanic Studies*, LXVI, 1989, pp. 88–90. Shaw cites Skármeta and refers to Agustín here.

[2] For a range of such views, see, for instance, John A. Brushwood, 'Sobre el referente y la transformación narrativa en las novelas de Carlos Fuentes y Gustavo Sainz,' *Revista Iberoamericana*, XLVII, 1981, pp. 49–54; J. Ann Duncan, *Voices, Visions and a New Reality: Mexican Fiction Since 1970*, Pittsburgh University Press, Pittsburgh, 1986; Malva E. Filer, 'La ciudad y el tiempo mexicano en la obra de Gustavo Sainz,' *Hispamérica*, XIII, 1984, pp. 95–102; Julie Jones, 'The Dynamics of the City: Gustavo Sainz's *La princesa del Palacio de Hierro*,' *Chasqui*, XII, 1982, pp. 14–23; and Raymond L. Williams, 'The Reader and the Recent Novels of Gustavo Sainz,' *Hispania*, LXV, 1982, pp. 383–7.

[3] Susan Purdie, *Comedy: The Mastery of Discourse*, Harvester Wheatsheaf, Hemel Hempstead, 1993, p. 5. The theoretical perspective on humour offered throughout largely follows Purdie. References to Lacan and Frye draw on Purdie's readings. See, for example: Jacques Lacan, *Ecrits: A Selection*, translated by A Sheridan and edited by J.-A. Miller, Tavistock, London, 1977; Northrop Frye, *Anatomy of Criticism*, Penguin, Harmondsworth, 1991.

[4] Gustavo Sainz, *La princesa del Palacio de Hierro*, Océano, Mexico City, 1982, p. 94.

[5]Brushwood's article makes a similar point.

[6]Though much of what is being said here accords with some of the views of Roberto González Echevarría, the observations in the preceding paragraph do not fully comply with his contention: 'Cuando el autor aparece en la obra ... lo hace como un personaje más de la ficción sin poderes superiores... En la última novela hispanoamericana el relato es más importante que el lenguaje o el narrador', quoted by Shaw (92). These observations also differ somewhat from Angel Rama's view, as summarised by Shaw, that 'there is an absence of distance between the youthful authors [of the post-Boom] and their often youthful characters, an (implicitly uncritical) identification between author and work' (91). See Roberto González Echevarría, *La ruta de Severo Sarduy*, Ediciones del Norte, Hanover, 1987, p. 250; and Angel Rama, *La novela latinoamericana 1920–1980*, Instituto Colombiano de Cultura, Bogotá, 1982.

[7]Gerald Martin, *Journeys Through the Labyrinth: Latin American Fiction in the Twentieth Century*, Verso, London and New York, 1989, p. 245.

[8]John Berger, *Ways of Seeing*, Penguin, London, 1972, p. 64.

# Chapter 8

# Clarice Lispector and *A hora da estrela*: 'Féminité' or 'réalité'?

One of the most striking features of the criticism of the work of Clarice Lispector is the extraordinary degree of vagueness that characterises much of the critical output. Earl E. Fitz, for example, in his book on Clarice, talks of her creation of the 'self-consciously introspective language novel' which he relates to a quest for 'authenticity of being' and in which her choice of 'a highly lyrical prose as her medium of expression … succeeds in bridging the gap between the inner and outer realms' thus giving 'one of the most complete expressions of [the] philosophical-cum-poetic vision of the human experience that we as yet have had in the world of Latin American letters.' In a similar vein, Benedito Nunes refers to

> esse *feeling* do fracasso da linguagem [que] acompanha, como um baixo-contínuo, o jogo de identidade da narradora, convertida em personagem, e de sua narrativa convertida num *espaço literário agônico*… A meditação apaixonada feita de lampejos intuitivos, e a ficção própriamente dita, sempre meditativa, feita de súbitas ilumin-ações, produzem-se recíprocamente, produzindo o movimento dubi-tativo, dramático, de uma *escritura errante*, autodilacerada, à procura de sua destinação, impelida pelo *vago objeto do desejo*, que desce ao limbo da vida impulsiva para subir a uma forma de *improviso* intér-mino, no qual parece abolir-se a distinção entre prosa e poesia, e que, fluxo verbal contínuo, sucessão de fragmentos da alma e do mundo, já não pode mais receber a denominação de conto, romance ou novela – *improviso* porque desenrolado, tal o *impromptu* musical, ao léu de múltiplos temas e motivos recorrentes …

As Nunes' words suggest, the problem lies not just with the critics but with the contemplative, plot-free, non-specific, abstract quality of Clarice's narrative itself. Not surprisingly, then, Debra Castillo has already remarked that 'puzzlement and a valiant effort to define this elusive type of nonsymbolic fiction dominate the criticism dedicated to Lispector.' For her, such critics find themselves 'almost always resting, helplessly, on an evaluation couched in the negative', finding it 'expedient to describe her work by what it is *not*', with the result that, for them, '"Clarice Lispector," both the person and the works published under that name, is the very figure of negativity, the mysterious and untouchable abyss of negativity as such.'[1]

Clarice herself has said that: 'I am incapable of "relating" an idea or of "dressing up an idea" with words. What comes to the surface is already expressed in words or simply fails to exist... . I should avoid using words. This might prove to be my solution.'[2] The difficulty, then, for the critic who wants to 'say something' about Lispector is that her works appear to say 'nothing' in any conventional sense of the term. This is, of course, ideal territory for Hélène Cixous and her concept of *écriture féminine* where 'vagueness' is allowed to acquire the respectability of theory. Thus, 'for Cixous', according to her translator Verena Andermatt Conley, 'Lispector insists on the effacement of the subject, which results in opening on a limitless perspective and undoing the frame of common or representable human experience', grasping through writing 'the sensory world', and 'this kind of writing, with no exchange or market value, with "no useful purpose", can be called *écriture féminine.*' The aforementioned vagueness or elusiveness of Clarice can therefore be explained or, better, explored in terms of 'an undoing of the hierarchies and oppositions that determine the limits of most conscious life.'[3] This Cixousian model or, rather, method is a convenient entry into the fictional world of Clarice Lispector, even if it will only ultimately lay bare its own limitations and perhaps those of the Brazilian author as well.

An appropriate starting point for a consideration from this perspective of Clarice's internationally best-known novel, *A hora da estrela*, is Macabéa, the – it is usually thought (by Cixous among others) – main protagonist of the work. Macabéa is a poor, badly educated, unhealthy and physically unattractive young woman from the barren north east of Brazil, who emigrates to the capital, Rio de Janeiro. On the one hand, Macabéa's anonymity, insignificance and nothingness are stressed: 'Como a nordestina, há milhares

de moças espalhadas por cortiços.... Não notam sequer que são
facilmente substituíveis e que tanto existiriam como não existiriam'; 'ela é virgem e inócua, não faz falta a ninguém.'[4] Yet at the
same time, the identity-less 'moça anônima' is revealed, startlingly,
more than halfway through the novel, to have a highly unusual and
dramatically individualising name. Indeed, attention is drawn to
the name Macabéa by her astonished boyfriend Olímpico de Jesus
(59–60). Moreover, the name is seen to stand in stark contrast to
his ('tinha como sobrenome apenas o de Jesus, sobrenome dos que
não têm pai' [60]) and also seems singular in comparison to those
of her roommates, 'as quatro Marias', whose names are all varia-
tions of Maria. If this is not enough, the obvious echo in the protagonist's name of the role of the Maccabees in the resistance to
hellenisation, and in the miracle of Hanukkah (particularly when set
against the Greek and Christian overtones of the names of Olímpico
de Jesus and the 'quatro Marias') gives a mystical or magical
dimension that sets her apart from anonymous everyday reality.[5]

The conjunction of anonymity and mystical singularity brings us
close to Cixous' notion of *écriture féminine*, in the sense that transcendence and authentic expression are achieved through the dissolution of difference, binary distinctions, the relationship between
Self and Other and, ultimately, of the traditional notion of the
unified self. In this sense, for Cixous, Macabéa 'is absolutely miser-
able, socially, culturally, but not at the level of the heart' for she is
full of 'infinite riches' (143). Hence though Macabéa 'era subter-
rânea e nunca tinha tido floração', at the same time 'ela era capim'
(46). Similarly, despite her withered ovaries, she is associated with
the process of parthenogenesis in which reproduction occurs without the conventional male–female exchange: 'era realmente de
espantar que para corpo quase murcho de Macabéa tão vasto fosse
o seu corpo de vida quase ilimitado e tão rico como o de uma
donzela grávida, engravidada por si mesma, por partenogênese'
(77). Macabéa, in other words, illustrates Cixous' goal of progressive impoverishment, of the achievement of inner wealth through
poverty – where poverty becomes a 'gift' in that it exists outside the
rational realm based on exchange value. Significantly therefore
Clarice's male narrator compares himself to his female character in
this way: 'Mas eu, que não chego a ser ela, sinto que vivo para
nada. Sou gratuito e pago as contas de luz, gás e telefone. Quanto
a ela, até mesmo de vez em quando ao receber o salário comprava

uma rosa' (48). This last reference hints at the mystic aspect of Cixous that has been identified by Anu Aneja and others.[6] The mystic ecstasy of self-erasure is implied in the narrator's remark that 'embora a moça anônima da história seja tão antiga que podia ser uma figura bíblica' (46) – itself an echo of the miraculous transformation of the Hanukkah oil in the story of the Maccabees. Macabéa herself is said to be in an 'estado de graça' (41) and close to sanctity in her emptiness: 'A maior parte do tempo tinha sem o saber o vazio que enche a alma dos santos. Ela era santa? Ao que parece' (54). The narrator thinks that 'talvez … nela haja um recolhimento e … na pobreza de corpo e espírito eu toco na santidade' (35). This grace or saintliness is a form of liberation, like the freedom of madness ('tinha a felicidade pura dos idiotas', it is said at one stage [87], and, elsewhere, 'tinha pensamentos gratuitos e soltos porque embora a toa possuía muita liberdade interior' [90]), beyond the rigidly imposed limitations of the external world. All of which aids a possible understanding of the title. At an early stage, commenting on the vacuity of his subject matter, the narrator warns his readers: 'que não se esperem, então, estrelas no que segue: nada cintilará, trata-se de matéria opaca e por sua própria natureza desprezível por todos' (30). Yet Macabéa becomes, irresistibly, the star or 'estrela' of this narrative, her lustrelessness becoming the very source of her lustre. Furthermore, the 'hour of the star' is also the hour of death: 'na certa morreria um dia como se antes tivesse estudado de cor a representação do papel de estrela. Pois na hora da morte a pessoa se torna brilhante estrela de cinema, é o instante de glória de cada um e é quando como no canto coral se ouvem agudos silbantes' (44). Hence her death at the end of the novel is evoked, partly, in terms of orgasmic sexuality, mysticism and epiphany. 'O abraço da morte', this 'profundo beijo … boca-a-boca na agonia do prazer que é morte', is like 'um gosto suave, arrepiante, gélido e agudo como no amor. Seria esta a graça a que vós chamais Deus?' (102–3). It is a 'doloroso reflorescimento tão difícil que ela empregava nele o corpo e a outra coisa que vós chamais de alma …' (104). Death, then, is a metaphor for, or approximation of, the ecstasy of the crossing of boundaries, the breaching of limits, the realisation of a new dimension. So death brings a 'silêncio' beyond language, logic or order: 'o silêncio é tal que nem o pensamento pensa…. Morrendo ela virou ar. Ar enérgico?' (105). Macabéa's life and story come to an end in an embrace or fusion with the essential, formless, transcendental dimension which she as a character appeared to incarnate.

The process described so far, however, is not limited to a mere anecdotal account of, or reflection on, the story of Macabéa. The narrative appears to be actually written in a way which embodies what Macabéa represents. The narrative thus becomes an enactment of what could be called *écriture féminine*. Maria José Somerlate Barbosa has pointed to 'the porosity and permeability of the text' and identified a number of instances of the blurring of distinctions or delimitations.[7] For example, there is no clear break between the 'real' and the 'fictional'. Though Macabéa clearly typifies a concrete social phenomenon in Brazilian reality (the dilemma of the immigrant *sertanejo* in the big cities), the narrator repeatedly reminds us that she is his fictional creation: the paradox remains that 'a história é verdadeira embora inventada' (26). But if Macabéa is the narrator's creation, he and she at times appear to be interchangeable: 'vejo a nordestina se olhando ao espelho e ... no espelho aparece o meu rosto cansado e barbudo. Tanto nós nos intertocamos' (37). His narration, in fact, purportedly about her, is often really about him. A typical stylistic feature is his promise that 'limito-me a contar as fracas aventuras de uma moça numa cidade toda feita contra ela', followed almost immediately by the apology: 'desculpai-me mas vou continuar a falar de mim ...' (29). In some ways her story actually is the same as his: 'Ainda bem que o que eu vou escrever já deve estar na certa de algum modo escrito em mim' (35). And at the end he asserts that: 'acabo de morrer com a moça' (105). Of course, in any case, the male narrator, supposedly called Rodrigo S. M., is the female author Clarice Lispector. The 'autor' of the 'dedicatória do autor' (note the masculine form) is, we are told, 'na verdade Clarice Lispector', while the title page (which contains a multiple list of titles to which Rodrigo S.M. refers during the course of his narration) contains a bold print reproduction of the signature of Clarice Lispector. If this is not enough, the revelation that 'eu em menino me criei no Nordeste' (26) identifies the speaker with Macabéa: yet Clarice herself grew up in the north-east, suggesting that she is Macabéa as much as Rodrigo is. The automatic separation between male and female and between author, narrator and character is thoroughly ruptured. And on top of all this Barbosa has noted a similar pattern of beclouding distinction in relation to expressions of certainty and uncertainty, direct and indirect speech, popular and erudite language, references to time and the frequent inclusion of elements connoting fluctuation (such as commercials, the radio station and the mirror). She also notes, finally, that when Macabéa *dies*, she is lying in a *foetal* position.

The foregoing remarks may go some way towards accounting for the perplexing quality of Clarice's writing. That writing seeks somehow to eclipse the logic and structure of conventional prose or language and come close to giving voice to a non-binary or semi-otic experiential rather than explanatory vision of life. From this point of view, it is important to notice that the novel is as much, if not more, 'about' Rodrigo's attempt to write a novel, to 'write Macabéa', as it is about the 'nordestina' herself. The quest for an appropriate language is thus one of the central ideas of the text. Aneja, exploring the relationship between Cixous' *Vivre l'Orange* and Clarice's *A paixão segundo G.H.*, comments that 'Lispector, approaching a language that seeks to simulate the silence before all speech, shows that there is a place where silence and speech are one, where no difference remains between presence and absence' (196). In a number of ways *A hora da estrela* seems both to theo-rise and attempt to practice this philosophy. 'A verdade é sempre um contato interior e inexplicável', says the narrator. 'A minha vida a mais verdadeira é irreconhecível, extremamente interior e não tem uma só palavra que a signifique' (25). And so, 'esta história será feita de palavras que se agrupam em frases e destas se evola um sentido secreto que ultrapassa palavras e frases' (28–9). This elusive, secret form will effectively embody the content of the narrative: 'Por que escrevo? Antes de tudo porque captei o espírito da língua e assim às vezes a forma é que faz conteúdo' (32). A simple illustration of this is the novel's peculiar opening sequence where, as has already been suggested, the interplay of the 'dedi-catória do autor' and the phrase 'na verdade Clarice Lispector' together with the problematically multiple sequence of titles formalises the absence of boundaries. Moreover, this opening emphasises references to music and neutrality of colour as well as to death and transfiguration. For example, Strauss's *Death and Transfiguration* is mentioned in relation to 'a vibração das cores neutras de Bach' (21). Later, it is said of Macabéa, who undergoes a transformative death at the novel's close, that 'o sustrato último da música era a sua única vibração' (68). Cixous herself, in com-menting on Clarice, says that 'I want to work on the colour gray,

on dust and on mud, on matter that can be transformed into gold
...' (144). Writing the story of Macabéa, then, is a process of engen-
dering a new and more authentic language which may break apart
rigidly denotative linguistic forms and lead to some kind of mystic
or ecstatic sensation of communion or epiphany. Hence the narrator's project is compared to the as yet unknown experience of tast-
ing the tastelessness of the sacred host: 'comer a hóstia será sentir
o insosso do mundo e banhar-se no não' (34). Writing this way
becomes a process of almost religious transfiguration or 'passion':
'é paixão minha ser o outro' (45). This passion and union with the
other is finally consummated in the quasi-mystical *jouissance* that
is the fusion of writer and character in death and silence at the end
of the novel. The novel therefore ends with what might seem to be
a positive affirmation: the final one word paragraph – 'Sim' (106).
Underlining the sense of wholeness and completion, this takes us
back to the beginning of the narrative proper which started with a
reflection on the 'Yes' which began a universe which never began,
in a timeless time when 'havia o nunca e havia o sim' (25). In this
way, an undelimited nothingness is turned into a powerful and
meaningful expression of positive experience.

So far so good. However, a reading of Clarice Lispector in this
way depends on an unqualified acceptance of the assumptions
underlying Cixous' concept of an *écriture féminine*. Such a reading
begins to fall apart somewhat if one has the impertinence to subject
it to the 'logic' of what one might call a *lecture masculine*. The
contradiction of developing an essentialist notion of 'feminine'
writing from the basis of an anti-essentialist notion of 'gender' is an
obvious one.[8] This is reflected in the very dualism of the 'moça
anônima' with a name like Macabéa, which we previously saw as
central to a Cixousian reading of the text. The anonymity of the
helpless 'nordestina' shows her to be a product of very specific
social, economic, political, geographical, and gendered forces,
while the special inner life of Macabéa makes her into an emblem
of quintessentially 'feminine' qualities. (One might be tempted to
complicate matters further by turning it around and arguing that
the idea of anonymity suggests an essentially 'feminine' identity
while the individualising name Macabéa suggests she is a gendered
creation of social forces.) The question arises then as to how far
'contradiction' is a challenge to binary logic, patriarchy and social
hierarchy and how far it is simply a matter of 'plain contradiction'.

The 'transgressive' writing of Rodrigo S. M., despite its repeated use of the word 'vós' to address the reader, may in the end communicate very little to the reader. Indeed, the supposedly positive outcome is not at all clear. From the opening page of the narrative proper a reference to its musical style is followed immediately by an assertion of the absence of happiness in the world – for both writer and 'nordestina' (25). And by the end it is not necessarily easy to accept Macabéa's grotesque and painful death as a sublime experience. There is little self-realisation for the young woman. Though she repeats to herself 'eu sou, eu sou', 'Quem era, é que não sabia' (103). Does she really achieve transcendence in death by becoming 'ar enérgico'? 'Nao sei', says the narrator (105). One conclusion drawn, in fact, is that 'a vida é um soco no estômago' (102). In any case, the drama of any potential climax is comprehensively undermined by the peppering of the final page with bizarre, inconsequential and banal questions or remarks like: 'Qual é o peso da luz?' or 'Não esquecer que por enquanto é tempo de morangos' (106). Is Clarice's revolutionary new language little more than just vagueness after all?

There are many examples in the novel of lack of communication through language: the radio station which broadcasts a series of pings to mark the time and snippets of useless information (both of which Macabéa enjoys though they mean nothing to her), commercials, the hot air of political speeches, and the comic *non sequiturs* and misunderstandings in the absurd dialogue involving Olímpico de Jesus, the doctor, or the fortune-teller madama Carlota. All of this may be meant to contrast with the authentic language the narrator seeks, but really it often simply underlines and parallels the arbitrariness of Rodrigo S. M.'s (or Clarice's) narrative strategy. Right from the start we have the idea of a misleading or confused narrative which is never what it says it is. The 'dedicatória' is not really a 'dedicatória' and the title page does not fix the title, while both, positing a male narrator, state that they are written by a woman. The narrative proper then begins with the observation that 'tudo no mundo começou com um sim ..., mas sei que o universo jamais começou' (25), setting the tone for much of what follows. One of its main structural features is its persistent failure to deliver what it promises: repeated assurances that the plot concerning Macabéa is about to begin are followed by quasi-philosophical digressions or the re-focusing of attention on the narrator. *A hora*

*da estrela* will not shine, the reader is told, and will have no stars
(30). This may have already seemed odd in the context of the early
reference to 'cores neutras', itself undermined by the promise of
'uma história em tecnicolor' (22). And despite all the allusions to
music and musicality, 'é que a esta história falta melodia cantabile'
(30). Indeed, it equally promises silence yet reveals that 'a história
será ... acompanhada pelo violino plangente ...' (390). Moreover,
the abstract tone is contradicted by the constant claim that this is a
story about hard facts, though in reality it contains very few facts
at all. Related to this are the regular reminders that this is 'narrativa tão exterior e explícita' (26), that 'proponho-me a que não seja
complexo' (26) and that 'pretendo ... escrever de modo cada vez
mais simples' (28). The facts that do emerge about Macabéa do not
enjoy much solidity either: she is described by the narrator as both
typical of society and a misfit in society, she is simultaneously glori-
fied by him and denigrated by him. The relation of Rodrigo S. M.
to Macabéa raises the question of narratorial, and perhaps by
extension authorial, control. The narrator lurches constantly
between assertiveness and self-doubt. He stresses his role as inven-
tor and creator, yet admits that he does not even know the protagonist's name (33) or how her story will end (30). Revealingly, he
asserts that 'só escrevo o que quero ... – e preciso falar dessa
nordestina' (31). This is echoed by his words at the time of
Macabéa's death: 'Estou tão puro que nada sei. Só uma coisa eu sei:
não preciso ter piedade de Deus. Ou preciso?' (103).

One final point about the narrator is that the text not only problematises his relationship to Macabéa but also his relationship to
the author Clarice Lispector and perhaps, more interestingly, hers
to him. The 'dedicatória do autor' and the title sequence show that
behind the desire to write a controlled 'masculine' narrative lies a
female author. The logic of a masculine discourse is undone by the
narrative's embodiment of an *écriture féminine*. At one stage,
Rodrigo S.M. tells the reader that the narrator 'teria que ser homem
porque escritora mulher pode lacrimejar piegas' (28). But the
reader already knows that the author is 'na verdade Clarice
Lispector'. Thus, from a Cixousian viewpoint, the undoing of
Rodrigo's narratorial project by Clarice Lispector is a metaphor for
the limitations and failure of a 'masculine' world view and its
replacement by a more authentic 'feminine' consciousness.
Unfortunately, this is merely a return to the realm of contradiction.

The dissolution of the distinction between author and narrator, male and female, may seem to point to the achievement of authorial effacement, self-erasure and the transgression of a binary logic. Yet at the same time the presence of the real author's signature and the declaration that the author is '*na verdade* Clarice Lispector' indicates a very strong authorial presence. Clarice may therefore be seen to be reinstating a pattern of dominance and hierarchy at the very point that her writing creates the illusion of dissolving it.

This last consideration leads us on to what is the thorniest problem in relation to both Cixous and Lispector: that is, the relationship between an essentialist *écriture féminine* and material reality, and between an aesthetic literary production and social reality. Though Cixous' work is often encompassed under the heading of 'theory', many of her critics see her writing as very much a non-theoretical practice. If Conley views Cixous' utopian project as expressing 'the importance of art for social change' (xv), Ann Rosalind Jones, for example, calls the French *féminité* movement 'fuzzy and fatal to constructive political action'.[9] This dilemma is crucially present in *A hora da estrela*, usually considered as an attempt to write a form of 'literature of social engagement' (DiAntonio, 164), where a 'fuzzy' narrative seeks to explore the huge social issue of the plight of the north-eastern immigrant. In fact, Rodrigo's narrative often seems to imply that the material reality he appears to want to transcend is what really matters after all. The replacement of the typically aware and introspective female Lispectorean narrator with a middle-class narrator trying to come to terms with a painfully unaware woman who is a social outcast may dramatise the struggle of the artistic intellectual with material issues. Thus the supremely poetic and unclear 'dedicatória' reveals that 'esta história acontece num estado de emergência e de calamidade pública' (22). Rodrigo's 'privileged' 'art' therefore is driven by a sense of moral and social obligation: 'o que escrevo é mais do que invenção, é minha obrigação contar sobre essa moça entre milhares delas' (27). The aching truth of social reality ('Fico abismado por saber tanto a verdade', he says [74]), leads him to want to change his 'modo de escrever' (31) and fulfill his duty of exposing his well-off readers to this reality (33). Hence the obsessive emphasis on facts and the repeated interplay between 'fato' and 'ato', the implication being that writing has to go beyond reflection and encourage concrete social change.

The point is that the novel never really fully completes the transition from meditation to engagement, as the foregoing 'fuzzy'
'feminine' reading would appear to indicate. Instead – and this
maybe reveals a level of honesty that distinguishes Clarice from
certain male Latin American writers – the narrative dwells guiltily
on the gap between the intellectual and society. So, while exalting
Macabéa's transcending of difference, the narrator recognises the
very real needs of her and the social group she represents: 'ela vive
num limbo impessoal, sem alcançar o pior nem o melhor. Ela
somente vive, inspirando e expirando. Na verdade – para que mais
que isso? O seu viver é ralo. Sim. Mas por que estou me sentindo
culpado? E procurando aliviar-me do peso de nada ter feito de
concreto em benefício da moça' (38). He even feels guilt for not
sharing her real-life suffering: 'parece-me covarde fuga o fato de eu
não a ser' (54). The fact is that he recognises that his intellectual or
artistic posture is a betrayal of material reality. He asks himself,
'por que trato dessa moça quando o que mais desejo é trigo pura-
mente maduro e ouro no estio?' (40), recognising his urge to flee
into the world of 'o figurativo' when faced by the temptation to
'cair de quatro em fatos e fatos' (37). The very basis of his writing
is fraudulent: 'Antecedentes meus de escrever? Sou um homem que
tem mais dinheiro do que os que passam fome, o que faz de mim de
algum modo um desonesto' (33). This is why the narrator/author
dedicates the book to his/her own humble north-eastern past which
contrasts so strongly with their comfortable present: 'dedico-me à
saudade de minha antiga pobreza, quando tudo era mais sóbrio e
digno e eu nunca havia comido lagosta' (21).

There is more than a hint of guilt in this dedication at the
author's own betrayal of the subaltern classes in her literal and
metaphorical enjoyment of 'lobster'. The reason for this guilt is that
the novel, through its very 'fuzziness', 'femininity' if you will, and
sheer ambiguity does very little in real terms to address the social
question which is at its centre but peripherally diffused at the same
time. As Jean Franco has suggested, 'the epiphany that critics
inevitably underscore in Lispector's writing is achieved in full
awareness of the savage heart that gives life to the aesthetic: that
savagery is represented not by the cockroach or the beggar or the
working girl, but by those who occupy the centre thanks to the
marginalisation of the Other.'[10] Rodrigo S. M. is aware that the
consumers of his narrative will be middle-class aesthetes (34): 'faço

aqui', he further says, 'o papel de vossa válvula de escape e da vida massacrante da média burguesa' (46). This is typical, to varying degrees, of authors like Donoso, Fuentes, Puig, Vargas Llosa and others, and may be the central dilemma of the modern Latin American novel as a whole. The middle-class author and reader can be radical in the comfort and security of his or her study or armchair, while the allure of the level of social or political commentary in such works is rendered safe and consumable by the posturing or even playfulness of problematising the knowability of reality and literature's relation to it. At a wider cultural level, as George Yúdice, Jean Franco, and Juan Flores have already noted, this relates to 'the meaning of pluralism as the ideology of contemporary neoliberalism. Pluralism camouflages itself behind an egalitarian mask, whereas it in fact neutralises class conflict and the claims of the new social movements' (ix).

All of this relates once more, of course, to questions concerning the relationship of High and Low art. Thanks partly to the association with Suzana Amaral's film version of the novel, *A hora da estrela* is often thought to interest itself in the world of popular culture. This is true insofar as there is a shift towards a character from the popular classes and a number of references to the culture of consumption, but the elusive, fragmented and introspective style of the novel, dwelling often on the dilemma of its own cultivated narrator, sets it far apart from the 'popular'. The word 'estrela' in the title does hint that the narrative will echo the tone of a popular movie and indeed the narrator informs his readers that his text will eschew flashy complexities and follow instead a pattern similar to that of a conventional movie: 'Relato antigo, este, pois não quero ser modernoso e inventar modismos à guisa de originalidade. Assim é que experimentarei contra os meus hábitos uma história com começo, meio e "gran finale" seguido de silêncio e de chuva caindo' (27). Yet this is clearly not the type of narrative that Rodrigo S. M. produces. The problem is that it is Macabéa who is linked to the popular and the Low, while it is the narrator (and perhaps author) who remains connected to the serious and the High.

On one level, this distance between narrator and character reflects the intellectual's awareness of how the masses are manipulated and exploited by popular or mass culture. At one stage Rodrigo S. M. defines 'felicidade' as a 'palavra ... inventada pelas nordestinas que andam por aí aos montes' (25), suggesting that popular culture, consumerism and capitalism encourage the masses to adapt a false 'technicolour' view of the world. The most striking image of this manipulation is that of Coca-Cola:

> ... o registro que em breve vai ter que começar é escrito sob o patrocínio do refrigerante mais popular do mundo e que nem por isso me paga nada, refrigerante esse espalhado por todos os países. Aliás foi ele quem patroçinou o último terremoto em Guatemala. Apesar de ter gosto do cheiro de esmalte de unhas, de sabão Aristolino e plástico mastigado. Tudo isso não impede que todos o amem com servilidade e subserviencia. Também porque – e vou dizer agora uma coisa difícil que só eu entendo – porque essa bebida que tem coca é hoje. Ela é um meio da pessoa atualizar-se e pisar na hora presente. (38)

An apparently biting attack on North American economic and cultural imperialism, the reference alludes to the destruction of national and individual identity, implying that people can today only achieve identity in shared consumption, not through shared giving. Coca-Cola therefore represents the opposite of Cixousian self-erasure and a barrier to fulfillment. Such crushing of individuality by a mass consumer culture is embodied in Macabéa's female friends. The fact that one of the four Marias sells Coty face powder in a store and that they are all always 'cansadas demais pelo trabalho que nem por ser anônimo era menos árduo' (47) is a reflection of the annulment of individual identity in favour of mass identification, as is the fact that Olímpico is so impressed by the way Glória's natural look is displaced by her dying of her hair blonde (76). In a similar way, Macabéa identifies with the glamorous model of Hollywood film stars. She used to identify, as a young girl, with a picture of Greta Garbo ('Greta Garbo, pensava ela sem se explicar, essa mulher deve ser a mulher mais importante do mundo' [82]) and yearns, more than anything else, to look like Marilyn Monroe. Of particular interest is the type of movie that Macabéa enjoys: 'gostava de filmes de terror ou de musicais. Tinha predileção por mulher enforçada ou que levava um tiro no coração' (75–6). The formulaic genres underline the allure of given roles while the pleasure she experiences in identifying with the woman-as-victim brings out the processes through which mass culture encourages the internalisation of a constructed social and sexual identity. Moreover, as in Puig, there is emphasis on the inevitable sense of frustration and failure generated by the tragic gap that exists between socially-created aspiration and social reality. Such a gap can be seen in Macabéa's desire to look like Marilyn Monroe (in herself an image of a similar gap). An incredulous Glória points out the chasm that exists between the real Macabéa and her dream (82) echoing an earlier, more graphically depicted experience involving Macabéa alone:

> Já que ninguém lhe dava festa, … daria uma festa para si mesma. A festa constitiu em comprar sem necessidade um batom novo, não cor-de-rosa como o que usava, mas vermelho vivante. No banheiro da firma pintou a boca toda e até fora dos contornos para que os seus lábios finos tivessem aquela coisa esquisita dos lábios de Marilyn Monroe. Depois de pintada ficou olhando no espelho a figura que por sua vez a olhava espantada. Pois em vez de batom parecia que grosso sangue lhe tivesse brotado dos lábios por um soco em plena boca, com quebra-dentes e rasga-carne … (79)

Rodrigo S. M.'s critique of popular culture, however, unavoidably involves a distancing of himself from it and, by extension, from Macabéa, the very figure with whom he (and the author) in some sense seek to identify. This is reflected in the opposition, for example, between classical music (allusions to which fill the novel's complex narrative and by which that narrative is said to be inspired and with which it is repeatedly parallelled) and popular music. At one stage, Macabéa recalls for the sake of Olímpico a beautiful song she once heard on Rádio Relógio:

> Eu também ouvi uma música linda, eu até chorei.
> — Era samba?
> — Acho que era. E cantada por um homem chamado Caruso que se diz que já morreu. A voz era tão macia que até doía ouvir. A música chamava-se 'Una Furtiva Lacrima'. Nao sei por que eles nao disseram lágrima.
> 'Una Furtiva Lacrima' fora a única coisa belísima na sua vida … (67)

The protagonist's language here comically reveals her ignorance and cultural 'inferiority'. Yet at the same time the implication is that behind the inescapable cultural baggage of her class, she has an innate sense of good taste. This feeling is reinforced by the juxta-position of her appreciation of beautiful music with a pointer to the largely discreditable Olímpico's enslavement to the mass cultural model of the samba. This taste for 'good' music identifies Macabéa with the narrator and the author, then – but only in their own High cultural terms. Thus the musical contact between the aesthete and the 'nordestina' reaffirms the distance between them at the same moment that it appears partially to dissolve it. In any case, a few lines earlier Macabéa was demonstrating similar enthusiasm for Rádio Relógio's pings and commercials. This ridicules her sense of taste, but also perhaps that of the narrator insofar as there is a suggestion that each form (pings, commercials, Caruso) has an equal or similar effect. The weakening of the distinction between popular and High culture therefore problematises the critique of popular culture from the High cultural perspective.

This relates to the tension between the abstract and the material. Peculiarly, Rodrigo feels that in order to write about Macabéa he has to withdraw from the material world into the world of 'o figurativo', abandoning even his interest in soccer (the perfect symbol of popular mass culture in a Brazilian context in particular) (37). Why withdrawal from the world of the masses should bring him closer to them remains extremely unclear. The point may well be that all this contradiction is another indication of guilt in the face of the unbridgeable distance between the role of the intellectual and the plight of the masses. Hence the very pages of this high-art novel actually seem to hint that popular culture is in fact closer to the emotional reality of everyday life. Macabéa's life *is* 'literatura de cordel' (48). It *is* 'melodrama' (100). Her death *is* 'a hora de estrela de cinema de Macabéa' (102). This *is* a story written in technicolour after all. Or at least perhaps it should be: for it seems that what the content demands the form does not deliver. The gap between the two worlds remains unbridged.

In fairness to Clarice Lispector her work at least reveals an awareness of this quandary. The impression remains, however, that a novel like *A hora da estrela* is neither wholly satisfactory as *écriture féminine* nor as social comment, since both sides of the equation seem to cancel each other out. The 'dedicatória do autor' contains the claim that 'meditar não precisa de ter resultados: a meditação pode ter como fim apenas ela mesma' (21–2). The subsequent narrative both embodies that notion and reveals it to be perverse. Rodrigo S.M.'s journey through his narrative and Macabéa's journey through life both come to an end with the final words of the novel. The reader joining them on that journey may well feel that he or she has gone along with them for the sake of the ride. The journey has been going nowhere and the blank space at the end is nothing more than a blank space.

## Notes

¹Earl E. Fitz, *Clarice Lispector*, Twayne, Boston, 1985; Benedito Nunes, 'Clarice Lispector ou o naufrágio da introspecção', *Remate de Males*, IX, 1989, p. 68; Debra Castillo, *Talking Back: Toward a Latin American Feminist Criticism*, Cornell University Press, Ithaca and London, 1992, pp. 186, 186–7.

²Quoted by Castillo, p. 191.

³The quotations are from the introduction to Hélène Cixous, *Reading with Clarice Lispector*, edited, translated and introduced by Verena Andermatt Conley, University of Minnesota Press, Minneapolis and London, 1990. All quotations from Cixous are also from this text. Conley comments that 'Cixous refers to Lispector as "Clarice", in an obviously poetic and political gesture insisting on an intimacy beyond language that avoids labeling the author as a dead fact' (ix). Of course, it is a convention to refer to Brazilian authors by their first name, a convention that will be followed here.

⁴Clarice Lispector, *A hora da estrela*, Francisco Alves, Rio de Janeiro, 1992, p. 28.

⁵Judah the Maccabee and his followers defeated the armies of the king Antiochus Epiphanes who had decided to force all the peoples under his rule to hellenise. Eventually the Maccabees liberated Jerusalem and reclaimed the temple from its defilement by the Greeks. The story goes that they lit the temple menorah with a small cruse of oil containing only enough for one day. The miracle of Hanukkah is that the menorah burned for eight days. See Michael Strassfeld, *The Jewish Holidays: A Guide and Commentary*, Harper and Row, New York, 1985. For further commentary in relation to Clarice Lispector, see, for example, Robert E. DiAntonio, *Brazilian Fiction: Aspects and Evolution of the Contemporary Narrative*, University of Arkansas Press, Fayetteville and London, 1989; and Nelson H. Vieira, 'A expressão judaica na obra de Clarice Lispector', *Remate de Males*, IX, 1989, pp. 207–9. It is interesting to note in this respect that Macabéa is at one stage described as 'tão antiga que podia ser uma figura bíblica' (46).

⁶Anu Aneja, 'The Mystic Aspect of *L'Écriture Féminine*: Hélène Cixous' *Vivre l'Orange*', *Qui Parle*, III, 1989, pp. 189–209.

[7] Maria José Somerlate Barbosa, '*A hora da estrela* and the Tangible Reality of Fiction', *Romance Languages Annual*, I, 1989, pp. 379–83. This is one of a number of useful articles by the same author on this and similar themes.

[8] The contradictions of Cixous' position are lucidly explored by Toril Moi in her well-known *Sexual/Textual Politics*, Routledge, London and New York, 1985. As the French word 'féminin' translates as 'female' and 'feminine', English usage will vary with, broadly speaking, the word 'feminine' connoting essentialism. A similar problem is posed by the adjective 'masculin'. A further difficulty is that *écriture féminine* does not necessarily – though in practice it often does – refer to 'female' writing as much as to a 'feminine' style of writing.

[9] Ann Rosalind Jones, 'Writing the Body: Toward an Understanding of *L'Écriture Féminine*', in *The New Feminist Criticism: Essays on Women, Literature, and Theory*, ed. Elaine Showalter, Pantheon-Random House, New York, 1985, p. 371; quoted by Susan Canty Quinlan, in *The Female Voice in Contemporary Brazilian Narrative*, Peter Lang, New York, 1991, p. 16.

[10] Jean Franco, 'Going Public: Reinhabiting the Private', in *On Edge: The Crisis of Contemporary Latin American Culture*, eds. George Yúdice, Jean Franco, and Juan Flores, University of Minnesota Press, Minneapolis and London, 1992, p. 76. The references in this quotation are to situations and phrases from several works by Clarice Lispector.

# Chapter 9

# Isabel Allende and *La casa de los espíritus*: Tyrants and trash

One author who is certainly post-Boom (in the sense of coming after the Boom), though probably not especially postmodern (in the sense of playfully complex), and who is definitely 'popular' (in the sense of widely readable) is Isabel Allende. Yet she is frequently criticised. In an article published in *Ideologies and Literature*, for instance, Gabriela Mora roundly attacks her on the grounds that the Chilean author reproposes in her fiction traditional negative female stereotypes and fails to equip her female characters with a serious political consciousness. Mora concludes – having spotted some unacceptable traces of individualism in the form of allusions to the idea of destiny – that, behind Allende's superficial revisionism, there lurk 'fundamentos más insidiosos que amarran a las gentes a creer en esencias e inmutabilidades'.[1] In other words, Isabel has committed the crime of liberal humanism, which, of course, if true, would put her in pretty bad odour with post-structuralist and feminist critics alike. Unfortunately, too, Allende's public persona has sometimes done little to allay such fears. In a 1988 interview in the magazine *Mother Jones*, she gave a very bourgeois picture of the new-found idyllicism of her life as a Californian housewife. She tells us how, having parted with her largely agreeable husband, she then fell head-over-heels with the handsome North American, William:

> And then somebody introduced us. William had read my second book, *Of Love and Shadow* [*sic*], and he had liked it very much and he had wanted to meet me. And so we just looked at each other and fell in love immediately. In the first meeting.... Well, I think Frank Sinatra was singing 'Strangers in the Night' in the restaurant and maybe that helped. And then we had a wonderful pasta.

Soon she was packing her bags to rejoin him in the USA and not to return home to live in Venezuela. The text of the interview is adorned by a photograph of Isabel in a rather glamorous pose, twirling around with a colourful shawl in the air (calling to mind the image of Beatriz Beltrán, the sharply satirised middle-aged, middle-class, looks-and-fashion-conscious mother of the protagonist of *De amor y de sombra*).[2] Add to this image her appropriation of the conventions of popular and romantic fiction, the apparently wavering ending of *La casa de los espíritus* and the repeated suggestions of borrowings from García Márquez, and we are left with what might seem a terribly ideologically suspect standard-bearer for women's fiction in Latin America.

The problem is that Isabel Allende's popular success has made her (quite legitimately) a media figure. At the 1987 Hamburg IberoAmericana Festival, while her compatriot José Donoso – until the appearance of *La casa de los espíritus* in 1982, the undisputed major modern Chilean novelist – was giving a reading of the German translation of his *Casa de campo* in a cramped bookshop in the peripheral suburb of Begedorf, Allende's fans were filling the seats of the city's large theatre, the Deutsches Schauspielhaus. Not surprisingly, the star treatment lavished upon her has tarnished her image in certain academic circles. And, as far as feminist criticism is concerned, there is little point – on a stylistic plane – in looking for manifestations of Irigaray's *parler femme* or Cixous' *écriture féminine* or in seeking stylistic parallels with, say, Clarice Lispector's *A hora da estrela* or the African–American Toni Morrison's *Beloved*. Allende's style aims to be more transparent. For her, writing is not 'about good literature but about telling a story', it is 'un ancho canal de comunicación'.[3] Indeed, the effect of her work is to invert the García Márquez model rather than to imitate it. Despite the Colombian's public political posture and despite Gerald Martin's efforts (brilliantly argued, it must be said) to reduce his fiction to clear social messages,[4] *Cien años de soledad* remains largely ineffective as a political novel precisely because of its ambiguous, playful and magical nature. The magic of literature is somewhat different for Allende: 'Eso tiene de maravilloso un libro', she says: 'establece un vínculo entre quien lo escribe y quien lo lee. Es la magia de las palabras'. Putting it plainly, she goes on:

> Los escritores somos intérpretes de la realidad. Es cierto que caminamos en el filo de los sueños, pero la ficción, aun la más subjetiva,

tiene un asidero en el mundo real. A los escritores de América Latina
se les reprocha a veces que su literatura sea de denuncia. ¿Por qué no
se limitan al arte y dejan de ocuparse de problemas irremediables?,
les reclaman algunos. Creo que la respuesta está en que conocemos
el poder de las palabras y estamos obligados a emplearlas para
contribuir a un mejor destino de nuestra tierra.

Allende's aim is to provide 'una voz que habla por los que sufren y
callan en nuestra tierra': in other words, to push the marginal into
the mainstream. It is ironic that Luis Harss's landmark collection of
conversations with Latin American writers from the 1960s is called
*Into the Mainstream*. If this was to celebrate the Latin American
novel's coming of age, the 'mainstream' into which most of its practitioners had entered, it might be argued, was a rather narrow bourgeois or academic one. The strength of a novel like *La casa de los
espíritus*, on the other hand, is that what it lacks in richness and
multiplicity, it gains in sheer emotional and political power. And, as
we shall see, a fundamental textual feature of the novel seems to be
the displacement of the master discourse of the Boom in favour of
a more directly politicised discourse of the post-Boom. This politicisation includes sexual politics and brings us closer to a Kristevan
model of marginality based on all 'that which is repressed in
discourse and in the relations of production. Call it "woman" or
"oppressed classes of society", it is the same struggle, and never the
one without the other'.[5] Though Allende's early work may not betray
the same *jouissance* on a linguistic or stylistic level as Kristeva's
French avantgarde texts, it does reveal an awareness of basic issues
in the feminist debate and a degree of intellectual engagement with
them. And if the allegedly ambivalent ending of *La casa de los
espíritus* is a liberal form of Utopianism, this is not a million miles
away from the position of a number of French feminist thinkers
and is, in any case, combined with a harrowing exposé of real material oppression to act as a counterbalance. The complaints of Mora,
then, if of a certain allure, are perhaps ultimately irrelevant and
unjustified. Allende does not inhabit what has been called the
'rococo realm of the academy',[6] but has done the rounds of the
American universities circuit: as a popular writer she does not need
to satisfy Mora's criteria, as a serious one she rises to their challenge.

Jean Gilkison has argued that the portrayal of women in *De
amor y de sombra* tends to undermine that novel's political impact.[7]
Nonetheless, it seems plain that *La casa de los espíritus* at least

attempts to establish a connection between the women's struggle and the class struggle. As Toril Moi has pointed out, marginalised groups like women and the working classes are actually central to the process of reproduction and the capitalist economy: 'it is precisely because the ruling order cannot maintain the *status quo* without the continual exploitation and oppression of these groups that it seeks to mask their central economic role by marginalising them on the cultural, ideological and political levels' (171). The main strategy in this programme of marginalisation (and this is the principal argument of Moi's *Sexual/Textual Politics*) is the creation of an illusion of a unified individual and collective self, a given universal world order in which male, white, middle-class, heterosexual experience passes itself off as 'nature'. It is not surprising, therefore, that the discourse of the patriarch Esteban Trueba is replete with the language of order. One short randomly-chosen sentence contains the words 'excentricidades', 'madurara', 'equilibrado' and 'sostén'.[8] In a typical elision, we are told that Trueba 'representaba mejor que nadie los valores de la familia, la tradición, la propiedad y el orden' (273). Thus bourgeois and capitalist values are made to appear synonymous with 'order'. With regard to women, Nívea's feminism is said to be 'en abierto desafío a la ley de Dios' (11), 'contra la naturaleza' and likely to produce 'una confusión y un desorden que puede terminar en un desastre' (65). This is exactly Trueba's view of the peasant and working classes. His 'teoría de los fuertes y los débiles' is 'la naturaleza', 'la realidad' and 'cómo es el mundo' (264). Indeed the oppression of women is repeatedly placed in a wider context of the oppression of the lower classes. For example, Pedro Segundo García's passive acceptance of his lot is seen in essentialist terms by Trueba as 'la timidez propia de la gente del campo' and, echoing the conventional role of the submissive woman with no independence or mobility, he speaks for all marginalised groups when he acknowledges to his master: 'entendimos, patrón... . No tenemos donde ir, siempre hemos vivido aquí. Nos quedamos' (52). The parallel is continued into the graphic account of Trueba's violent rape of Pancha García. The vocabulary employed in the description of the rape ('fiereza', 'incrustándose', 'brutalidad', 'sangrientas') contrasts sharply with the young girl's total lack of resistance. Her passivity is not just a reflection of her position as a woman, but also her poverty and class status. Trueba's first words after the deed are: 'Desde mañana quiero que trabajes en la casa' (58). Her mother and grandmother had likewise been the enforced sexual and domestic servants of the 'casa patronal'. In this way the economy of ownership is mirrored in sexual relations and Trueba frequently talks of women in terms of property: as a sort of cattle (27), as a kind of consumer good to be purchased (37) or as something to be possessed totally (117). The link is reinforced by the dual perspective of Pedro Segundo García on Trueba and his wife Clara: 'La apreciaba tanto como odiaba a Esteban Trueba' (149). The inference is that the women's and workers' struggles are an interconnected reaction against patriarchy. It is significant in this respect that, as the central female characters develop their own sense of identity as women, they achieve an increasing degree of solidarity with the underprivileged classes.

Of course, awareness is the first step towards resistance and, for this reason, one of the novel's principal tasks is to unmask the 'natural' as the learned. A young peasant grows up knowing 'su lugar en el mundo' (133), so that a relationship between the classes cannot take place 'porque esa posibilidad no estaba en el orden natural del mundo' (156). In fact Pedro Segundo denies to his son the possibility of social change for them: 'Siempre ha sido así, hijo. Usted no puede cambiar la ley de Dios' (147). Interestingly, Pedro Tercero grows up to invert the language of the natural order, arguing for 'leyes más justas y repúblicas como Dios manda' (154). The point is that 'nature' and 'order' are concepts appropriated by the dominant classes to preserve the prevailing hierarchy of power relations and that identity, therefore, is something which is socially constructed. As Simone de Beauvoir said of the 'second sex', 'One is not born a woman; one becomes one' (Moi, 92). The Nana hints at this harsh moulding into the values of the Symbolic Order when she claims that 'hay muchos niños que vuelan como las moscas, que adivinan los sueños y hablan con las ánimas, pero a todos se les pasa cuando pierden la inocencia' (15). She is herself a small but crucial figure in the novel's theory of identity. In a passage which recalls the depiction of the 'viejas', the old nursemaids and servants of Donoso's *El obsceno pájaro de la noche*, the Nana's life is summarised: 'Había nacido para vivir de sentimientos y tristezas prestadas, para envejecer bajo el techo de otros, para morir un día en su cuartucho del último patio, en una cama que no era suya y ser enterrada en una tumba común del Cementerio General' (114). She is characterised (as a servant and woman) in terms of lack, an absence, with no individual identity of her own. Like Humberto Peñaloza in Donoso's novel, she literally becomes 'nobody' as her identity is marginalised. Trueba's sister, Férula, is a similar case. Existing only to serve others (her mother, Trueba, Clara), she becomes sheer absence when, like Donoso's 'viejas', she is banished from her brother's house to a convent and supplements her own effective non-existence with a series of bizarre wigs and costumes (another possible borrowing from the 'disfraz'/'máscara' motif of *El obsceno pájaro de la noche*). Insofar as the Nana is concerned, it is significant that she has no individualising name, a feature shared with the string of peasant characters with names like Pedro García, Pedro Segundo García, Pedro Tercero García. These marginal characters are effectively reduced to the level of supplement to the greater reality that is socially created by the ruling classes, their vital supportive role neutralised by a process of false naturalisation.

The obvious link between the Nana and *El obsceno pájaro de la noche* also brings to mind Donoso's Peta Ponce and the motif of the witch. The crushing of identity is based on fear of the potential power of those sectors whose centrality to the interests of the dominant group requires their marginalisation. In Allende's novel, Esteban Trueba wants his house to be 'un reflejo de él', with 'un aspecto de orden y concierto, de pulcritud y civilización' (87), though under the influence of Clara it becomes 'un laberinto encantado imposible de limpiar, que desafiaba numerosas leyes urbanísticas y municipales' (88). This reflects Jerónimo de Azcoitía's desire, in Donoso's novel, to replace any 'exuberancia natural' in his estate with 'estrictas formas geométricas'.[9] But don Jerónimo's sense of order disintegrates as his wife Inés falls increasingly under the influence of the nursemaid and witch-figure Peta Ponce. Peta's residence lies at the edge of Jerónimo's symmetrical world in 'un desorden de construcciones utilitarias sin pretensión de belleza: el revés de la fachada', all of which 'hizo tastabillar [*sic*] su orden al reconocer en la Peta Ponce a una enemiga poderosa' (181, 183). Similarly, the edge of Esteban Trueba's country estate is the point where 'la casa perdía su señorial prestancia y empezaba el desorden de las perreras, los gallineros y los cuartos de los sirvientes' (40). Servant, woman or witch, then, are all terms which connote the possible rupture of a secure order. The creation of the notion of 'witch' is a means of exteriorising and normalising such a fear via a perverse form of sublimation and so weakening the threat by turning it into a negative, a taboo. All social structures grow, up to a point, out of a need to explain, to impose order (witches were essentially 'created' to explain otherwise inexplicable disasters) and, as Sharon Magnarelli observes, the real sin of witches was their alleged knowledge, that is recognition of the dark, chaotic side of life and hence embodiment of the threat to order.[10] So, in *La casa de los espíritus*, the priest, padre Restrepo, identifies the peculiarities of the child Clara with demonic possession, the phrase 'hasta ese día, no habían puesto nombre a las excentricidades de su hija menor' (14) hinting at the need to name, explain, naturalise and neutralise. She is later seen as 'una criatura algo estrafalaria' because she is 'poco apta para las responsabilidades matrimoniales y la vida doméstica' (83). Dr Cuevas (the voice of science and reason) even diagnoses her silence (actually 'su último inviolable refugio') as 'una enfermedad mental' (105). Rosa, la Bella – echoing the hyperbole of Remedios la Bella's role as an extreme if unwitting *femme fatale* in *Cien años de soledad* – is also seen as threatening because of her beauty and femininity. She is twice referred to as a 'sirena' (12, 36) and we are told that 'su belleza atemorizaba' (28). Just as, following Magnarelli's line of thought, Eve is created from Adam's rib, so man projects his sexuality on to woman, seeing her as the provoker of his unruly desire. But the witch or the *femme fatale* is not the only manifestation of patriarchy's (ir)rationalisation of a perceived danger. A link with politics is again apparent in the way Esteban Trueba turns any potential alteration of the ruling order into an example of the red peril of communism. At one stage he refers to 'la monstruosidad de que todos nacen con los mismos derechos' (65) and his ranting about 'commie subversives' and Soviet spies recalls the allegorical transformation, in the minds of the landowners, of the natives into 'antropófagos' (i.e. communists) in Donoso's *Casa de campo*. The child Wenceslao lays bare the true operation of the power structures and naturalising processes at work here when he describes the cannibals/communists as 'una fantasía creada por los grandes con el fin de ejercer la represión mediante el terror, fantasía en que ellos mismos terminaron por creer' and 'una ficción con que los grandes pretenden dominarnos cultivando en nosotros ese miedo que ellos llaman orden'.[11]

A further feature of patriarchy is that, in its identification of itself with the natural order, it seeks to efface any trace of ideology in its own allegedly neutral position, assigning ideology to the extremes of 'cranky' theories like Marxism or feminism. It is no surprise, therefore, that Esteban Trueba's first-person discourse attempts to portray the landowner in liberal, common-sense terms. The 'yo' person signals a faith in an essential, unified self, a source of power and control, as opposed to the general passive mass of women and peasants whose lives he can mould 'con mi propia mano'. Indeed Trueba states clearly: 'Yo era como un padre para ellos' (53). He is the source and centre of everything and in his patriarchal role he can justify his power by casting himself in the role of father–provider. Hence he furnishes a comprehensive account of his programme of training, feeding, housing and caring for the health of his workforce, concluding that, 'Sí, he sido un buen patrón, de eso no hay duda' (55). Needless to say, this is, once again, a strategy designed exactly to perpetuate the marginalisation of a group that is central to the landowner's needs. Education is a selective form of control: 'tenía la ambición de que todos los niños y adultos de las Tres Marías debían aprender a leer, escribir y sumar, aunque no era partidario de que adquirieran otros conoci-mientos, para que no se les llenara la cabeza con ideas inapropiadas a su estado y condición' (59). Feeding and health care are a means of ensuring that the peasants 'crecieran fuertes y sanos y pudieran trabajar desde pequeños' (59). Liberation here is actually a subtle form of repression: Pedro Segundo's potential for rebellion is disabled by his own recognition of his boss's achievements, leaving him with 'una mezcla de miedo y de rencorosa admiración' (61). What basically happens is that, like many women, the peasants internalise their perceived inferiority and accept their dependency as a natural state. In describing the positive changes he has person-ally introduced, Trueba comments of the peasants that: 'Eran gente buena y sencilla, no había revoltosos. También es cierto que eran muy pobres e ignorantes' (53–4). In other words, their naturally compliant nature is really a function of their deliberately generated ignorance, so that they become a blank page upon which the *patrón* can inscribe the hidden agenda of a seemingly quidditative order. As Trueba says, 'Fue necesario que yo llegara para que aquí hubiera orden, ley, trabajo.... Sin mí estarían perdidos. Si vamos al fondo de las cosas, no sirven ni para hacer los mandados, siempre lo he dicho: son como niños' (64).

In a specifically Latin American context, Trueba's world view restates the basic values underlying the Spanish conquest and the emergence of the civilisation-versus-barbarism ethic in the post-Independence subcontinent of the nineteenth century (and its survival into the twentieth). The Independence movement in general was, despite its liberationist rhetoric, largely aimed at furthering the interests of the well-off *criollo* classes, and, in many ways, the enlightened pursuit of 'civilisation' by Sarmiento *et al.* was an extension of this. Trueba clearly sees himself as bringing civilisation to a backward countryside but, as *Cien años de soledad* has already shown, the civilisation-versus-barbarism notion was a myth which was passed off as reality. Trueba's obsession with 'civilisation' is reflected in his fascination with science and his favouring of European and North American customs and practices. His sister Férula incarnates a largely anti-countryside, anti-Latin American stance. She thinks that the child Blanca has 'malos modales' because 'parece un indio' (100), and she wants to 'vivir como cristiana', away from this 'purgatorio de incivilizados' (104). Inadvertently echoing the twin beliefs of biological determinism and scientific positivism, she feels trapped 'en una región inhumana, donde no funcionaban las leyes de Dios ni el progreso de la ciencia' (104). Yet Esteban's alternative 'civilisation' is frequently mocked or subverted. The much-admired European Jean de Satigny – whose 'sentido práctico propio de los de su raza' is contrasted with 'aquellos bárbaros aborígenes' (191) – is actually involved in raping the country of its talent and natural treasures, is engaged in a plainly barbaric trade in chinchilla skins and turns out to be a ridiculous dandy and fond of what his erstwhile admirers would probably regard as dubious sexual proclivities. Trueba's decision to visit a North American hospital 'porque había llegado a la prematura conclusión de que los doctores latinos eran todos unos charlatanes más cercanos al brujo aborigen que al científico' (216) has to be compared with old Pedro García's fixing of his master's broken bones in such a way that 'los médicos que lo revisaron después no podían creer que eso fuera posible' (145) (the old man – though he does not always get it right – similarly rids the estate of a plague of ants in the face of the helplessness of foreign modern technology). Trueba also wants to have his house built on the model of 'los nuevos palacetes de Europa y Norteamérica' (87), with a 'jardín versallesco' to offset the native tendency towards 'una selva enmarañada donde proliferaban variedades de plantas y flores ...' (200). However, it is said that Clara, the woman Trueba idolises, 'creció como una planta salvaje, a pesar de las recomendaciones del doctor Cuevas, que había traído de Europa la novedad de los baños de agua fría y los golpes de electricidad para curar a los locos' (75). Clara's 'madness' (or 'barbarism') is, in fact, nothing more than the exuberance of a true Latin American condition which should not be distorted by alien values, hence Nívea's readiness to 'amarla sin condiciones y aceptarla tal cual era' (74–5).

At the same time, woman, to Trueba's mind, is a key factor in the drive towards civilisation. In the important third section of the second chapter, where he outlines his patriarchal philosophy, Trueba realises that he himself is 'convirtiéndose en un bárbaro' (56). The solution comes to him when 'su sentido práctico le indicó que tenía que buscarse una mujer y, una vez tomada la decisión, la ansiedad que lo consumía se calmó y su rabia pareció aquietarse' (56). While this may seem to cast the woman in the typically gentle, feminine, supportive role, it does also show the falsehood of the male patriarchal notion of order, in the sense that Trueba depends on the woman to overcome his own barbarism. So, union with a woman will be a positive development that will civilise him and his environs. Yet the irony is that he simply takes a woman: he rapes Pancha García. The episode, though upsetting, is a witty commentary on the civilisation-versus-barbarism theme and its inherent contradictions. Significantly, however, it is the influence of Pancha which opens up Trueba to the more worthwhile aspects of 'civilisation'. His commands turn into a 'súplica' and in his happiness with her:

> le mejoró por un tiempo el mal humor y comenzó a interesarse en sus inquilinos... . Se dio cuenta, por primera vez, que el peor abandono no era el de las tierras y los animales, sino de los habitantes de los Tres Marías, que habían vivido en el desamparo desde la época en que su padre se jugó la dote y la herencia de su madre. Decidió que era tiempo de llevar un poco de civilización a ese rincón perdido entre la cordillera y el mar. (58–9)

Woman here is the source of positive action, but man thinks he is. In practice, the 'civilisation' that Trueba brings is one which serves his own purposes but which comes to be indistinguishable from the natural order of things, the way of the world. By the end of the novel, though, he is finding it difficult to 'seguir sosteniéndose en precaria estabilidad sobre un mundo que se le hacía trizas.... Ya no tenía las ideas tan claras y se le había borrado la frontera entre lo que le parecía bueno y lo que consideraba malo' (350). In effect, the novel subverts the entire premise on which it superficially appears to be based: in the end it is Esteban Trueba who is living in a fantasy world rather than his supposedly eccentric wife Clara.

The evaluation of the alternative world of Clara and the other female characters is a much thornier problem than the exposition of the gaps and inconsistencies of the patriarchal discourse. Pointing out the errors is always easier than providing the right answers, but then this has always been the traditional role of literature. Isabel Allende here seems to oscillate between a kind of female essentialism, a radical deconstruction of essentialism and a more concrete political materialism. As an author rather than a systematic thinker, she may end up with a cocktail of all three, but with an overall taste that combines broadly consistent elements. This is, after all, a political work written in a popular tone with the ultimate goal of touching an emotional nerve and jolting the reader into a new awareness. The popular or mass-market dimension means that there is little pretence of producing an open-ended feminine[12] language of so-called 'other bisexuality' à la Cixous nor much evidence of the ruptures and breaks in symbolic language talked of by Kristeva. Nonetheless, some ideas associated with both thinkers can be detected at what one imagines would be, for Allende, the more important level of content.

Esteban Trueba can be identified with Cixous' 'Realm of the Proper', while the female characters would be matched to the 'Realm of the Gift'. Trueba, as an ambitious landowner, is clearly linked to property, self-projection, hierarchy and so on. His driving fear of communism is a fear of expropriation of land and power (or, for Cixous, the loss of the attribute or castration). Women, needless to say, do not share this fear and can oppose masculine culture (based on dominance) with the 'Realm of the Gift' (based on giving and exchange). In the female characters of *La casa de los espíritus* such generosity is reflected in their sexuality and their charitable works, both of which, to different extents in differing cases, break down hierarchies and class divisions. The distinction is not unlike that of Annie Leclerc between desire and pleasure.[13] Trueba, for whom sexual and economic desire are much the same thing, always *wants* to own or possess an 'object', while the women's thought is based on pleasure or *jouissance* (for instance, Blanca revelling in her domestic pursuits or Clara in her world of spirits or all of the central women characters in their creative arts). This ideal of female *jouissance*, though, suggests an essential feminine spirit, located in a sort of pre-Oedipal state. Indeed Allende's self-professed belief in a 'feminine solidarity' passed on from mother to daughter and excluding men (Levine and Engelbert, 18) contains faint echoes of Cixous' notion of the mother as the origin of the source and voice in all female/feminine texts. Hence the bond between Nívea and Clara, 'estableciendo un vínculo tan fuerte, que se prolongó en las generaciones posteriores como una tradición familiar' (78) and repeated specifically in Clara's relationship with Blanca (117), Clara's own pregnancy in which she finds herself 'volcándose hacia el interior de sí misma, en un diálogo secreto y constante con la criatura' (93) and her belief in 'una memoria genética' (156) which allows mothers to pass on their 'locuras' (or special qualities) to their daughters. Hence too the evolving pattern of light imagery in the chain of names (Nívea-Clara-Blanca-Alba), implying that the world view of each is informed and enriched by that inherited from the mother. This perhaps explains in part the use of water imagery in relation to women. The mermaid-like Rosa with her 'belleza de fondo de mar' (32) is like 'un habitante del agua' (12) and Trueba feels the urge to 'hundirme en sus aguas más profundas' (39). Clara meantime 'navegaba hábilmente por las agitadas aguas de la vida social y por las otras, sorprendentes, de su camino espiritual' (237). For Cixous, water is the essential feminine element, reflecting a closed womb-like world flowing through the female writer and keeping her in touch with the mother's voice.

Clara, living in her world of silence and spirits, is the most obvious example of this essentially feminine world. Her retreat into silence is a kind of retreat into the 'semiotic' or 'imaginary' unity with the mother, a challenge to the Symbolic Order (which, according to Lacan, is associated with the Law of the Father and is when language is acquired). Both instances of her self-immersion into silence involve solidarity with another woman and a rejection of masculine control. The first follows the symbolic 'rape' of Rosa by the representative of scientific knowledge, Dr Cuevas, in the form of her autopsy (described in a way connoting assumptions of male 'ownership' of the female body). The second comes after Trueba strikes her in response to her defence of Blanca's relationship with Pedro Tercero García. Clara's silent world undermines patriarchal binary thought, being a world where 'el tiempo no se marcaba con relojes ni calendarios ..., el pasado y el futuro eran parte de la misma cosa y la realidad del presente era un caleidoscopio de espejos desordenados donde todo podía ocurrir ..., donde no siempre funcionaban las leyes de la física o la lógica' (78–9). The world of the spirits is an essentially female space where women meet to 'invocar a los espíritus e intercambiar cábalas y recetas de cocina' (115) and which excludes men, being 'una dimensión desconocida a la que él [Trueba] jamás podría llegar' (119). It relates also to a species of *écriture féminine*. Clara's imaginative mind is set against Trueba's scientific rationalism: she loves to read, write and entertain poets, and when her husband removes all radios to keep the news from her, she simply discovers the truth through her intuitive powers (110–1). And though Allende's text makes no attempt to reproduce Clara's own style, it is made plain that the protagonist's 'cuadernos de anotar' are written in an experiential, non-chronological format (380), at one stage defying conventional logic (124). In Cixous' terms she is (perhaps) in the free space of the Lacanian Imaginary: 'the speaking/writing woman is in a space outside time (eternity), a space that allows no naming and no syntax' (Moi, 114).

There are a number of problems with this interpretation, however, and it would be highly reductive to rely too heavily on such a reading. For a start, it may seem inconsistent to oppose the patriarchal notion of a (false) natural order with a theory of an essential feminine nature (or, for that matter, an essentialist view of the innocent peasant or native Latin American). Having said that, at the level of an exposé of the workings of patriarchy, the text is not necessarily anti-essentialist in any strict sense: in many ways it seems simply to be arguing that 'true nature' (which is unruly) has been replaced by a counterfeit nature (which is ruly but artificial). This opens the way to a simplified version of the Kristevan concept of 'bisexuality' (though, of course, Kristeva herself is no essentialist). From this point of view, the promotion of the female sex ('stage two' feminism) should give way to a more generalised weakening of gender divisions and dissolution of binary distinctions ('stage three' feminism). Though this does not lead to any real semiotic theory of writing in Allende, the deconstruction of rigid binary oppositions (right/wrong, appropriate/inappropriate, sane/mad, mine/yours and so on) does involve a reinterpretation of societal structures in a way which binds the question of woman's position to wider political or ideological questions. So, Clara's spiritualism is not purely and essentially feminine: one character – though, perhaps, admittedly being presented humourously – 'tenía la teoría de que esta condición estaba presente en todos los seres humanos, especialmente en los de su familia, y que si no funcionaba con eficiencia era sólo por falta de entrenamiento' (21). All human beings have the potential to dissolve or at least loosen up the binary divisions that separate them. This is the significance of the hybrid figures that are portrayed in Rosa's sewing, Blanca's pottery and Alba's painting. In a similar way, Blanca's fairy tales tell of 'un príncipe que durmió cien años, ... doncellas que peleaban cuerpo a cuerpo con los dragones, ... un lobo perdido en el bosque a quien una niña destripó sin razón alguna' (269). This also aids an understanding of the roles of the male children Jaime and Nicolás, sometimes thought to be poorly integrated into the text. They are equally marginal and antistereotypical. Despite being trained in the traditional art of upperclass manhood (117), the initially more conventional Nicolás becomes an outrageous-looking member of an Eastern religious group and Jaime abandons sexual and social norms by becoming 'un sentimental incorregible', a timid bookworm, a socialist and a friend of Pedro Tercero García (168).[14] As Allende herself has said, 'men and women are not really so different' but are 'mutilated' by social 'education' and 'rigid roles' (Levine and Engelbert, 19). These characters represent a plea for the slackening of those rigid class and gender roles. And this is really the key to the entire narrative structure of the novel. Esteban Trueba's first-person narrative is mixed in with a third-person narrative by a female narrator. Sandra Boschetto has commented that 'la mediación metatextual será un intento por parte de la autora de reconciliar oposiciones, de fundir diferencias para crear una sola realidad totalizadora e incluyente, texto en blanco'.[15] This is perhaps the nearest the novel gets to textual 'bisexuality' as it were. But more meaningfully, Trueba's first-person narration regularly refers to the variant viewpoints of 'mi nieta', while the third-person narration of the family history is Alba's account, into which her own first-person perspective intervenes. Thus the novel revolves around a dialectic between Trueba and Alba, inaugurating a *rapprochement* between previously opposite sexes, age groups and sociopolitical loyalties. And hence the centrality of Trueba. Though some see it as a weakness to have a male character as the structural backbone of a feminist novel, his centrality is the centrality of patriarchal binary logic which is in opposition with the 'bisexuality' of the other members of his family. Yet the 'bisexual' pole invades and subverts the patriarchal pole. Trueba, as we shall see, undergoes a learning process and by the end of the novel he has moved towards Alba's position. And if Alba's epilogue seems a rather corny plea for mutual love, the basis of her appeal lies in the desired erasure of binary conflict which gives the text much of its cohesion.

While all this may seem rather utopian, the learning process does also enjoy a more concrete, material manifestation in *La casa de los espíritus*. Early on in the novel, Rosa's idealised, romanticised view of the young Trueba's exploits in the gold mines is said to be totally at odds with the harsh reality he has to face (13). This is an early hint at the potentially suspect nature of a 'feminine' world view which does not take account of material factors. From this perspective, Clara's silence and spiritualism needs to be re-interpreted. The two occasions she goes silent (discussed earlier) are, in fact, quite different. The first is ostensibly a traumatic reaction to the shock of Rosa's autopsy: it is a retreat from reality and into 'un universo inventado para ella, protegida de las inclemencias de la vida, donde se confundían la verdad prosaica de las cosas materiales con la verdad tumultuosa de los sueños' (78–9). This is paralleled by her spiritualism up to and in adult life, described as 'su tendencia a evadir la realidad y perderse en el ensueño' (123). The second silence, however, disrupts this pattern. It is not so much a retreat as an act of rebellion. The crucial changes come in the fifth and sixth chapters. The earthquake wakes her up from 'una larga infancia ... sin obligaciones', exposing her to 'necesidades básicas, que antes había ignorado' and making her spiritualism seem irrelevant (148). She becomes a working woman instead of 'un ángel vestido de blanco' (155). This change is heralded by the freeing of the birds and the disappearance of the spirits:

> Abrieron una por una las jaulas de los pájaros y el cielo se llenó de caturras, canarios, jilgueros y cristofué, que revolotearon encegueci-dos por la libertad y finalmente emprendieron el vuelo en todas direcciones. Blanca notó que en todos esos afanes, no apareció fantasma alguno detrás de las cortinas, no llegó ningún Rosacruz advertido por su sexto sentido, ni poeta hambriento llamado por la necesidad. Su madre parecía haberse convertido en una señora

común y silvestre.
    — Usted ha cambiado mucho mamá — observó Blanca.
    — No soy yo, hija. Es el mundo que ha cambiado — respondió
Clara. (151)

This may be a symbolic liberation of a material feminist and class
consciousness. She travels alone for the first time, realises that 'ya
no contaba con su marido, con Férula o con Nana' (148) and initiates her clearly significant friendship with the peasant Pedro
Segundo García, to whom she is said to move closer as she now
drifts away from the patriarchal Trueba (159–60). The final break
with Trueba comes when he hits her following her open denunciation of his sexism, classism and hypocrisy. The blow sends her reel-
ing into the arms of Pedro Segundo García and she never speaks to
Trueba again: a conscious decision to reject patriarchal values and
an acknowledgement of the material reality of class struggle.

In fact, the evolution of the feminism of all the main female
protagonists is inextricably bound up with a similarly developing
progressiveness and consciousness of material issues. Taking them
chronologically, Nívea is a suffragette, but one who wears a fur
coat and classy shoes to preach equality to a group of comfortless
workers and discusses her campaign over tea and pastries in the
Plaza de Armas (77–8). Her daughter Clara recognises that it
should be more than just a question of trying to 'tranquilizarnos la
conciencia' and that the poor 'no necesitan caridad, sino justicia'
(247); she defies her husband, spurns fashion and jewellery and has
a friendship with a peasant. Her daughter Blanca continues her
mother's charitable works, stands up to her father's authority,
raises an illegitimate child and – going a stage further than Clara –
has a lasting affair with Pedro Tercero García, a peasant leader,
revolutionary singer and member of a Marxist government.[16]
Finally, her daughter Alba joins the student political movement, has
a relationship with a guerrilla leader and ends up a victim of
torture. She becomes the most fully integrated with the interlinked
class, political and women's struggles. She finds solidarity with her
fellow prisoner, the working-class Ana Díaz, whose non-individu-
alising name associates her with the masses at large. As it happens,
Ana used to distrust Alba because she was a 'burguesa'. Alba's
'education' is now complete, therefore, and is symbolically crowned
by her positive encounter with ordinary women in a prison camp
and, later, in a shanty town. And so, importantly, she puts Clara's

non-chronological notes into order and writes a coherent history of her family (263). The material world, perceived through a feminist and politically aware perspective, has displaced the 'feminine' world of the spirits.

The relationship of Alba's text to Clara's text brings us back to the question of style and tone. It is taken as a given by now, in the present work, that from, roughly, the late sixties/early seventies, the Latin American novel began to experience a shift away from complex, even tortuous narrative forms towards more popular forms, often (though not always) relatively straightforward and sometimes, too, more directly political: a shift from the Boom to the post-Boom. The new novel had acquired an official air, lapsing into stereotype and a kind of heavy neo-classicism. The re-evaluation of popular culture (meaning, again, broadly speaking, mass culture rather than a form of indigenism) by writers considered here, like Puig, Cabrera Infante, the later Donoso and Vargas Llosa brought a wind of change (of sorts at least). Puig notes a connection between the previous valuation of popular culture and the valuation of women. Women, he says, especially in the Hispanic world, are rather like 'géneros menores': 'se goza con ellas pero nadie se las respeta'.[17] Hence in Allende's novel, which is firmly aimed at a wide market embracing a sizeable middle-brow audience, in the transition from spiritualism to materialism, from Clara's less penetrable text to Alba's accessible text, there is a re-enactment of the shift from Boom to post-Boom in a way which establishes a parallel between emancipation and narrative form. This is something of an inversion of the (by this stage) conventional view that formal textual disruption is revolutionary in political terms because it challenges the bourgeois, capitalist or patriarchal order. As Antonio Skármeta – one of the figures closely associated with the post-Boom – has said of the new novel (in a way applicable perhaps also to certain aspects of Cixous and to Kristeva's theories of writing): 'Creo que la literatura del boom ha hecho más por cubrir que descubrir'.[18] There is certainly ambiguity and even inconsistency in *La casa de los espíritus* but those who accuse Allende of ideological impurity or a masculinist aesthetics miss the point of this wish to translate notions of a feminine essence or consciousness into the more concrete and broadly-based arena of social and political reality, to address serious and difficult questions but simultaneously communicate with a larger public.

At this point, the question of the relationship of *La casa de los espíritus* to *Cien años de soledad* becomes unavoidable. The similarities are obvious: in both novels Latin American history is explored via a lengthy family saga punctuated by bizarre or fantastic occurrences; the style (in its use of time and display of so-called Magical Realism) is alike in some ways; and there are some specific parallels such as those between Rosa, la bella and Remedios la Bella or tío Marcos' obsession with progress and inventions and that of several members of the Buendía family. But the most crucial point of contact is that between Alba's work with her mother's 'cuadernos de anotar' and that of various Buendías with Melquíades's parchments. There are key differences here, though. Clara's scripts are quite dissimilar to those of Melquíades. His are deliberately obscure (they are written in Sanskrit, verse and secret code) and are notoriously difficult to decipher. Clara's are certainly non-chronological. However, this is justified on the grounds that they represent an intuitive feminine space which merely needs to be channelled into a more material direction: Alba's task is therefore simply one of ordering and rendering useful an eminently decipherable text. Though Martin makes the claim that 'nothing, surely, could be clearer' for his feasible but highly reductive reading of Aureliano's cracking of the code of Melquíades' manuscripts as a political awakening (Martin, 231), it seems an inescapable conclusion that this ending is much less satisfactory in concrete sociopolitical terms than the position in which Alba finds herself vis-à-vis Clara's notebooks. Why are Aureliano and Macondo destroyed at this point of realisation? Is the text he deciphers the same as the one we are reading? Is he discovering his own fictionality and, if so, what can the novel say to us about reality? If the novel is a reflection on history and reality, why is it so dependent on a 'magical' world view for its appeal? And why is that view both celebrated and undermined? *Cien años de soledad* is redolent with possibilities and associations, but for that very reason maintains an inevitably ambivalent relation to reality. Allende's novel, on the other hand, is, for Peter Earle, a 'celebration of reality'.[19] It refers pretty unequivocally to a specific (Chilean) reality instead of taking refuge in a quasi-allegorical unreality. Indeed it appears explicitly to reject the García Márquez approach. Clara, we are told, 'no era partidaria de repetir los nombres en la familia, porque eso siembra confusión en los cuadernos de anotar la vida' (233) – perhaps a swipe at the obfuscation of

García Márquez with his litany of José Arcadios and Aurelianos? And Alba sifts through her mother and grandmother's correspondence in order to preserve the facts, 'salvándolos de la nebulosa de los hechos improbables' (219) – perhaps a criticism of an excessive tendency towards fantasy?

This position is supported by a narrative structure which appears to overturn the magical element. The magical strand is converted into a realist strand, as has already been seen in relation to the evolution of Clara as a character, a process summed up in Alba's allusion to 'un mundo mágico que se acabó' (78). The book is made up of fifteen chapters (including the epilogue). The middle chapter, the eighth, 'El conde', is clearly a kind of pivotal interlude: it takes place in a different geographical location, is marginal to the mainstream of the action, and is the only chapter not to be divided into a series of sub-sections. After this chapter, the symmetrical centre of the novel, there is a marked structural shift. Chapter Nine starts with the birth of Alba and ends with the death of Clara: the world of magic is over and a grim new realism is ushered in. The change in the house of the spirits will be sharp: 'Alba sabía que su abuela era el alma de la gran casa de la esquina. Los demás lo supieron más tarde, cuando Clara murió y la casa perdió las flores, los amigos transeúntes y los espíritus juguetones y entró de lleno en la época del estropicio' (250). The chapter ends with Jaime's diagnosis 'Mamá ya se fue' and the next one starts immediately with the title 'La época del estropicio', explaining that 'la muerte de Clara' means that 'los tiempos cambiaron', giving way to 'deterioro' and 'ruina' (262). Significantly, the next chapter is called 'El despertar'. The remainder of the book is an only tokenly veiled account of the election of Allende, the Pinochet coup and the appalling aftermath. The final chapter before the epilogue is 'La hora de la verdad'. Alba now comes face to face with a horrific reality (torture and repression). Material change will now be all important.

This structural pattern does not really mean the negation of Clara's position by that of Alba. Clara's spiritualism, on one level, simply represents happy times which are destroyed by natural and political cataclysms. The world of the spirits, in other words, is the sort of ideal place the world should be. In the meantime, the positive force of Clara's spiritualism needs to be harnessed on a practical and political level. Yet if Clara is associated with magic, Esteban Trueba is equally living in a fantasy: the fantasy of a patriarchal natural order. But his fantasy world is also subverted by reality in the form of the arrest of Alba: he realises 'al fin que había llegado la hora de la verdad, después de casi noventa años de vivir bajo su propia ley' (353). The title of Allende's second novel *De amor y de sombra* could be a gloss on the first. Structurally 'amor' is overthrown by 'sombra', but there has always been a shadow hanging over love, and even now love survives despite the shadow: if people can learn (Alba) and change (Trueba), then perhaps one day 'sombra' will be overthrown by 'amor'.

The interplay between love and shadow and between magic and reality suggests a final feature of the structural pattern of *La casa de los espíritus*: the relationship of the circle and the straight line. It is a commonplace in García Márquez criticism to talk of the circular structure of *Cien años de soledad*.[20] But circularity and progressive politics are strange bedfellows. In *La casa de los espíritus* there is a narrator in the present trying to recuperate the past and reconstruct a link through to the present: this implies both a straight line and a learning process. This is reflected in turn in the evolution in the feminism and politics of the central line of female characters discussed earlier. Alba's name is 'el último de una cadena de palabras luminosas que quieren decir lo mismo' (234), but the chain Nívea-Clara-Blanca-Alba indicates a progression in the positive image of whiteness, culminating in Alba, a kind of new dawn or new hope amidst the darkness and despair. Yet this is set against a series of instances or images of circularity. For example, despite Clara's distaste for the duplication of names, there are some classic García Márquez-style repetitions, such as Férula's assumption of the role of the Nana and the recurrent children's games with the books from tío Marcos' trunk (91). More specifically, the novel sets up a pattern of circularity in which a victim becomes a victimiser. Férula sacrifices her life to look after her mother, while her brother Esteban Trueba enjoys a freedom of which she is envious: before long she is manipulating and victimising her brother (45–7, 92), though she, of course, becomes his victim too. Trueba's greed and arrogance has its roots in his poverty as a child or youth (48, 201): emblematic of this is the humiliating episode of the 'café vienés' at the Hotel Francés, which scars him for life (45–6). Victimising others, Trueba ensures the repetition of the circle. Esteban García, a kind of Frankenstein's monster, resents the wealth and power of the grandfather who created his bastard father and dreams of revenge (170). Alba, who 'encarnaba lo que nunca tendría, lo que él nunca sería' (253), is in turn raped by him. This raises another central circular or repeated motif of *Cien años de soledad*, incest. Though incest can be identified with solitude and non-solidarity in García Márquez, it is often celebrated in a bawdy, earthy way as, for example, with the final couple Aureliano Babilonia and Amaranta Ursula. Here there is nothing marvellous about incest: it is an unequivocal image of a distorted society. So, circularity and repetition in the style of García Márquez are associated with negative and destructive forces, while the straight line of female development is positive and progressive. This may be the function of the del Valle family's tree. In a repetitious 'rito de iniciación', all the male members of the family wanting to start wearing long trousers had to climb the tree to prove their worth – until cousin Jerónimo falls and is killed and Nívea intervenes and orders that the tree be cut down. Rodrigo Cánovas has identified the tree with the family tree.[21] Yet this is the point at which the circular male ritual is stopped and a female dynasty begins. In the same chapter Clara decides to speak again, announcing her marriage. The only offspring of this marriage to produce a child will be the female, Blanca; her daughter is pregnant at the end of the novel. Thus a productive female line displaces a circle of sterile male activity, culminating in Blanca and Alba's role in the disintegration of a hitherto hermetic integrated phallic male self as their experience forces the patriarch Trueba out of his false circle and into the world of 'verdad'. Once more, this ties to the level of class and politics. The moving turning-point of Trueba's embrace with Pedro Tercero García (a positive development) follows the more-or-less exact (though inverted) repetition of a dialogue between them that had taken place some time earlier: the circular trap has been punctured (345, 319). The peasant names, Pedro García, Pedro Segundo García and Pedro Tercero García, echo the reduplication of names in *Cien años de soledad*, suggesting they are caught in a hopeless circle of oppression. But their names contain the seeds of numerical progress (Segundo, Tercero), linking them to the forward-moving female chain. As Allende herself has commented, 'nada es un callejón sin salida, es que siempre al final hay una respuesta, hay una salida, hay una solución' (Cortínez, 81).[22]

The epilogue of the novel may now seem more acceptable. Even if there is an element of fudge and some toying with the buzz notions of the new novel, Mora's judgement that it represents 'una postura conservadora' (55) is somewhat harsh. True, the final pages do talk of repetition and predetermination: 'Sospecho que todo lo ocurrido no es fortuito, sino que corresponde a un destino dibujado antes de mi nacimiento y Esteban García es parte de ese dibujo ...' (379). But surely this is a reference to the Frankenstein idea – that oppressive patriarchal systems will inevitably breed their own monsters which will one day turn around and bite. Trueba and the system he represents have brought disaster upon themselves. However, Alba realises that this apparently cyclic pattern, this 'trazo tosco y torcido', has a hidden meaning, that 'ninguna pincelada es inútil' and that, when the 'rompecabezas' is deciphered, 'el resultado sería armonioso' (379). Putting it simply, people can learn from the past and there is hope. It is equally true that the last line of the novel takes us back to the first. Yet this does not close the text in a vicious circle of inevitability. The last line is from Clara's diaries, from which Alba has learned a positive lesson. If directed along proper avenues, writing can overcome confused, circular patterns and help us to 'ver las cosas en su dimensión real y ... burlar a la mala memoria' (379). In other words, the last sentence underlines Alba's vital political function as a mainstream testimonial writer: she will retrace the family history in an accessible form so that people can learn from it. Alba's role in the 'rompecabezas' is to replace the stifling circle of a false order with the straight line of learning and truth:

> Clara ... le surgió, además, que escribiera un testimonio que algún día podría servir para sacar a la luz el terrible secreto que estaba viviendo, para que el mundo se enterara del horror que ocurría paralelamente a la existencia apacible y ordenada de los que no querían saber, de los que podían tener la ilusión de una vida normal, de los que podían negar que iban a flote en una balsa sobre un mar de lamentos, ignorando, a pesar de todas las evidencias, que a pocas cuadras de su mundo feliz estaban los otros, los que sobreviven o mueren en el lado oscuro. (362–3)

This, also, is the role of Isabel Allende. Popular culture can, without doubt, be exploited as an agent of oppression, but it can also be liberating. Its value, when used appropriately, is that it can distil relatively complex concepts into a readily-digestible form: essentially, the process that has been described here. Thus, when old

Férula, ticking off Trueba for his ostentation, comes out with the sort of naive-sounding hackneyed cliché conventionally thought typical of her social–sexual role, she is actually crystallising the argument of the novel and an important historical truth: 'tanto despilfarro era seguramente pecado mortal y Dios iba a castigar a todos por gastar en chabacanerías de nuevo rico lo que estaría mejor empleado ayudando a los pobres' (87). Similarly, a simple song by Pedro Tercero García about chickens and foxes (in which the once-timid chickens get together to scare off the sly fox) has a far greater political impact than the more recondite messages of the Socialist Party 'panfletos' that he tirelessly distributes (157). So, those academics who mistrust Isabel Allende because of the mainstreamism of her work may be effectively mirroring the sentiments of Esteban Trueba with his loathing of 'la música popular' (203) and his prohibition of radios that transmit 'canciones subversivas' and 'comedias y folletines' (274). The supposedly trashy world of women, peasants and popular culture can be seen to challenge the official tyrannies of patriarchy, capitalism and cultural supremacism. Thus the various theoretical positions rehearsed in *La casa de los espíritus* are condensed into a concise but simple philosophy of love in the closing pages. Alba says: 'Me será muy difícil vengar a todos los que tienen que ser vengados, porque mi venganza no sería más que otra parte del mismo rito inexorable. Quiero pensar que mi oficio es la vida y que mi misión no es prolongar el odio, sino sólo llenar estas páginas …' (379). She has set herself free from aimless circularities (social, political, sexual and artistic) and chosen to use her writing to communicate a clear and powerful message of love. This may well be one of the most effective ways of trashing tyrants of all the novels discussed in this book. It is precisely the relatively uncomplicated 'mass' or, at least, wide appeal of *La casa de los espíritus* that sets Isabel Allende apart from many other practitioners of the Latin American new novel and marks her as one of those writers from beyond the Boom who does actually manage something approaching a reconciliation of politics with the popular.

## Notes

[1]Gabriela Mora, 'Las novelas de Isabel Allende y el papel de la mujer como ciudadana', *Ideologies and Literature*, II, no. 1, 1987, p. 60.

[2]Douglas Foster, 'Isabel Allende Unveiled', *Mother Jones*, XIII, no. 10, 1988, pp. 42–6. It should be pointed out that, since then, Isabel Allende has, sadly, experienced great personal tragedy in her life in the form of the premature death of her daughter.

[3]Linda Levine and Jo Anne Engelbert, 'The World Is Full of Stories', *Review*, XXXIV, 1980, p. 20; Isabel Allende, 'La magia de las palabras', *Revista Iberoamericana*, LI, 1985, p. 451: the remaining quotations in this paragraph come from the same page.

[4]Gerald Martin, *Journeys Through the Labyrinth: Latin American Fiction in the Twentieth Century*, Verso, London, 1989, pp. 218–35.

[5]Julia Kristeva, 'La femme, ce n'est jamais ça', *Tel Quel*, LIX, 1974, pp. 19–24 (24). Quoted in Toril Moi, *Sexual/Textual Politics: Feminist Literary Theory*, Routledge, London, 1990, p. 164. The theoretical positions outlined in this essay are largely drawn from Moi's excellent survey. The main references are to Hélène Cixous and Julia Kristeva, particularly, in the latter case, *La Révolution du langage poétique*, Seuil, Paris, 1974, in which she examines avantgarde and modernist writers.

[6]Gene H. Bell-Villada, *García Márquez: The Man and His Work*, University of North Carolina Press, Chapel Hill, 1990, p. 208.

[7]Jean Gilkison, 'The Appropriation of the Conventions of Romance in Isabel Allende's *De amor y de sombra*', paper given at the conference of the Association of Hispanists of Great Britain and Ireland, Belfast, 1991. I am grateful to the author for providing me with a copy of her persuasively-argued paper.

[8]Isabel Allende, *La casa de los espíritus*, 18th ed., Plaza y Janés, Barcelona, 1985, p. 203.

[9]José Donoso, *El obsceno pájaro de la noche*, 6th ed., Seix Barral, Barcelona, 1979, p. 230.

[10]'José Donoso's *El obsceno pájaro de la noche*: Witches Everywhere and Nowhere', in Sharon Magnarelli, *The Lost Rib: Female Characters in the Spanish-American Novel*, Associated University Presses, London, 1985, 147–68. The general comments on witches here draw on Magnarelli's stimulating analysis.

[11]José Donoso, *Casa de campo*, 3rd ed., Seix Barral, Barcelona, 1980, pp. 34, 130.

[12]The problem of the word 'feminine' here is the same as in the previous chapter. The French word 'féminin' translates as 'female' and 'feminine'.

Usage here will vary according to context. Broadly speaking, 'feminine' is preferred to 'female' where possible essential qualities of the sex are being considered. The adjective 'masculin' poses a similar problem.

[13]Annie Leclerc, extract from *Parole de femme*, Grasset, Paris, 1974, in *French Feminist Thought: A Reader*, ed. Toril Moi, Basil Blackwell, Oxford, 1987, pp. 73–9.

[14]Mario A. Rojas, in '*La casa de los espíritus*, de Isabel Allende: un caleidoscopio de espejos desordenados', *Revista Iberoamericana*, LI, 1985, pp. 917-25, usefully discusses the tendency to 'obliterar las rígidas dicotomías que polarizan la diferenciación genérica' (921). In particular, he notes hints of androgyny in the portrayal of Jaime and other characters (216). Similar points could be made about the later Nicolás.

[15]Sandra M. Boschetto, 'Dialéctica metatextual y sexual en *La casa de los espíritus* de Isabel Allende', *Hispania*, LXXII, no. 3, 1989, p. 530. The overall argument of Boschetto's well-written article is the familiar and, in this case, irrelevant one that the text is merely a 'signo representando otros signos, significantes apuntando a otros significantes' (526).

[16]There are obvious shades of Víctor Jara here, though he died in the repression that followed the coup. Mora complains that Pedro Tercero García's escape to and success in Canada devalues his political significance (57).

[17]M. Osorio, 'Entrevista con Manuel Puig', *Cuadernos para el Diálogo*, CCXXXXI, 1977, p. 52. Chapter 2, of course, suggests that Puig does not, however, always expound a coherent view of popular culture or reconcile it adequately with politics or the aesthetics of the new novel.

[18]Verónica Cortínez, 'Polifonía: entrevista a Isabel Allende y Antonio Skármeta', *Revista Chilena de Literatura*, XXXII, 1988, p. 80.

[19]Peter G. Earle, 'Literature as Survival: Allende's *The House of the Spirits*', *Contemporary Literature*, XXVII, 1987, pp. 543–4.

[20]Of course, not all critics would reduce *Cien años de soledad* to a circular structure. See my survey of the various critical positions in my *Cómo leer a Gabriel García Márquez*, Júcar, Madrid, 1991.

[21]Rodrigo Cánovas, 'Los espíritus literarios y políticos de Isabel Allende', *Revista Chilena de Literatura*, XXXII, 1988, p. 122.

[22]A slightly less convincing case of the circle-v-straight line is that of Tránsito Soto. Marjorie Agosín, in 'Isabel Allende: *La casa de los espíritus*', *Revista Interamericana de Bibliografía*, XXXV 1985, pp. 448-58, has argued that Clara uses her femininity as a means of self-advancement when she turns silence (traditional feminine coyness and passivity) into a weapon and an act of defiance (450 ff). In a similar way, Tránsito Soto uses her

female sexuality to progress from small-town whore to wealthy star turn of a top brothel in the capital. This linear development is matched by a circular inversion. Trueba lends the money to start her off on her, he thinks, laughable ambition, but he ends up begging her to help him free Alba. The right-wing senator is now out of favour with the dictatorship, while she (a former member of a co-operative) is in a position of influence with the government. Trueba's full-circle turnabout may represent the inevitable come-uppance of an unjust system, but the prostitute remains a dubious symbol of emancipation.

# Bibliography of works cited

**Adelstein**, Miriam, ed., *Studies on the Works of José Donoso*, Edwin Mellen Press, Lewiston/Queenston/Lampeter, 1990.

**Agosín**, Marjorie, 'Isabel Allende: *La casa de los espíritus*', *Revista Interamericana de Bibliografía*', XXXV, 1985, pp. 448–58.

**Aiken**, Susan Hardy, *et al.*, 'Trying Transformations: Curriculum Legislation and the Problem of Resistance', *Signs*, XII, 1987, pp. 255–75.

**Allende**, Isabel, *La casa de los espíritus*, 18th ed., Plaza y Janés, Barcelona, 1985.

——, 'La magia de las palabras', *Revista Iberoamericana*, LI, 1985, pp. 447–52.

**Alonso**, Carlos J., '*La tía Julia y el escribidor*: The Writing Subject's Fantasy of Empowerment', *PMLA*, CVI, 1991, pp. 46–59.

——, *The Spanish American Regional Novel*, Cambridge University Press, Cambridge, 1990.

**Alvarez-Borland**, Isabel, 'Identidad cíclica de *Tres tristes tigres*', *Revista Iberoamericana*, LVII, 1991, pp. 215–33.

**Aneja**, Anu, 'The Mystic Aspect of *L' Ecriture Féminine*: Hélène Cixous' *Vivre l'Orange*', *Qui Parle*, III, 1989, pp. 189–209.

**Bacarisse**, Pamela, *The Necessary Dream: A Study of the Novels of Manuel Puig*, University of Wales Press, Cardiff, 1988.

——, *Impossible Choices: The Implications of the Cultural References in the Novels of Manuel Puig*, University of Wales Press, Cardiff, 1993.

**Bakhtin**, Mikhail, *Problems of Dostoevsky's Poetics*, Ardis, Ann Arbor, 1973.

——, *Rabelais and His World*, MIT Press, Cambridge, 1968.

**Barbosa**, Maria José Somerlate, '*A hora da estrela* and the Tangible Reality of Fiction', *Romance Languages Annual*, I, 1989, pp. 379–83.

**Barthes**, Roland, *Essais critiques*, Seuil, Paris, 1964.

——, *S/Z*, Seuil, Paris, 1970.

**Beardsell**, Peter R., '*Don Segundo Sombra* and *Machismo*', *Forum for Modern Language Studies*, XVII, 1981, pp. 302–11.

**Bell-Villada**, Gene H., *García Márquez: The Man and His Work*, University of North Carolina Press, Chapel Hill, 1990.

**Berger**, John, *Ways of Seeing*, Penguin, London, 1972.

**Bernard**, Maité, 'Verdad y mentira del escribidor en *La tía Julia y el escribidor* de Mario Vargas Llosa', *Tropos*, XVII, 1991, pp. 33–46.

**Bevan**, David, ed., *Literature and Revolution*, Rodopi, Amsterdam and Atlanta, 1989.

**Beverley**, John, *Against Literature*, University of Minnesota Press, Minneapolis and London, 1993.

**Boldy**, Steven, 'Julio Cortázar: *Rayuela*', in Philip Swanson, ed., *Landmarks in Modern Latin American Fiction*, Routledge, London and New York, 1990, pp. 118–40.

**Bordwell**, David and Kristin Thompson, *Film Art*, Addison-Wesley Publishing Co., Reading/Menlo Park/London/Amsterdam/Don Mills/Sydney, 1980.

**Boschetto**, Sandra M., 'Dialéctica metatextual y sexual en *La casa de los espíritus* de Isabel Allende', *Hispania*, LXXII, 1989, pp. 526–32.

**Brushwood**, John S., 'Sobre el referente y la transformación narrativa en las novelas de Carlos Fuentes y Gustavo Sainz', *Revista Iberoamericana*, XLVII, 1981, pp. 49–54.

**Cabrera Infante**, Guillermo, *La Habana para un infante difunto*, Seix Barral, Barcelona, 1979.

——, 'The Invisible Exile', in John Glad, ed., *Literature in Exile*, Duke University Press, Durham and London, 1990, pp. 34–40.

——, *Tres tristes tigres*, Seix Barral, Barcelona, 1965.

**Cano Gaviria**, Ricardo, *El buitre y el ave fénix: conversaciones con Mario Vargas Llosa*, Anagrama, Barcelona, 1972.

**Cánovas**, Rodrigo, 'Los espíritus literarios y políticos de Isabel Allende', *Revista Chilena de Literatura*, XXXII, 1988, pp. 119–29.

**Castillo**, Debra, *Talking Back: Toward a Latin American Feminist Criticism*, Cornell University Press, Ithaca and London , 1992.

**Castillo-Feliú**, Guillermo I., *The Creative Process in the Works of José Donoso*, Winthrop Studies on Major Modern Writers, Rock Hill, 1982.

**Castro-Klarén**, Sara, *Understanding Mario Vargas Llosa*, University of South Carolina Press, Columbia, 1990.

**Cervantes**, Miguel de, *Don Quijote de la Mancha*, Juventud, Barcelona, 1971.

Cixous, Hélène, *Reading with Clarice Lispector*, edited, translated and introduced by Verena Andermatt Conley, University of Minnesota Press, Minneapolis and London, 1990.

——, 'The Laugh of the Medusa', in Elaine Marks and Isabelle de Courtivron, eds., *New French Feminisms*, University of Massachusetts Press, Amherst, 1980, pp. 245–64.

Close, A.J., *Miguel de Cervantes: Don Quijote*, Cambridge University Press, Cambridge, 1990.

Cornejo Polar, Antonio, ed., *José Donoso: la destrucción de un mundo*, Fernando García Cambeiro, Buenos Aires, 1975.

Cortínez, Verónica, 'Polifonía: entrevista a Isabel Allende y Antonio Skármeta', *Revista Chilena de Literatura*, XXXII, 1988, pp. 78–89.

Dapaz Strout, Lilia, 'Más allá del principio del placer del texto: Pascal, Puig y la pasión de la escritura: "El misterio de la celda siete"', *Hispanic Journal*, LI, 1983, pp. 87–99.

Darío, Rubén, *Poesías completas*, Aguilar, Madrid, 1961.

Di Antonio, Robert E., *Brazilian Fiction: Aspects and Evolution of the Contemporary Narrative*, University of Arkansas Press, Fayetville and London, 1989.

Doane, Mary Ann, *Femmes Fatales: Feminism, Film Theory, Psychoanalysis*, Routledge, London and New York, 1991.

Donoso, José, *Casa de campo*, 3rd ed., Seix Barral, Barcelona, 1980.

——, 'Dos mundos americanos', *El mercurio (Artes y letras)*, 14 Nov. 1982, p. 1.

——, *El jardín de al lado*, Seix Barral, Barcelona, 1981.

——, *El obsceno pájaro de la noche*, 6th ed., Seix Barral, Barcelona, 1979.

——, *Historia personal del 'boom'*, Anagrama, Barcelona, 1972.

——, *La misteriosa desaparición de la marquesita de Loria*, Seix Barral, Barcelona, 1980.

Dreyfus, Hubert, L. and Paul Rabinow, *Michel Foucault: Beyond Structuralism and Hermeneutics*, 2nd ed., University of Chicago Press, Chicago, 1983.

Duncan, J. Ann, *Voices, Visions and a New Reality: Mexican Fiction Since 1970*, Pittsburgh University Press, Pittsburgh, 1986.

Durán, Gloria, 'The Fuentes Interviews in Fact and in Fiction', *Mester*, XI, 1982, pp. 16–24.

Earle, Peter G., 'Literature as Survival: Allende's *The House of the Spirits*', XXVIII, 1987, pp. 543–54.

Ezquerro, Milagros, *Essai d'analyse de 'El beso de la mujer araña' de Manuel Puig*, Institut d'études hispaniques et hispano-americaines,

Université de Toulouse–Le Mirail, Toulouse, 1981.

Faris, Wendy B., *Carlos Fuentes*, Frederick Ungar, New York, 1983.

Fernández Moreno, César, ed., *América latina en su literatura*, Siglo XXI, Mexico, 1972.

Fiddian, Robin, 'A Prospective Post-script: Apropos of *Love in the Times of Cholera*', in Bernard McGuirk and Richard Cardwell, eds., *Gabriel García Márquez: New Readings*, Cambridge University Press, Cambridge, 1987, pp. 191–205.

——, 'Carlos Fuentes: *La muerte de Artemio Cruz*', in Philip Swanson, ed., *Landmarks in Modern Latin American Fiction*, Routledge, London and New York, 1990, pp. 96–117.

Filer, Malva E., 'La ciudad y el tiempo mexicano en la obra de Gustavo Sainz', *Hispamérica*, XIII, 1984, pp. 95–102.

Fitz, Earl E., *Clarice Lispector*, Twayne, Boston, 1985.

Foster, Douglas, 'Isabel Allende Unveiled', *Mother Jones*, XIII, 1988, pp. 42–46.

Foucault, Michel, *Les Mots et les choses*, Gallimard, Paris, 1966.

——, 'The Subject and Power', in Hubert L. Dreyfus and Paul Rabinow, *Michel Foucault: Beyond Structuralism and Hermeneutics*, 2nd ed., University of Chicago Press, Chicago, 1983, pp. 208–26.

Franco, Jean, 'Going Public: Reinhabiting the Private', in George Yúdice, Jean Franco, and Juan Flores, *On Edge: The Crisis of Contemporary Latin American Culture*, University of Minnesota Press, Minneapolis and London, 1992, pp. 65–83.

——, *Spanish American Literature Since Independence*, Ernest Benn, London, 1973.

——, 'The Critique of the Pyramid and Mexican Narrative After 1968', in Rose S. Minc, ed., *Latin American Fiction Today*, Montclair State College and Hispamérica, Takoma Park, n.d., pp. 49–60.

Frye, Northrop, *Anatomy of Criticism*, Penguin, Harmondsworth, 1991.

Fuentes, Carlos, *La cabeza de la hidra*, Argos Vergara, Barcelona, 1979.

——, *La nueva novela hispanoamericana*, Joaquín Mortiz, Mexico, 1969.

——, *Myself with Others*, Picador, London, 1988.

García Márquez, Gabriel, *Cien años de soledad*, 50th ed., Sudamericana, Buenos Aires, 1978.

García Ramos, Juan Manuel, *La narrativa de Manuel Puig (Por una crítica en libertad)*, Secretariado de publicaciones de la Universidad de La Laguna, La Laguna, 1982.

García Serrano, M. Victoria, 'Un pre-texto problemático: la advertencia de *Tres tristes tigres*', *Hispanófila*, XXXIV, 1991, pp. 89–92.

Gass, W. H., 'The First Seven Pages of the Boom', *Latin American Literary Review*, XXIX, 1987, pp. 33–56.

Gazarian Gautier, Marie-Lise, 'A Conversation between José Donoso and Marie-Lise Gazarian Gautier', in Guillermo I. Castillo-Feliú, *The Creative Process in the Works of José Donoso*, Winthrop Studies on Major Modern Writers, Rock Hill, 1982, pp. 1–13.

Geisdorfer Feal, Rosemary, *Novel Lives: The Fictional Autobiographies of Guillermo Cabrera Infante and Mario Vargas Llosa*, University of North Carolina Press, Chapel Hill, 1986.

Gerdes, Dick, *Mario Vargas Llosa*, Twayne, Boston, 1985.

Gilkison, Jean, 'The Appropriation of the Conventions of Romance in Isabel Allende's *De amor y de sombra*', paper given at the Association of Hispanists of Great Britain and Ireland, Belfast, 1991.

Glad, John, ed., *Literature in Exile*, Duke University Press, Durham and London, 1990.

Gnutzmann, Rita, *Cómo leer a Mario Vargas Llosa*, Júcar, Madrid, 1992.

González Echevarría, Roberto, *Alejo Carpentier: The Pilgrim at Home*, Cornell University Press, Ithaca and London, 1977.

——, *La ruta de Severo Sarduy*, Ediciones del Norte, Hanover, 1987.

Guibert, Rita, 'Guillermo Cabrera Infante: conversación sobre *Tres tristes tigres*', in Julio Ortega, *et al.*, *Guillermo Cabrera Infante*, Fundamentos, Madrid, 1974, pp. 19–46.

Gutiérrez-Mouat, Ricardo, *José Donoso: impostura e impostación*, Hispamérica, Gaithersburg, 1983.

Gyurko, Lanin A., 'Individual and National Identity in Fuentes' *La cabeza de la hidra*', in Rose S. Minc, ed., *Latin American Fiction Today*, Montclair State College and Hispamérica, Takoma Park, n.d., pp. 33–48.

Hall, Kenneth E., *Guillermo Cabrera Infante and the Cinema*, Juan de la Cuesta, Newark, 1989.

Harper, Ralph, *The World of the Thriller*, The Press of Case Western Reserve University, Cleveland, 1969.

Herrero, Javier, 'Carlos Fuentes y las lecturas modernas del *Quijote*', *Revista Iberoamericana*, XLV, 1979, pp. 555–62.

Janes, Regina, 'No More Interviews', *Salmagundi*, XLIII, 1979, pp. 87–95.

Jones, Ann Rosalind, 'Writing the Body: Toward an Understanding of *L'Ecriture Féminine*', in Elaine Showalter, ed., *The New Feminist Criticism: Essays on Women, Literature and Theory*, Pantheon-Random House, New York, 1985, pp. 361–77.

Jones, Julie, 'The Dynamics of the City: Gustavo Sainz's *La princesa del Palacio de Hierro*', *Chasqui*, XII, 1982, pp. 14–23.

Kafalenos, Emma, 'The Grace and Disgrace of Literature: Carlos Fuentes' *The Hydra Head*', *Latin American Literary Review*, XV, 1987, pp. 141–58.

Kerr, Lucille, *Reclaiming the Author: Figures and Fictions from Spanish America*, Duke University Press, Durham and London, 1992.

——, *Suspended Fictions: Reading Novels by Manuel Puig*, University of Illinois Press, Urbana, 1987.

King, John, ed., *Modern Latin American Fiction*, Faber and Faber, London, 1987.

Koldewyn, Phillip, '*La cabeza de la hidra*: residuos del colonialismo', *Mester*, XI, 1982, pp. 47–56.

Kristeva, Julia, 'La femme, ce n'est jamais ça', *Tel Quel*, LIX, 1974, pp. 19–24.

——, *La Révolution du langage poétique*, Seuil, Paris, 1974.

——, 'Le mot, le dialogue et le roman', in *Semiotiké*, Seuil, Paris, 1969.

Lacan, Jacques, *Ecrits: A Selection*, translated by A. Sheridan and edited by J.-A. Miller, Tavistock, London, 1977.

Leclerc, Annie, *Parole de femme*, Grasset, Paris, 1974.

Levine, Linda, and Jo Anne Engelbert, 'The World Is Full of Stories', *Review*, XXXIV 1980, pp. 18–20.

Lévy, Isaac Jack, and Juan Loveluck, eds., *Simposio Carlos Fuentes: Actas*, University of South Carolina Press, Columbia, n.d.

Lewis, Marvin A., *From Lima to Leticia: The Peruvian Novels of Mario Vargas Llosa*, University Press of America, Lanham and London, 1983.

Lipski, John M., 'Paradigmatic Overlapping in *Tres tristes tigres*', *Dispositio*, I, 1976, pp. 33–43.

Lispector, Clarice, *A hora da estrela*, Francisco Alves, Rio de Janeiro, 1992.

Ludmer, Josefina, '*Tres tristes tigres*: órdenes literarios y jerarquías sociales', *Revista Iberoamericana*, XLV, 1979, pp. 493–512.

Magnarelli, Sharon, 'Disappearance Under the Cover of Language: The Case of the Marquesita de Loria', in Miriam Adelstein, ed., *Studies on the Works of José Donoso*, Edwin Mellen Press, Lewiston/Queenston/Lampeter, 1990, pp. 102–29.

——, 'The Diseases of Love and Discourse: *La tía Julia y el escribidor* and *María*', *Hispanic Review*, LIV, 1986, pp. 195–205.

——, *The Lost Rib: Female Characters in the Spanish-American Novel*, Associated University Presses, London and Toronto, 1985.

——, *Understanding José Donoso*, University of South Carolina Press, Columbia, 1993.

**Malcuzynski**, M.-Pierrette, '*Tres tristes tigres*, or the Treacherous Play on Carnival', *Ideologies and Literature*, III, 1981, pp. 33–56.

**Marks**, Elaine and Isabelle de Courtivron, eds., *New French Feminisms*, University of Massachusetts Press, Amherst, 1980.

**Martin**, Gerald, *Journeys Through the Labyrinth: Latin American Fiction in the Twentieth Century*, Verso, London and New York, 1989.

——, 'Mario Vargas Llosa: Errant Knight of the Liberal Imagination', in John King, ed., *Modern Latin American Fiction*, Faber and Faber, London, 1987, pp. 205–33.

——, 'On "Magical" and Social Realism in García Márquez', in Bernard McGuirk and Richard Cardwell, eds., *Gabriel García Márquez: New Readings*, Cambridge University Press, Cambridge, 1987, pp. 95–116.

——, Review of Philip Swanson, *José Donoso: The 'Boom' and Beyond*, *Bulletin of Latin American Research*, VIII, 1989, pp. 130–1.

**Martín**, José Luis, *La narrativa de Vargas Llosa*, Gredos, Madrid, 1974.

**Martínez**, Z. Nelly, 'José Donoso', *Hispamérica*, XXI, 1978, pp. 53–74.

**McCracken**, Ellen, 'Vargas Llosa's *La tía Julia y el escribidor*: The New Novel and the Mass Media', *Ideologies and Literature*, III, 1980, pp. 54–69.

**McGuirk**, Bernard and Richard Cardwell, eds., *Gabriel García Márquez: New Readings*, Cambridge University Press, Cambridge, 1987.

**Merrim**, Stephanie, 'A Secret Idiom: The Grammar and Role of Language in *Tres tristes tigres*', *Latin American Literary Review*, VIII, 1980, pp. 96–117.

——, 'Through the Film Darkly: Grade "B" Movies and Dreamwork in *Tres tristes tigres* and *El beso de la mujer araña*', *Modern Language Studies*, XV, 1985, pp. 300–12.

——, '*Tres tristes tigres*: antimundo, antilenguaje, antinovela', *Texto crítico*, XI, 1985, pp. 133–52.

**Millington**, Mark I., 'Voces múltiples en Cabrera Infante', paper given at the Primer Congreso Anglo–Hispano, Huelva, 1992. Subsequently published in Alan Deyermond and Ralph Penny, eds., *Actas del Primer Congreso Anglo-Hispano*. Tomo II: *Literatura*. Castalia, Madrid, 1993, pp. 353–62.

**Mimoso-Ruiz**, Duarte, 'Aspects des "media" dans *El beso de la mujer araña* de Manuel Puig (1976) et *La tía Julia y el escribidor* de Mario Vargas Llosa (1977)', *Les Langues Néo-latines*, LXXVI, 1982, pp. 29–47.

**Minc**, Rose S., ed., *Latin American Fiction Today*, Montclair State College and Hispamérica, Takoma Park, n.d.

**Minta**, Stephen, *Gabriel García Márquez: Writer of Colombia*, Jonathan Cape, London, 1987.

Moi, Toril, ed., *French Feminist Thought: A Reader*, Basil Blackwell, Oxford, 1987.

——, *Sexual/Textual Politics*, Routledge, London and New York, 1990.

Monaco, James, *How to Read a Film*, Oxford University Press, Oxford and New York, 1977.

Montenegro, Nivia and Enrico Mario Santí, 'A Conversation with José Donoso', *New Novel Review*, I, no. 2, 1994, pp. 7–15.

Mora, Gabriela, 'Las novelas de Isabel Allende y el papel de la mujer como ciudadana', *Ideologies and Literature*, II, 1987, pp. 53–61.

Mulvey, Laura, 'Visual Pleasure and Narrative Cinema', *Screen*, XVI, 1975, pp. 6–18.

Muñoz, Elías Miguel, 'La utopía sexual en *El beso de la mujer araña* de Manuel Puig', *Alba de América*, July–December 1984, pp. 49–60.

Nelson, Ardis L., *Cabrera Infante in the Menippean Tradition*, Juan de la Cuesta, Newark, 1983.

——, '*Tres tristes tigres* y el cine', *Kentucky Romance Quarterly*, XXIX, 1982, pp. 391–404.

Nochlin, Linda, *Women, Art, and Power and Other Essays*, Harper and Row, New York, 1988.

Nunes, Benedito, 'Clarice Lispector ou o naufrágio da introspecçao', *Remate de Males*, IX, 1989, pp. 63–70.

Oliveira Filho, Odil José de, 'A voz do narrador em *O beijo da mulher aranha*', *Revista de Letras*, XXIV, 1984, pp. 53–60.

Ortega, Julio, *Poetics of Change: The New Spanish American Narrative*, University of Texas Press, Austin, 1984.

——, *et al.*, *Guillermo Cabrera Infante*, Fundamentos, Madrid, 1974.

Osorio, M., 'Entrevista con Manuel Puig', *Cuadernos para el diálogo*, CCXXXI, 1977, pp. 51–3.

Oviedo, José Miguel, '*La tía Julia y el escribidor*, or the Coded Self-portrait', in Charles Rossman and Alan Warren Friedman, eds., *Mario Vargas Llosa: A Collection of Critical Essays*, University of Texas Press, Austin and London, 1978, pp. 166–81.

Pellón, Gustavo, 'Manuel Puig's Contradictory Strategy: Kitsch Paradigms *versus* Paradigmatic Structure in *El beso de la mujer araña* and *Pubis angelical*', *Symposium*, XXXVII, 1983, pp. 186–201.

Pereira, Amalia, 'Interview with José Donoso', *Latin American Literary Review*, XV, 1987, pp. 57–67.

Pérez Blanco, Lucrecio, 'Acercamiento a una novela de denuncia social: *La misteriosa desaparición de la marquesita de Loria* de José Donoso', *Revista de Estudios Hispánicos*, XVI, 1982, pp. 399–410.

Pérez Galdós, Benito, *Obras completas*, Aguilar, Madrid, 1961.

Pérez Luna, Elizabeth, 'Con Manuel Puig en Nueva York', *Hombre de Mundo*, III, no. 8, 1978, pp. 69–78 and 104–7.

Polo García, Victorino, 'De *Tres tristes tigres* a *La Habana para un infante difunto*, un espejo para el camino', *Revista Iberoamericana*, LVIII, 1992, pp. 557–66.

Promis Ojeda, José, 'La desintegración del orden en la novela de José Donoso', in Antonio Cornejo Polar, ed., *José Donoso: la destrucción de un mundo*, Fernando García Cambeiro, Buenos Aires, 1975, pp. 13–42.

Puig, Manuel, *Bajo un manto de estrellas*, Seix Barral, Barcelona, 1983.

——, *El beso de la mujer araña*, 2nd ed., Seix Barral, Barcelona, 1981.

Purdie, Susan, *Comedy: The Mastery of Discourse*, Harvester Wheatsheaf, Hemel Hempstead, 1993.

Quinlan, Susan Canty, *The Female Voice in Contemporary Brazilian Narrative*, Peter Lang, New York, 1991.

Rama, Angel, *La novela latinoamericana 1920–1980*, Instituto Colombiano de Cultura, Bogotá, 1982.

Reedy, Daniel R., 'Del beso de la mujer araña al de la tía Julia: estructura y dinámica interior', *Revista Iberoamericana*, XLVII, 1981, pp. 109–16.

Ricardou, Jean, *Nouveau problèmes du roman*, Seuil, Paris, 1978.

——, *Pour une théorie du nouveau roman*, Seuil, Paris, 1971.

Riley, E. C., *Don Quixote*, Allen and Unwin, London, 1986.

Rodríguez Monegal, Emir, *El arte de narrar*, Monte Avila, Caracas, n.d.

Rojas, Mario A., '*La casa de los espíritus* de Isabel Allende: un caleidoscopio de espejos desordenados', *Revista Iberoamericana*, LI, 1985, pp. 917–25.

Rossman, Charles and Alan Warren Friedman, eds., *Mario Vargas Llosa: A Collection of Critical Essays*, University of Texas Press, Austin and London, 1978.

Rowe, William, 'Liberalism and Authority: The Case of Mario Vargas Llosa', in George Yúdice, Jean Franco, and Juan Flores, *On Edge: The Crisis of Contemporary Latin American Culture*, University of Minnesota Press, Minneapolis and London, 1992, pp. 45–64.

——, and Vivian Schelling, *Memory and Modernity: Popular Culture in Latin America*, Verso, London and New York, 1991.

Sagarzazu, María Elvira, 'New Concerns for the Novel: A Latin American Viewpoint', in David Bevan, ed., *Literature and Revolution*, Rodopi, Amsterdam and Atlanta, 1989, pp. 163–9.

Sainz, Gustavo, *La princesa del Palacio de Hierro*, Océano, Mexico, 1982.

Sarduy, Severo, 'El barroco y el neobarroco', in César Fernández Moreno, ed., *América latina en su literatura*, Siglo XXI, Mexico, 1972, pp. 167–84.

——, 'Notas a las notas a las notas ... a propósito de Manuel Puig', *Revista Iberoamericana*, XXXVII, 1971, pp. 555–67.

Shaw, D. L., 'Concerning the Interpretation of *Cien años de soledad*', *Ibero-Amerikanisches Archiv*, III, 1977, pp. 318–29.

——, *Nueva narrativa hispanoamericana*, Cátedra, Madrid, 1981.

——, Review of John King, ed., *Modern Latin American Fiction*, *Modern Language Review*, LXXXIV, 1989, p. 510.

——, 'Towards a Description of the Post-Boom', *Bulletin of Hispanic Studies*, LXVII, 1989, pp. 87–94.

Showalter, Elaine, *Sexual Anarchy: Gender and Culture at the Fin-de-siècle*, Penguin, New York, 1990.

——, ed., *The New Feminist Criticism: Essays on Women, Literature and Theory*, Pantheon-Random House, New York, 1985.

Siemens, William L., 'Guillermo Cabrera Infante and the Divergence of Revolutions: Political versus Textual', in David Bevan, ed., *Literature and Revolution*, Rodopi, Amsterdam and Atlanta, 1989, pp. 107–19.

——, *Worlds Reborn: The Hero in the Modern Spanish American Novel*, West Virginia University Press, Morgantown, 1984.

Smith, Paul Julian, *The Body Hispanic*, Oxford University Press, Oxford, 1989.

Smyth, Edmund J., ed., *Postmodernism and Contemporary Fiction*, Batsford, London, 1991.

Souza, Raymond D., *Major Cuban Novelists: Innovation and Tradition*, University of Missouri Press, Columbia and London, 1976.

Strassfield, Michael, *The Jewish Holidays*, Harper and Row, New York, 1985.

Swanson, Philip, *Cómo leer a Gabriel García Márquez*, Júcar, Madrid, 1991.

——, *Jose Donoso: The 'Boom' and Beyond*, Francis Cairns, Liverpool and Wolfeboro, 1988.

——, ed., *Landmarks in Modern Latin American Fiction*, Routledge, London and New York, 1990.

——, 'Structure and Meaning in *La misteriosa desaparición de la marquesita de Loria*', *Bulletin of Hispanic Studies*, LXIII, 1986, pp. 247–56.

——, 'Una entrevista con José Donoso', *Revista Iberoamericana*, 53, 1987, pp. 995–8.

Tittler, Jonathan, 'Carlos Fuentes', *Diacritics*, September 1980, pp. 46–56.

Vargas Llosa, Mario, *La tía Julia y el escribidor*, Seix Barral, Barcelona, 1977.

Vieira, Nelson H., 'A expressão judaica na obra de Clarice Lispector', *Remate de Males*, IX, 1989, pp. 207–9.

Waugh, Patricia, *Metafiction*, Routledge, London and New York, 1984.

Williams, Raymond L., 'The Reader and the Recent Novels of Gustavo Sainz', *Hispania*, LXV, 1982, pp. 383–7.

Williamson, Edwin, 'Magical Realism and the Theme of Incest in *One Hundred Years of Solitude*', in Bernard McGuirk and Richard Cardwell, eds., *Gabriel García Márquez: New Readings*, Cambridge University Press, Cambridge, 1987, pp. 45–63.

Wilson, Jason, 'Guillermo Cabrera Infante: An Interview in a Summer Manner with Jason Wilson', in John King, ed., *Modern Latin American Fiction*, Faber and Faber, London, 1987, pp. 305–25.

Yúdice, George, '¿Puede hablarse de postmodernidad en América Latina?', *Revista de Crítica Literaria Latinoamericana*, XXIX, 1989, pp. 105–28.

——, Jean Franco, and Juan Flores, eds., *On Edge: The Crisis of Contemporary Latin American Culture*, University of Minnesota Press, Minneapolis and London, 1992.

# Index